BROKEN

How far would you go for a dog that you love?

Michelle Stark

FIRE ANT PRESS

www.fireantpress.com

Issued in print and electronic formats

ISBN: 978-1-0689386-0-3 (pbk.) ISBN: 978-1-0689386-0-3 (ebk.)

First Edition: [November, 2024]

Cover Design by Nayomi A (@maxphotomaster)

For permissions, please contact: Fire Ant Press, www.fireantpress.com

Disclaimer: This is a work of nonfiction. The events described herein are based on the author's experiences. The author and publisher have made every effort to ensure the accuracy and completeness of the information contained in this book. However, the author and publisher assume no responsibility for errors, inaccuracies, or omissions, or for damages that may result from the use of the information contained herein. Some names and identifying details have been changed to protect the privacy of individuals. The content of this book is not intended to constitute legal advice. Readers should seek their own legal counsel regarding any legal matters discussed in this book. This publication is protected under Canadian copyright law and is subject to the exclusive jurisdiction of the courts of Canada.

This book is dedicated to Maple and Raisa—two sensitive souls who were born into the most beautiful yet fragile of bodies. This story is woven from our shared journey, and it belongs to them as much as it does to me.

To live in this world
you must be able
to do three things:
to love what is mortal;
to hold it
against your bones knowing
your own life depends on it;
and, when the time comes to let it go,
to let it go.

"In Blackwater Woods" by Mary Oliver

PROLOGUE

T HERE WAS ONLY ONE thing I knew for certain as I left Tony's Live Bait Shop that morning: I was going to be late for court.

I had been pacing in front of the shabby little shack, growing more impatient by the minute, when the old man rolled up in his weather-beaten golf cart.

"Good morning young lady," he greeted me with a chipper voice. With a shaky hand, he pulled a foam keychain out of the golf cart's ignition, and fumbled with the many keys until he found the right one to unlock the windowless door. Holding it open with a grand gesture, he invited me inside.

"Morning," I said, turning sideways and carefully shuffling past him, trying my best not to touch him or the door. As I entered, he looked me up and down, probably wondering why his first bait-buying customer of the day was dressed in a navy pinstriped suit and high-heels.

Once inside, I strode purposefully past a few bubbling tanks of minnows to get to the grubby white fridge. It had a sign on the door that read, "Dew Worms, $2.99 per dozen." I held my breath as I opened the door, bracing for a bad smell.

The old man had barely gotten himself behind the counter before I set the white Styrofoam container of worms down in front of him. I extended my hand offering him the exact change in an open palm. As his thick fingers struggled to pick up the coins, I smiled politely, while in my head I was screaming, "Hurry up!"

The old man commented on the nice weather as he handed me the receipt. I wished him a good day and rushed out of the shop, singing "thank you" as the screen door banged behind me.

Once back on the highway, I looked over to the passenger seat beside me where a tall perchless birdcage was being held in place by a seatbelt. Looking back at me from the bottom of the cage was Solomon, the baby starling. He was all nestled up in a piece of red fleece blanket that I had shaped into a nest. At that point in time, I didn't know he was a starling. I rescued him a few days earlier from a city parking lot, where he was hunkered down on the concrete at the same level as the shoes of the busy humans who surely would have stepped on him if I hadn't intervened. Or at least that's what I told myself - that I had no choice really.

Solomon, who was named after one of my files, was so ugly that he was cute. With pink and grey puckered skin, he was featherless apart from a few tufts of fluff that looked like eyebrows, and some random grey fuzz on his back. His enormous bright yellow beak looked much too big for the size of his head.

I didn't know what to feed a baby starling. This was prior to the Internet. So, on the advice of a neighbour who seemed to know everything about anything, I had been mashing up worms with a fork (while gagging) and using an eye dropper to feed them to him. A baby bird that young needed to eat every few hours, which is why I needed a lot more worms than I was able to find outside. It was also why Solomon had been coming to work with me.

Arriving at my office, I stepped out of the elevator directly into my firm's lobby and almost walked right into the senior partner. Mumbling an apology while avoiding eye contact, I sidestepped, assuming he was getting on the elevator to go to court. I positioned the birdcage behind my back and tried to whiz by him as quickly as I could, but he moved in front of me and uttered the one sentence that had the power to make me remember every single time I had been in trouble in my whole life:

"Michelle. I need to talk to you."

Had he been waiting for me? The fact that he used my first name made me nervous. He, along with the other partners, normally just called me "Student," and I wasn't entirely sure until that moment that he even knew what my name was.

Even though he was a small man (almost my size and I am petite), I was terrified of him. I was an articling student beginning my yearlong requirement of working in a law firm before being called to the Bar. He was my assigned mentor and was responsible for deciding whether I would be hired back to the firm as an associate. Fledgling lawyer jobs were scarce at the time, so he was in control of my professional destiny. I had just graduated from Osgoode Hall Law School in Toronto and was hoping to practise at his firm in Hamilton after I finished my articling requirement.

"Ummmm, can it can wait? I don't want to be late for court," I replied, knowing from his hard stare and one raised eyebrow that he had definitely noticed the birdcage.

"No," he answered, arms still crossed, staring me down. He was still not allowing me to get any further into the office.

"It has been brought to my attention that you have been putting worms in the staff refrigerator. The secretaries have complained. This cannot continue."

I exhaled, "Yep, no problem."

I glanced over at the receptionist who was staring down at her folded hands on her desk, trying to hide a smirk. The whole office was going to know about this encounter by the time I got back from court. Law firm culture is divided into two distinct groups – the lawyers and the staff. As an articling student, the staff didn't accept me because they considered me a lawyer. Not yet a lawyer, I wasn't accepted by that half of the firm either. I was in law firm limbo, with no office allies of my own.

The senior partner then stepped aside, permitting me to hurry past him to get to my cubby-hole of an office, where I said hello to my shared assistant, stashed the baby bird under my desk, and hoofed it as quickly as was humanly possible in high-heeled shoes to the courthouse.

It was time to switch gears from starlings to small claims court.

1

PRELUDE TO PUREBREDS

NOBODY EVER ASKS ME why I don't have children. I find this really strange. In my younger years, I suppose people might have assumed I was focusing on my career. As I grew older, maybe they thought there was a medical issue or a painful personal story behind it. Whatever the reason, I am thankful that I don't have to explain my decision, because the truth is, I'm not really sure why myself. All I know is that I have felt this way ever since I was a child.

To clarify from the outset, my ambivalence towards becoming a mother isn't rooted in any negative experiences from my own upbringing, which on the whole was pretty average, and mostly happy.

I grew up in the small Ontario village of Waterdown. My parents are retired and still live in the house where I was raised – a modest ranch-style bungalow that was built in the 1960's. My mom was a schoolteacher and my dad worked as a manager for a public utility in the nearby city of Hamilton, which is about an hour west of Toronto.

I am the oldest of three children and the only girl. Like all the Starks, I am small in stature and as a little girl I was one of the shortest kids in my class. Skinny with long brown hair and bangs that were always cut a bit too short by my mother, I loved the colour pink, wearing dresses, and doing gymnastics on our big front lawn. But most of all, I loved animals. I was that little girl who said hello to the birds in the trees, hand-fed peanuts to squirrels, rescued toads from window wells, and was always asking strangers, "Can I pet your dog?"

While I never dreamed of being a mother to any human children, my maternal instincts towards animals were always very strong and began at an early age. Growing up, I was constantly on the lookout for creatures in distress; frequently bringing home lost dogs, stray cats and sometimes even orphaned wildlife. My innocent enthusiasm for animal rescue always incited chaos in the Stark household, given that my youngest brother was, and still is, severely allergic to anything with fur or feathers.

Jeff grew up relying on asthma inhalers and antihistamines to survive everyday life. I have vivid recollections of being ordered to roll up car windows as we drove by farm animals on windy days, otherwise he would get so itchy that he would knuckle-rub his eyes until they became puffy enough that my dad would tease him by asking where he was going with his "bags packed."

My incessant desire for a pet was constantly clashing with Jeff's compromised immune system, which resulted in a significant amount of parental anxiety. This is probably how it came to be that I owned an enormous collection of stuffed animals and eventually an enormous collection of fish. And even a reptile.

It all started with Blackie and Goldie, two flashy fantail goldfish that lived in a bowl on my white French Provincial style dresser. Right from the get-go, I felt extremely sad about their cramped quarters and it didn't take me long to successfully lobby my parents for an upgrade to their accommodation. As my enthusiasm for aquatic pets grew, my parents indulged it, and it didn't take long for my tiny pink bedroom to become cluttered with a table full of bubbling fish tanks, one of which provided lodging for a newt named Olivia. Most of the kids I knew had a dog or a cat, or at least a hamster or gerbil. My pets weren't cuddly but I considered them my friends and I loved them all dearly.

Despite providing me with lots of little lives to love, my parents were never able to fully eradicate my one true desire. While I was grateful for all of my aquarium friends, what I still really wanted was a dog. In fact, I was so obsessed with the idea that I never truly accepted Jeff's allergies as a legitimate reason for why I couldn't have one.

My fervent pleas and relentless petitions for a canine companion became my personal anthem. Any "free to good home" dog advertised on the grocery store bulletin board would ignite relentless begging that would eventually end in tears when I was told "enough is enough" by my dad. My entreaties grew even more impassioned during the time leading up to Christmas, when I always doubled-down on my requests for a puppy. This was of course because I was being egged on by those quintessential television commercials depicting a fluffy golden retriever puppy bursting out of a big box with a red bow on it, to the delight of some very lucky children.

Over the years, I never gave up trying to convince my parents that we needed to get a dog. In fact, as I got older I started looking for more creative ways to change their minds.

My campaigning involved reading up on the subject to demonstrate my unwavering commitment to being a good dog owner. This was of course an enjoyable task, since I loved books almost as much as I loved dogs.

The Waterdown Library was located in a beautiful stone Victorian building rumoured to be inhabited by a ghost. There were old gravestones mounted on a wall beside a clunky elevator that took unexplained trips when empty, which for some reason didn't freak me out, because I loved old buildings too, especially haunted ones. I would sit for hours cross-legged on the red carpet in the aisle between the tall bookshelves, browsing through the pages of every dog book. I especially loved leafing through the "Encyclopedia of Dog Breeds," which profiled the various types of dogs in alphabetical order under the general categories of Sporting Group, Hound Group, Working Group, Terrier Group, Toy Group, Non-Sporting Group, and Herding Group.

Every breed listed in the Dog Encyclopedia seemed exotic to me, since almost all of the dogs in my town were mixed breeds that people referred to as mutts or Heinz 57s. The dogs of Waterdown were all unique, since none of them were purebred anythings. Ralph had the colouring of a Doberman but was much smaller and shaggy. Muffin was a small dog with a tube-shaped body, long skinny legs, wiry beige terrier fur and a tail that was as curly as a corkscrew. Tramp was shaped like a beagle but had no spots. The mutts of Waterdown often looked scruffy, and I think at least one of them was even named Scruffy.

Every weekday my father brought home the Hamilton newspaper from his office in the city. I enjoyed browsing the "Pets" section of the Classified Ads, where Canadian Kennel Club registered purebred puppies were advertised for sale. This is how, even as a kid, I knew that purebred dogs were expensive. I thought you had to be rich or famous to own a "show dog," a belief which was reinforced when I got to see one of the most exotic breeds in the world.

I was 11 years old when my grandparents, who were wintering in Florida, took me to see the "The Greatest Show on Earth." The Ringling Brothers Barnum & Bailey Circus featured jungle cats jumping through rings of fire and bears riding motorcycles. My brothers loved the tiger shows, but it was the circus dogs that made the biggest impression on me. When a glamorous lady in a hot pink sequined outfit led a troupe of tall white dogs into the ring, I didn't need the program to tell me what they were. I recognized them from the Dog Encyclopedia: a breed called borzoi, also known as Russian wolfhounds. The surreal-looking dogs were as tall as ponies with incredibly long noses, doleful eyes and impossibly skinny bodies. They were the canine equivalents of runway models and I was mesmerized as they moved around the ring so gracefully, giving the appearance that they were floating on air.

I adored those exotic borzoi dogs, but I would have been just as happy with any dog to call my own. Back at home my heart was captured by a much less glamorous but very iconic brand of dog. On Thursday nights at 7:30 p.m. my brothers and I would sit in our wood-paneled rec room to watch reruns of my favourite show, "The Littlest Hobo." It was a Canadian series about a stray German shepherd dog that went from town to town helping people. I daydreamed about a dog like Hobo showing up and befriending me. The crazy thing is, my prayers were answered, and eventually one did.

One wintry weekend day, a dog that looked almost exactly like the Littlest Hobo showed up when I was playing outside. Thinking that fate had orchestrated the encounter, I believed that this dog was meant to be mine. We roamed the forest and streets as if we owned the world. Eventually, her owner came looking, and as he pulled the young dog by the scruff of her neck into his Jeep, he told me (because I asked) that her name was Duchess, and that she was an Alaskan malamute/German shepherd crossbreed (because I also asked). She had wandered away from his horse farm, which was about a 15-minute walk from my house.

A few days later, Duchess was back, and once again, we embarked on adventures together that danced between reality and my childhood imagination. Again, her owner came to retrieve her, this time talking to my parents.

Over the next few weeks, Duchess routinely broke free to come and find me. Sometimes I would find her waiting for me outside our front door when I got up in the morning, or she would be there when I got off the school bus. My parents allowed me play with her until it started to get dark, and then I would walk her back to the farm, where her owners would tie her back up to her doghouse. It was an ideal arrangement really, since Duchess wasn't allowed in our house because of Jeff's allergies, and her owners didn't seem to have the time for her and were probably happy that someone was exercising their rambunctious young pup for them. It was almost like I had my own dog, and I was the happiest I had ever been in my life.

Duchess and I had many adventures in between her escapes and her eventual returns home. We were inseparable when she was loose. I fell deeply in love with my canine guardian who seemed to silently understand the language of my young dog-loving heart, as no one ever had. I considered her my dog and I am pretty sure she considered me her person. In fact, it was because of Duchess that I became a lawyer.

Early one morning Duchess got loose and was waiting for me in the alcove at the front door of our house. Sunday was the only day of the week that my father had a Toronto newspaper delivered. When the papergirl approached our door, she must have startled the dog, or maybe Duchess was just protecting our house - we will never know. There was no "attack" per se, but Duchess jumped on the papergirl, leaving marks on her skin where her nails scratched her.

Even though my parents thought the girl was more frightened than injured, they brought her a box of chocolates as an apology. Under normal Waterdown circumstances, that neighbourly gesture alone would have been the end of it, but the papergirl's mother just happened to be a clerk in a law firm in the city.

The local animal authority showed up at our house and interrogated us. A short time later, we (along with the owners of Duchess) were served with legal papers for personal injury damages, and I was subpoenaed to testify in court. It was terrifying.

It was during this stressful time that Duchess disappeared. My parents told me that she had been sent by her owners to live on a farm in another town, but I knew what really happened to her, and it made me sad and angry. It was such a tumultuous and confusing time for me. I was just a young girl and didn't know how to process or even acknowledge my feelings of extreme grief over losing my best friend. What manifested instead was anger: anger towards the papergirl and her family, anger towards myself for not running away with Duchess before they could take her away; but most of all, I felt a seething anger towards what I perceived was a grave injustice that had resulted in my beloved dog losing her life.

Dreaming of becoming a lawyer was the only way that the younger version of myself was able to feel like I had any control over a situation that was so far out of my control. The seeds of ambition had been sown. I didn't want this type of injustice to happen to any dog ever again. I wanted to be the voice for the dogs who had no voice in the justice system. I wanted to be the guardian of their rights.

And long after the pain that arose from the loss of Duchess had faded, the dream of becoming a lawyer stayed with me, driving me to be academically disciplined and focused. That pursuit directed the course of my life from that point on.

2

HARDWOOD AND HOUNDS DON'T MIX

H AVE YOU EVER HAD one of those years when numerous monumental things happen to you? For me, it was the year that I was asked into the partnership of my law firm, bought a house, and started dating the man who would become my husband.

Seven years had passed since I articled at the firm where I was hired back as an associate. While I had achieved my childhood career goal, the work I ended up doing on a daily basis had absolutely nothing to do with the reason that motivated me to become a lawyer in the first place.

As a civil litigator, I occasionally defended dog bite cases; the most memorable of which involved a dog named Judas who bit an intruder's penis. But it was never the dog that I was defending. It was the owner of the dog - or more precisely, it was their insurance company. By the time I received the file, as was the case with Judas, the dog had already been euthanized, and the only thing I was fighting about was money. My clients weren't even people – they were corporations, and the majority of my files involved injuries that resulted from motor vehicle accidents. This certainly wasn't the life I had imagined for myself when I decided to become a lawyer.

Almost all the lawyers at my firm were middle-aged white men. Every day at noon, they would gather in the foyer of our office on the 11th floor and walk together to a restaurant for lunch as a group — a small herd of dark suits and overcoats that frequented windowless steak houses with names like *The Sirloin Cellar*.

Even though I had no desire to eat a big expensive meal in the middle of the day, I was still expected to join this daily ritual unless I was out of town for a court appearance. Early on, it was made clear to me that being present at these daily outings was just as important to my career advancement as winning at court. To avoid having my male colleagues think

I wasn't a team player—or worse, labeling me a prude, I attended the lunches, laughed at their offensive jokes and ordered alcoholic drinks I didn't want. To make matters worse, I often had to work late to make up for the billable hours I missed while lunching with the leaders of the firm.

I knew something was up on the day I was invited to dine alone with the man who had been my articling principal (the same scary senior partner who interrogated me about the worms in the refrigerator). I was still somewhat afraid of him. Well, maybe afraid isn't the right word to use. I guess by then I was just merely intimidated, which might explain why, when he asked me to join the partnership on the basis of a handshake alone, I felt obligated to say yes, right there in that moment.

I say obligated because I wasn't entirely sure it was what I actually wanted. Not to mention the fact that I had to borrow a lot of money to "buy in" to the partnership. It had taken me years to pay off my student loan, which had necessitated my moving back in with my parents for a few years, which felt weird, given that I was in my late 20's and was practising law. I had also just purchased a house, so I already had a big debt owing to the bank in the form of a mortgage. "Not to worry," said the scary senior partner, "We will co-sign your loan."

I was nervous. However, the door to the old boys' club had been opened just a crack to let me in, and questioning the "gentleman's agreement" would have made me look ungrateful. After all, as they liked to remind me, I was only the second woman to ever make partner in a firm that had been around for almost 60 years. It was the next logical step in my career, so declining or delaying the offer didn't really seem like an option.

I celebrated my new status because it made my family proud. I was told that one of the perks of becoming a partner was golfing at prestigious private courses while entertaining clients. This didn't feel like a perk to me as I wasn't a schmoozer and I didn't like golfing. That being said, it was during one of these outings that I received the biggest perk of all – a chance meeting with a handsome golf course superintendent (greenskeeper) named Tim.

Soon after we met, Tim took me on a dinner date, and then another, and it didn't take long before we were an item. With a dark crew cut, concrete jaw and dramatic eyebrows, Tim towered over me at 6'3". He had a quiet confidence about him, and in button down Polo shirts and chinos, he was groomed as conservatively as his golf course, looking more like a golf pro than someone who worked outside on the grounds.

Tim was raised by Dutch immigrant parents and grew up on a farm, which is probably why he was so different from the other young men I had previously dated. Old-fashioned in a good way; he was a hard worker, a straight talker, and the most dependable, uncomplicated and capable person that I had ever met. Right from the start our relationship was almost perfect. I say almost because there was still one big hurdle standing in the way ... only one of us wanted a dog.

Tim owned a delightful little beagle named Ozzy. She was a skinny white hound with brown spots and amber almond-shaped eyes, ridiculously long ears, and a tail that never stopped wagging. Ozzy had a gentle nature but boundless energy and strong instincts to follow her nose. Running away, chasing rabbits, and getting really dirty were three of her special talents. She went everywhere with Tim, running free all day at the golf course and then lounging around as a house pet in the evenings with Tim and his two messy bachelor roommates.

Ozzy's houndy personality, while endearing, was not at all well suited to visiting the fancy house that I had recently purchased.

My new house was completely different from the 1960's era bungalow that I grew up in. It was a two and a half story Tudor Revival located on a beautiful tree-lined street in an upscale neighbourhood. Nestled below the escarpment and within walking distance to downtown Hamilton, the house stood among stately stone and brick mansions that were built for the heavy-hitters of the past. I adored it.

My house wasn't as big as the others, but it was just as grand. At almost a hundred years of age, it still had all of its original features like leaded glass windows, gumwood wainscoting, and an impressive wood panelled entrance foyer. Its traditional attributes elicited deep emotions in me, I think because it symbolized the life that I had been working so hard for; the physical embodiment of my childhood ambitions which showed the world that I had "made it" - that the small-town kid, the first in her family to go to university, had become a successful professional.

Owning this house made the daily grind of being a lawyer almost bearable, but my demanding job didn't allow me the time I needed to look after any house, let alone a big old one. I ended up paying people to cut my grass, wash my windows, and keep the inside spotlessly clean. It felt like an extravagance, but the scary senior partner insisted that my billable time was much too valuable to be spent on such mundane tasks, so almost all of the money that I earned went to maintaining my house and paying the mortgage and taxes.

Somehow Tim must have understood how I felt about my house, even though we never talked about it. As a result, we did some questionable things when his hound was visiting my house with him. For instance, we lined my antique furniture with aluminum foil to deter Ozzy from jumping up on it. We put socks over her paws to stop her nails from scratching the gleaming hardwood floors. Sometimes we even locked her in the damp unfinished basement so she wouldn't bark at the professional people walking by with their well-bred civilized city dogs. Our efforts weren't working though, and everyone was miserable, especially poor Ozzy.

When Tim moved in with me, the dog situation came to a head. Whenever the front door opened, Ozzy would bolt out and run away. Not that I could blame her. I still loved animals and I loved Ozzy too (when she wasn't in my house), but at that time in my life I loved my house more. That mini-mansion and all that it stood for were so important to me that I couldn't bear the thought of anything, including a dog that Tim loved, to sully any part of its perfection. The irony is not lost on me that what I had longed for most as a child had become a stumbling block in what was otherwise an ideal relationship – the best one I had ever had.

Luckily, Tim's parents saved the day. They still lived on the farm where Tim grew up, and they agreed to adopt Ozzy into their dog-loving household. Now that I have dogs of my own, I realize what a huge sacrifice he made for me. Truth be told, I feel like a jerk even recounting this story now, but karma did eventually end up taking care of me in the dog department.

3

THE LAP OF LUXURY

T HE FIRST FEW YEARS after Tim and I got married, we were both so busy building our careers that we weren't thinking much about dogs at all. I was completely immersed in urban life as a young professional and Tim was working long hours establishing a new golf course in the Greater Toronto area.

Most of my days were spent in courtrooms and boardrooms. It was an adversarial existence, filled with tension and conflict. I didn't mind the hard work, the constant scrutiny or the long hours. It was the lack of certainty that really stressed me out. Providing legal advice to clients in such an unpredictable and high stakes system always felt a bit like gambling to me. Trials are time consuming, costly, and risky for those on both sides of the lawsuit. Using alternative ways to resolve disputes involves less risk, but both parties are usually unhappy with the results. Legitimately injured people never feel like they are being compensated enough for their injuries, while insurance companies (my clients) always feel like they are paying too much.

Oddly enough, while the practice of law itself wasn't suiting my soul, I did thoroughly enjoy all of the trappings that went along with it. I loved the tradition – the robes, the libraries and the ceremonies. I dined and socialized in historic places like The Hamilton Club, whose "fine bones" and "discerning membership" dated from 1873. The annual Lawyers' Picnic took place at the Tamahaac, "the most private of clubs," where prominent citizens have played tennis and shot clay pigeons for over a century. I spent many evenings in The Great Hall of the Hamilton Golf and Country Club, rubbing shoulders with the likes of Lincoln Alexander, the famous former Lieutenant Governor of Ontario. These were places that I would never have had access to, if it weren't for my job.

Another perk of my profession involved travel. When I had to go out of town for court appearances, conferences, or firm retreats, I always stayed at high-end luxury hotels. The novelty of doing this never wore off, I think because when I was growing up, the vacations my family took usually involved staying in tents, trailers or roadside motels.

Every year I attended a civil litigation conference in Quebec. The two-day event was held in a historic hotel built in the 1930's. Le Château Montebello is reportedly the largest log building in the world and was one of Canada's grand railway hotels. Though I was there to work, it always felt like a mini-vacation because I was able to spend unprogrammed time relaxing in the rustic but luxurious lobby, which featured a three-story atrium built around a massive stone fireplace.

I always arrived a day early, which gave me extra time to enjoy the hotel. It was then that I would skim through the giant binder of conference materials, deciding which lectures I wanted to attend the following day. The reading was boring, but doing it while sitting in front of a six-sided fireplace and sipping a $30 glass of champagne that had just been delivered from the "Bar Le Foyer" made the exercise a whole lot more enjoyable. In fact, it was while I was engaging in this annual ritual one fateful evening that I observed something intriguing - something that was quite small in size, but something that ended up making a big impact on me.

It was an animal that caught my eye as it high-stepped into the hotel lobby, tethered to a crimson leash that was attached to the wrist of a well-dressed middle-aged man. Deeply dark and steel grey in colour, its coat was so shiny that the light reflecting off it gave a metallic appearance. The little enchanter looked like a seal or an otter, but with long thin legs on which it pranced to the front desk with its head held high. Its long slim neck was adorned with a ruby red collar that accentuated its regal appearance and air of belonging.

It was quite simply the most exquisite creature I had ever seen. So exquisite in fact, that it was unclear to me at first whether it was even a dog.

I casually approached the owner. Well, I thought I was being casual, but it was probably pretty obvious to him that I had been moving all around the hotel lobby to get a better look at his glorious canine companion. I bet he was used to it though. With a dog like that trotting beside him, I am sure that he was stopped everywhere he went.

The well-groomed gentleman, whom I took to be a lawyer checking into the conference, told me that his dog was an Italian greyhound named Crumpet. I had seen greyhounds before, but never the much-miniaturized version. I asked if I could pet her and he said yes.

As I knelt down and held my hand out for her to sniff, Crumpet stood as erect and still as a statue. She didn't turn her head to sniff my hand. She didn't wag her tail, not even a little bit. In fact, the animal barely even acknowledged that I was kneeling beside her. She was the most dignified dog that I had ever met.

Crumpet's owner told me that she was odourless, very quiet in the house, and that yes, she was always this calm. After a few seconds of stroking her velvet fur, I thanked him and begrudgingly dragged myself away so that he could finish checking in.

Back on my lobby chesterfield I watched the distinguished gentleman in his cashmere coat as he headed towards the elevator, flanked on one side by the bellhop wheeling a brass birdcage-shaped luggage cart, and on the other by the charcoal nymph-dog that was moving in such a way that it reminded me of a racehorse being led to the starting gate of the Kentucky Derby. They disappeared into the elevator and I didn't see them again, though I ended up thinking about that dog constantly, so much so, that it distracted me from learning about mundane topics like "The Implied Undertaking Rule."

It didn't end when I got home, where I envisioned the presence of an Italian greyhound in my house. In the living room, I pictured her curled up on the sofa between us. In my study, I imagined her keeping me company on a fur-lined dog bed. Meeting that pint-sized pixie stirred something up inside of me that had lain dormant for years – the desire to own a dog. But while my childhood obsession had been abruptly reignited, my childhood tastes had changed. I was no longer that small-town girl who would have been happy with just any dog. The dog that I now dreamed about owning was a fancy one, just like Crumpet. The dog that I was picturing myself with was one fit for a lawyer; which of course meant a dog that came with a pedigree.

4

GOLDILOCKS GOES DOG SHOPPING

Some of Tim's fellow golf course superintendents had dogs that went to work with them. They had Labrador retrievers, border collies, and other outdoorsy breeds that fit their masculine self-image. This is why I fully expected to get some resistance when I revealed that the only type of dog I was truly considering was the kind I had met at the Chateau Montebello – an elegant little soul that wouldn't compromise our pristine house with its dogginess.

When I mentioned to Tim that I wanted an Italian greyhound, he was surprisingly enthusiastic. Confident in his masculinity, Tim didn't require a rugged type of dog to portray his manliness. He was just happy that I finally wanted a dog.

All of a sudden, I was ridiculously excited. Now it was real. I was finally going to have my own dog. I couldn't wait to start buying all the canine haberdashery: beautiful leashes, colourful collars and a regal dog bed for my new fancy friend. But, before I allowed myself to do any of this, I embarked on some online research to discover everything there was to know about the Italian greyhound breed. What I found out stopped me in my tracks.

It only took about five minutes of Internet searching to find out that fragility was the price that many Italian greyhounds pay for their sleek streamlined beauty. Websites like Wikipedia outlined how these slender dogs were quite prone to leg breaks. I checked a few online forums and was horrified to read the stories about snapped front legs and how expensive it was to repair them. I had never known a dog with a broken leg, but I did know that it was a situation that I didn't want to risk dealing with.

I was disappointed, but since I now had my heart set on getting a puppy, I wasn't giving up. I went back to the drawing board, determined to find another breed that would suit us. This time though, I imbued my mission with the same meticulousness I used when researching for a case. I bought dog magazines. I watched the Westminster Dog Show on television. I asked everyone I knew that had a dog about theirs. I even stopped people on the street to canvas them and pet their dogs. I quickly discovered that every single dog owner considered the breed they owned to be the zenith of canine excellence. Yet none of these breeds appealed to me. While I liked most of the dogs I met, there weren't any that captured my heart the way that the polite, refined dog in Quebec had. I still wanted a Crumpet.

I went back to searching the Internet again to see if I could find a breed similar to the Italian greyhound. I'm glad I did because it led me to discover the type of dog I knew I should be looking for. There was a whole group of elegant dogs called sighthounds. Also called gazehounds, they were said to be some of the most ancient breeds in the world. I recognized their physical traits from images in artwork and on tapestries: deep chests, slim waists, tall slender legs and long necks that taper to skinny pointed heads. Sighthounds were associated with the aristocracy because historically only nobility was allowed to own them.

Then it hit me. I remembered the circus borzoi from all those years back that I had fallen in love with. They were sighthounds! Tim was intrigued and seemed agreeable. That is, until he did his own research and found out that borzoi stand about six feet tall on their hind legs; tall enough to steal food off the top of the refrigerator. He liked how they looked, but he didn't like how big they were. While I was dreaming about how amazing it would be to walk one of those regal dogs around my neighbourhood, Tim was thinking about practical things, like how would we fit one in my small car, and how big was their poop?

Borzoi were out. But my heart was still set on sighthounds. I really liked the idea of adopting a retired racing Greyhound, after hearing that there one living in my neighbourhood. I contacted the owners and we arranged to meet in the park. As I saw them approaching from a distance, I could tell that something wasn't right. Their dog seemed to be limping. As it got closer, I noticed it was actually hobbling. On three legs!

The owners told us that greyhounds were prone to osteosarcoma, a type of bone cancer, which was the reason that their dog was a "tri-pawd." As soon as I got home, I found out that they were right. The National Greyhound Adoption Program (NGAP) website stated:

No one is perfect. Greyhounds, however, come pretty close. They are beautiful, elegant and gentle. They are the closest things to a perfect dog. Unfortunately, their ability to develop bone *cancer transcends that of almost all other breeds of dog. Osteosarcoma, or 'bone cancer', is an aggressive, life shortening cancer. There are options, but sadly, they often carry a poor prognosis and can be very expensive - think $5,000 to $15,000.*

An amputated leg was not something that I felt I could live with. Not to mention the $5,000 to $15,000 vet bill. I knew myself well enough to know that watching a noble creature like a greyhound hobble around on three legs would be unbearable for me. I scratched another sighthound off our list.

The next breed I looked into was the Scottish deerhound. I had seen one in the movie "Out of Africa" years earlier and always remembered the dignified charcoal-coloured dog with the wiry coat that belonged to the Baroness Blixen. The deerhound was a giant breed like the borzoi, but that wasn't why it was eliminated from consideration. I read that they were extremely prone to a life-threatening digestive syndrome called bloat, and that an alarming number of them die relatively young of cancer and heart disease.

I then looked up health information on a smaller sighthound breed, the saluki, and read articles that indicated the primary concern in this breed was their heart. Two different heart diseases were noted to occur in salukis. Heart cancer (cardiac hemangiosarcoma) was also said to be more common in salukis than in other breeds.

I was beginning to lose hope. I knew that just like people, there were health issues that could crop up in any individual dog at any time, but we wanted our new puppy to have the healthiest genetic background possible. I was starting to wonder if there was ever going to be a sighthound breed that didn't come with a lot of baggage in terms of health risks.

Just when I was almost ready to give up, I stumbled upon the description of a breed that ticked all of the boxes and didn't raise any red flags in terms of health risk deal-breakers. It wasn't listed in my Encyclopedia of Dog Breeds. I had never seen one while watching the Westminster Dog Show on television, or in any dog magazines. In fact, if it wasn't for the Internet, I doubt I would have discovered it at all.

The silken windhound was said to be a rare breed of dog, similar to a greyhound but smaller in size, with a long silky coat. Like greyhounds, they were born to run, but tended to be quiet when indoors. Essentially, they appeared to be a miniature version of the borzoi breed that I had fallen in love with so many years earlier.

The more I read, the better the news got. The silken windhound was touted as having exceptionally good health and a very long life. The website of the "International Silken Windhound Society" stated: "Typically, silken windhounds live very healthy, active lives.

While most live into their late teens, the oldest known silken windhound lived a few months past her 20th birthday."

Wow, a dog that lived to be over 20 years old? I had never even heard of such a thing. Tim's beagle lived to 14, which I considered to be an exceptionally long life for a dog; and she was pretty frail by the time she reached that age. Other websites about the silken windhound breed boasted similar endorsements. I couldn't find a bad review.

It all sounded a little too good to be true. But I wanted to believe it. Surely an expensive purebred dog from health-tested parents of a rare breed should be as healthy and long-lived as promised? We certainly thought so. And as such, our big decision had been made, based only on what we had read online.

We were going to get a rare, exotic, pedigree dog... a dog that would be free of health problems that might live for 20 years. We were going to get a silken windhound. What we didn't yet realize was just how difficult it was going to be to find one.

5

GLAMOUR IN THE GREAT WHITE NORTH

W HEN WE STARTED SHOPPING for a silken windhound, there was only one breeder listed in all of Canada. Located somewhere "up north," the kennel was called "Aquilo Silken Windhounds."

The website didn't offer any specific information about where exactly up north the kennel was, but it featured gorgeous professional-looking photographs, as well as a four-minute YouTube video curated to the Enya song "Lazy Days." The little movie was a marketing masterpiece, with depictions of otherworldly dogs set to mystical music. The mini-motion-picture included images of elegant hounds reposed on furniture, and video clips of the same dogs flying through the air at dog-racing events. There were also clips of the slender silky-coated dogs zipping through the woods in autumn, looking like magical creatures from a fairy tale.

The most exciting part of the Aquilo website was the one-line notification on the homepage stating that puppies were expected. I started checking the website daily for any news of puppies, and in about a month's time, there was a litter announcement and photos of the pups. There were seven of them. All but one were female. The litter was called "The Boreal Forest Litter."

I learned to unravel what had previously been a mystery regarding the crazy long pure-bred dog names that I noticed while watching the Westminster Dog Show. I discovered that some breeders use letters of the alphabet to name a litter, but most attach a theme and name the puppies according to that theme. All of the pups in the silken windhound litter had names that matched the "Boreal Forest" theme: Water Lily, Wild Clover, Silver Willow, Aurora Borealis, Autumn Beech, Chandos Lake, and Maple Breeze.

In the purebred dog world, each individual dog has both a registered name and a call name. The names of the puppies on the Aquilo website were their registered names. A call name is the unofficial name for the dog to be used on an everyday basis.

Pedigrees, registered names...all of this was pretty exciting stuff, and man, it sounded important. But it also sounded expensive. The price of the puppies was not mentioned on the Aquilo website. In fact, the price of silken windhounds wasn't mentioned anywhere on any of the websites that I visited. We had no idea if getting one would cost us $500 or $5000. The closest I came to finding a price was a statement from a breeder that the cost of a puppy was dependent on a number of things, and "they are worth paying for."

Even though we were dying to know how much one of these rare puppies might cost us, we weren't about to scuttle our chances of obtaining one by making any uncouth inquiries about price right off the bat. We decided instead to just let the breeder know that we would like to buy one of the puppies listed on the website. In order to do this, I had to fill out a form on the Aquilo website. There was no other contact information or method of reaching out to the kennel owners other than the form itself.

Kim, the breeder, emailed me back directly, advising that all of the puppies were already spoken for, but that we could add our names to the wait list for the next litter. I felt crushed. We finally found the perfect dog but now we couldn't get one.

I wrote Kim back, asking to be put on the waiting list for the next litter. She replied that that it would be a few years before she had puppies available again. I couldn't believe there was a waiting list for puppies that wouldn't be born for several years?

Tim and I talked it over and decided to wait. From that point on, I did no further research regarding dog breeds. We decided that the silken windhound was the breed for us, and since the Aquilo kennel was the only game in town, we would wait a few years for one of their rare and sought-after puppies.

Once again, Tim offered some practical advice. Perhaps we should drive to Kim's kennel and meet her dogs and the puppies so we would know exactly what we were waiting for.

When I emailed Kim to find out if this was possible, she responded, "Hi Michelle, nice to hear from you! I am working through details with a potential owner with the last little girl. She may come available if that home doesn't work out." And just like that, we were back in the silken windhound game!

Over the next few days, Kim the breeder wasn't offering up any further details about what was happening with the potential owner of the last puppy, or how likely it was that "the deal" might fall through. She did, however, ask us to fill out her puppy questionnaire, which she sent to me by email.

A puppy questionnaire is basically an electronic interview. I had seen similar forms on most of the silken windhound kennel websites and it appeared to me that all of the breeders were using the same template.

The questionnaire had the usual and understandable questions about where we lived and what kind of home we would provide for the puppy. But it also had questions like "Please indicate why you are interested in acquiring a silken windhound" - one of those open-ended questions that reminded me of writing an essay for an English exam, where the so-called "right" answer was completely subjective. What if I said the wrong thing?

We were also required to list the number of full-time residents in the household (ages, occupations, and the number of hours each spends at home on an average day), as well as any guests that would be visiting with frequency, and a description of their interactions with the household. A minimum of two personal references as well as a veterinary reference was required.

For the sake of the puppies, I was impressed with this in-depth screening tool, but it seemed overly intrusive to me, so instead of filling it out I sent a detailed email to Kim, telling her all about our lives and how a silken windhound would fit into it.

Hearing nothing back for a few days, I followed up, asking Kim if she had received my email. When she answered, she let me know that she had not yet been in touch with the remaining puppy buyer. I was dying. We knew we might potentially be getting one of the puppies, but which one? How much would it cost? The whole process had been so mysterious. I didn't want to sound like I was "hounding" her, but I was desperate for more information, so I sent her another email (but still didn't dare ask anything about the price for a pup).

Kim wrote back advising that "Aquilo Maple Breeze" was the puppy that "might" become available. The "expert" that had been flown in from the United States to evaluate the pups determined that Maple should go to a "show or breeding" home, however the puppy had developed an outie belly button, so now a pet home was preferred. Kim also wrote that Maple was "a balanced girl, beautiful expression, beautiful mover" and that she was going to grow up to be a "very elegant sighthound."

From the photographs on the website, I could see that Maple was a white dog with a few reddish/brown spots on her back and a brown mask over her face. Kim described her as "extreme white with brindle spots." The puppy, at eight, ten and twelve weeks old, was posed in what breeders call a stack, meaning that she was manipulated into standing still to be examined by a judge and/or photographed.

Maple looked unhappy in the photos. I couldn't blame her. I was used to seeing photographs of puppies playing and horsing around, not forced to pose standing still on a table. The terms Kim used to describe Maple were elusive to me, other than the elegant part, which of course I understood. What the heck did an "outie" belly button have to do with showing or breeding?

I wanted to pick up the phone and call, but I still didn't have a telephone number or any other contact information for Kim, other than her email address. Every time I tried to get some answers in this process, I only ended up with more questions. I emailed back and finally just directly asked if we were being considered.

Kim answered, "If you would still like, I can put your family down as next in line for Maple - I should know by the end of this weekend if she will be available."

I immediately answered yes, and indicated that either way we would like to visit the Aquilo kennel to meet Kim's dogs and the puppies, who were now already over three months old. Everyone I knew had picked up their puppies when they were around eight weeks old, though I suppose they weren't getting a rare exotic breed like we were (hopefully?) going to get.

I was in agony with all of the unanswered questions, and couldn't help myself from sending yet another email. Being a lawyer, of course I asked if there was a contract that I could review prior to our meeting, thinking that the contract may reveal the price of the puppy without me having to ask directly.

Once I reviewed the contract I had even more questions. Maple was being sold as a "companion" and therefore spaying was required. This was fine with us, as we had planned to do that anyway. But why did we have to wait until she was 18 months old? All the dogs that I knew were spayed much earlier than that. I had other questions. Were the pups house trained yet? And what about this "outie" belly button – did it have any health implications?

I made more inquiries, but still didn't ask about price, even though we were starting to panic a bit about what it might be.

Kim wrote back that the outie belly button was called an umbilical hernia and it wasn't a health concern, however it was an inherited condition, so Maple wasn't suitable for breeding. She also said that the pups were "somewhat" housebroken. Thankfully, she also agreed that we could visit the Aquilo kennel to meet the dogs and the puppies.

It felt like we were going on vacation. Only better. The Aquilo kennel was located in the heart of Ontario's iconic cottage country. We travelled the night before and stayed in a hotel in the closest city, which was still an hour's drive from Kim's place.

Despite the uncertainty, I was excited and kept telling myself that it was a treat to be away on a little adventure, even if the puppy didn't come home with us. Though I do have to admit that by this time I really had my heart set on Maple being ours. I was already picturing her in our house. And I loved her name. Maple. It was so Canadian.

I woke up early on the morning of our visit, feeling strangely nervous, almost as if I were going to a job interview. The further north we drove, the more dramatic the landscape looked. The trees were mostly cedars and hemlock, and there were massive boulders made of pink granite, some so large that the road was cut straight through them. The rugged beauty of the Canadian Shield was on full display, yet we still were unable to talk about anything else other than Maple. Tim turned the radio off as we got close to our destination so he could pay attention to the directions, which intensified my nervousness.

When we saw the rural marker with the house number sign, he slowed down to a crawl before turning left to enter a gravel driveway that went up a curvy hill to a house that was barely visible from the road.

As we approached the house, there were no signs of any dogs. I guess I was expecting dog runs and kennels, but this just looked like an ordinary, fairly new house in the country. We figured the dogs must be inside, which I thought was a good sign.

We got out of Tim's truck and knocked on the front door. Surprisingly, there was no barking in response to our knocks.

Kim answered the door with a huge smile on her face. Tall and slender with medium length curly brown hair and dimples, she looked to be about my age. She welcomed us into a rustic open concept house, where we immediately spotted two of the skinniest dogs that I had ever seen lying on a sofa and chair respectively. I lost my breath, but in a good way.

Kim introduced us to her dogs, Bacardi and Bella, prior to introducing us to her two young sons and her husband. Bacardi, who I knew from the website to be the mother of the puppies, eventually got down from the chair she was draped over, stretching luxuriously before calmly and slowly sauntering over to greet us.

I was taken aback at how small she was. She looked so much bigger in the photographs on the website. She was almost two dimensional, like an angelfish, with a long swan-like neck. I reached out to pet her, finding that she had the silkiest soft fur I had ever felt, which hung in tapers from her ears, the back of her legs and her tail. She was magnificent.

I stroked Bacardi's beautiful coat while we all chatted casually for about five minutes or so. Kim looked at me, smiled and said, "Do you want to meet the puppies?"

We nodded enthusiastically and she walked across the living room, to the edge of the kitchen, where she opened a gate at the top of a set of stairs that led to the basement. She whistled and called out "puppy puppy puppy" in a high-pitched voice. Seconds later, five puppies came bounding up the stairs. She told us that two of the pups had already gone to their new homes in the United States.

The baby silken windhounds were the most exotic looking puppies that I had ever seen, with legs looking much too long for the size of their bodies, and long slender pointy noses to match their legs. They had short but dense soft coats that felt like bunny fur. Their tails were so long they touched the ground but they weren't feathered with hair like the adult version, making them appear even longer.

It was quite something to have them all whipping around us in the living room. I felt like I was standing in water with a bunch of fish swirling around my legs. I was in heaven.

Bacardi and her puppies then followed us down the stairs, through a basement walkout door to a large fenced back yard where there was evidence of dog occupation in the form of dug holes and scattered dog toys. Once outside, the puppies were no longer interested in interacting with us. They all went off on their own in the yard to play and then eventually curled up next to one another in the dirt against the house, while Tim and I talked to Kim and her husband David.

Though we were talking mostly about the dogs, we found out that we had much in common with the couple, who were the country version of ourselves. If we had met under different circumstances, and lived closer, I just knew that we would be good friends.

After an hour or so, we said awkward good-byes and headed home, without a puppy, and without any more information about Maple's availability or the price.

"Enough is enough," Tim said, so the following day I sent an email to Kim, candidly asking if Maple was available, if we could have her, and what the price was. She replied almost immediately. Yes, we could have Maple, and the price was $1000 for a "companion" puppy, which I now know means pet quality as opposed to show/breeding quality. The purchase price had been reduced on account of the genetic defect — outie belly-button which would need to be surgically repaired. It was so much lower than we expected.

Through the quickest return email ever, I committed to buy Aquilo Maple Breeze. It was a done deal. We had secured our puppy. I was finally going to have a dog to call my own. My childhood dream was finally coming true, and I couldn't wait for our adventure into the purebred dog world to begin.

6

THE HONEYMOON PHASE

IN TYPICAL TYPE A fashion, I had everything ready before the puppy came home. Our family room featured a giant dog bed from Costco, a raised food and water dish, and a toy box full of rubber squeakies, ropes, and balls. The excitement of planning for a puppy had superseded my previous resistance to dog paraphernalia cluttering up my organized house. I couldn't wait for Maple to arrive.

Kim suggested that we should use a crate at night and for training. While I hated the idea, in the interest of keeping my new puppy safe and preventing my house from being destroyed, I bought the biggest one I could find. And man was it hideous – a giant cream-coloured plastic monstrosity. I didn't want the behemoth in my main living area, so I had Tim carry it upstairs and set it up in our bedroom.

It was a weekday when we made the eight-hour round trip to pick up our new family member. When we arrived, Kim insisted that we sit down to a spaghetti dinner with her family. It felt like we were visiting relatives. After dinner, while still sitting at the dining room table, we signed the contract and gave Kim our money, which felt weirdly transactional under the circumstances.

We were in a hurry to get back on the road, since we had a long drive ahead of us and Tim had to get up at the crack of dawn for work the following day. As we headed out the door with Maple cradled in Tim's arms, I looked over at Bacardi, the mother dog, but she didn't seem to give a care that we were taking her puppy away. Kim, on the other hand, was visibly upset, tearing up as we loaded Maple into our vehicle.

Kim's whole family lined up and glumly waved good-bye as we pulled out of the driveway. I never envisioned that getting a dog from a breeder would be like this - it felt so personal.

Maple, the leggy pup, was unsteady on her feet in the truck, but eventually curled up on my lap, looking more like a deer fawn than a dog. She was eerily silent, with no whimpering or whining. She vomited about 15 minutes into the drive and then hardly moved for the remainder of the trip, though it was clear that she was not content. Wide-eyed and occasionally trembling, she stared straight ahead at the dashboard of the truck, and didn't respond to our puppy talk or head pets.

I thought about how it must feel to be kidnapped by strangers and taken away from the only home she had ever known. This was a happy day for us, but a terrifying one for her. I assumed she would have greeted us with love and somehow knew that we were her new family. I hadn't factored in the fear she would experience as a result of being torn away from her "pack" for the first time. I wasn't mentally prepared for such an extremely sensitive sighthound. In all of my daydreaming about bringing home my first puppy, I hadn't considered the feelings of the dog. My daydream had been all about my own feelings.

Once home, I took Maple out of the vehicle and put her down on the front lawn so she could do her business. I had planned to take her for a short walk on her beautiful new red leather leash, but it became clear that Maple didn't know how to walk on a leash, and even if she did, she was too nervous to walk around at all. It was late, so we went inside, unpacked and got ready for bed.

I was pleasantly surprised that Maple didn't make any fuss about being placed into her crate, where she slept through the night without making a peep.

The next morning, after Tim left for work, I rolled over in bed to look at my new puppy. Big brown doe eyes were staring back at me. She looked impossibly vulnerable in her plastic prison, but we had agreed that our new dog wouldn't be allowed on any furniture, and certainly not on the bed. I leaned over and opened the door to the crate so I could pet her. In one fluid motion, Maple freed herself from the cage, slid up onto the bed, and moved in beside me under the covers, settling into the nook between my armpit and my waist. She then promptly fell asleep.

I was afraid to move, watching her chest moving up and down as I stroked her velvet fur. Then it happened. My heart melted. It had only been a matter of hours since she came home, but I already knew that my life had changed; that I would do anything to make this sensitive creature feel happy and loved. There was no way I was going to deny her the comfort of sleeping on the bed from now on, or on any piece of furniture for that matter. That evening, I had Tim move the crate into the basement.

Those first few months with Maple were wonderful. She was a young pup with an old soul. In the house she was serene, almost lazy. She never barked. She didn't even move around much, other than to commute from sofa to chair to bed, where she would blissfully sprawl out, and remain peacefully ornamental for hours on end.

She was the cleanest dog I had ever met. Her satin hair-like coat was always pristine, even without baths or brushing. Having no undercoat, she was almost odourless except when wet, and even then, her coat smelled pleasant, like wool sweaters. She never once had an accident in the house. Not one. In fact, she wouldn't even relieve herself in our small yard, always waiting until she was at least ten minutes away to "do her business." It felt like we had won the dog lottery.

In stark contrast to her inside demeanor, when Maple was loose outside, she behaved like a true canine athlete. She was so fast! It was a sight to behold watching her run free. With all four feet off the ground, it sometimes appeared as if she were flying. At mid-gallop, she looked just like the dog depicted on the side of the greyhound bus.

True to her sighthound nature, Maple was prey driven and would chase anything that moved. She was a silent serial killer, which made her a great goose-chaser at Tim's golf course. Much to my animal-loving horror, she also quickly grew into a skilled huntress of squirrels and other small wild creatures.

Walking Maple on a leash was like walking around with a celebrity. Everyone wanted to meet her. People would even stop their cars to comment on how beautiful she was, often mistaking her for a Russian wolfhound, an Afghan hound or a saluki. We were proud to tell everyone we met that she was a rare breed. Nobody had ever heard of a silken windhound. We were sometimes asked if she was a rescue, and there was always a look of disappointment on the faces of those who asked when we admitted that we had purchased her from a breeder.

Not everyone appreciated Maple's brand of canine beauty, though. There were many who thought that she looked weird. We had to endure people calling her the aardvark, Santa's Little Helper from the Simpsons, and even the flamingo with fur. And then there was the corny breed's name, silken windhound, which didn't help matters. One of our neighbours nicknamed her "the silken wind chime." Another referred to her as a Disney princess pony. My brothers often said to me "why don't you get a real dog?"

Most people were taken aback by her cat-like personality. Maple had a refined sense of manners. She was never pushy with people or other dogs. I loved this trait, but her aloofness didn't appeal to everyone. She never sought affection and didn't greet anyone, including us, with a tail wag or dog kisses. In fact, she never wagged her tail at all. When we would arrive home after a long day, she didn't even rise to greet us. The best Maple would do for a stranger was to stand still and allow them to pet her.

I thought she was elegant. Some people we met thought she was a snob. One of our good friends was convinced that she was deaf because she didn't acknowledge him when he called her name or whistled at her. She was like no dog I had ever met. And I loved her intensely. Tim did too.

Despite the detractors, we were proud, and I must say a bit smug about our rare pure-bred. It was easy to take a million pictures of her, and I lost some Facebook friends from over-posting them. I made a new page and only friended "dog people" who would appreciate frequent photographs and updates of my beautiful hound. I began collecting elegant velvet-lined martingale collars to accentuate her artistic beauty in the photographs.

We took Maple everywhere. At extended family gatherings our adult siblings would bring their kids. We always brought Maple. This worked out just fine when we went to events at Tim's parents' farm, but when we went to my family parties, my poor brother (and his son) always had to load up on allergy medication. This didn't stop us.

We even took Maple with us on vacation. A few months after we brought her home, we took her to my conference at the Chateau Montebello in Quebec, where she looked as regal, maybe even more so than that Italian greyhound that we had seen there years prior.

Our closest friends and family scoffed at how we had become so wrapped up in having a dog, yet, I am convinced that my relationship with Maple made me a better person. Practising law had hardened me emotionally, and loving Maple softened me back up. The selfless love that I felt for her shifted my focus from the material trappings of my professional life to the simple daily pleasures that came along with owning a dog. I spent way more time outside. I got a lot more exercise. I even talked to my neighbours – or at least the ones who were also out walking their dogs several times a day. Tim and I talked more too, sharing stories about what Maple did when the other wasn't around to witness it in person.

I hesitate to admit that right from the get go, even though we obviously knew she was a dog, we treated Maple like our child, and even though I never wanted to have kids, I quite naturally fell into the role of being a mother to this dog.

I began to gauge my own happiness on how happy Maple was. If she had a good time, then I had a good time. It brought me joy to attend an event where she was welcome and enjoying herself too. If we had to leave her at home, I didn't have as much fun. Before getting a dog, I was concerned about being tied down, but planning my day-to-day life around Maple felt more like a privilege than a chore. I adored everything about her, which reinforced my belief that all the research we did before choosing a dog breed had paid off. Maple was truly turning out to be our perfect dog.

7

FABLE ... A CAUTIONARY TALE

THE DAILY HIKING RITUAL we put into practice soon after bringing Maple home was a real game changer for all of us. In fact, of all the changes to our lives that happened as a result of getting a dog, this activity was unparalleled in its impact.

Located exactly half way between our respective workplaces, The Royal Botanical Gardens (RBG) turned out to be the perfect place to meet up after work. For an annual fee we gained access to miles and miles of trails that weaved through forests, open fields, and even shore lines. We never missed a day, rain or shine. Maple adored the long hikes and so did we. The simple act of setting aside this sacred time ended up deepening our own relationship by providing us with lots of opportunities to really talk to each other without the usual distractions of city life.

The RBG trails were never busy and because they were quite far from the road, we felt comfortable letting Maple be off leash there. She loved to run, and we loved watching her run: through creeks, over logs, through fields and swamps. Being free also gave her a chance to "do her business" in private, which was obviously the way she preferred, given that she was still refusing to relieve herself in our yard and even hesitated to do so while being walked on a leash.

The only downside to our daily hikes was the discovery that other dogs just didn't like Maple. Whenever we encountered another hiker with an off-leash dog, we would hear the dreaded words bellowed out, "he's friendly," followed by a dog barreling towards us. It would beeline for Maple, stiffen up, raise its hackles and then pummel her. Maple never fought back, so we often had to yell at or even kick the other dog, which inevitably caused problems between us and the other dog's owner.

I felt sorry for Maple that she had no friends. When I mentioned this to Kim on one of our regular phone chats, she told me it was a sighthound thing. She suggested that Maple would undoubtedly prefer the company of another sighthound, and she told me about a woman named Heather who lived in Hamilton that had a young silken windhound that might be a good playmate for Maple.

What? There was another silken windhound that lived so close to us? I was shocked. There were only a few silken windhounds in all of Canada at that time, and most of them were at Kim's kennel. Excited for Maple to have a new friend, I wasted no time in getting in touch with Heather and making arrangements to meet up at the RBG to go on a hike with our dogs.

It wasn't difficult to locate Heather's vehicle as I drove into the RBG parking lot that early autumn day. Her burgundy minivan had running greyhound dog decals on the windows. She waved at me from inside the van as I pulled my Smart Car into the adjacent parking spot. Before I had my door all the way open, Maple jumped over my lap and was out of the car with her nose to the ground. She ran right past Heather, who was holding out her hand for Maple to sniff. I apologized but Heather brushed it off, obviously used to the quirky sighthound personality.

Heather looked to be in her late twenties or early thirties. Her long blonde hair was pulled back in a tight ponytail which was sticking out of a black baseball cap. She was outfitted in several layers of sporty outdoor clothing and sturdy low-cut hiking boots. I noticed right away she had a lot of dog paraphernalia on her: a fanny-pack belted to her waist, a leash slung over her shoulder, a collapsible dog water bowl clipped to her belt, and a holster that held a bottle of water. Heather was equipped to scale a mountain. I on the other hand, was wearing a skort, a hoodie and flimsy running shoes.

I followed Heather to the back of her van; super excited to meet her silken windhound. Before she opened up the hatchback, she told me she was married but had no kids. She drove a minivan for the sole purpose of transporting her dogs. As the van's back door lifted, I saw two wire dog crates mounted permanently on wooden frames. There were blankets and what appeared to be a dog first aid kit tucked underneath them.

"Wow," I said as she proudly pointed to the special fans and water dishes attached to the sides of the crates. Each one had a pouch secured to the front with canine photo ID and a wad of paperwork folded behind it.

"I love this," I said, thinking how nice it would be to transport Maple this way. I wondered why there were two crates when there was only one dog?

Heather opened a safety clip and out jumped a slighter, black-coloured version of Maple. The dog shook itself off, and then sat obediently at Heather's side, waiting for a treat to be popped into his mouth.

The elegant black dog was outfitted in a similar style to Heather, with several layers of functional dog apparel. A wide durable collar held multiple tags and a bell, while the matching lime green working vest had zipped compartments and a handle on top. I approached the little hound to say hello, and was greeted calmly with a pointy nose pushed gently into my hand. He remained in a seated position.

Heather then surprised me by saying, "My silken windhound is at home recovering from a broken leg."

I must have looked confused, so she quickly added, "This is Puzzle. He's a longhaired whippet."

I had never heard of a longhaired whippet, and told her so. I would have sworn that the dog sitting in front of me was a silken windhound, if I hadn't been told otherwise.

At this point, Maple finally clued in that there was another dog and she cantered over to investigate. Puzzle remained obediently sitting beside Heather, looking up at her while Maple sniffed around. I was impressed. She pulled a treat from her belt bag, ordering Maple to sit, which surprisingly, she did. She then pulled out another one out and slid it into Puzzle's mouth, before giving a command that released both dogs from their seated positions so we could begin our hike.

"Let's go," Heather ordered, and both dogs bounded off ahead of us, surprisingly showing absolutely no interest in one another.

As we began walking, Heather told me that she had been involved in the organized dog world for almost 20 years, through greyhound rescue and dog sports like obedience, rally, and agility. Dogs were her passion. She was a dog trainer by night and an animal control officer with the local municipality during the day.

Puzzle remained obediently close to Heather as we walked. Maple, on the other hand, was off doing her own thing, and for the first time, I felt somewhat embarrassed by her lack of training. Heather proudly told me that the longhaired whippet was also a rare breed.

"How did you end up with two rare breeds?" I asked.

"It all started with Puzzle," she replied, and then she began telling me the story of how she and her husband ended up owning a longhaired whippet. Heather loved sighthounds and she loved dog sports. She discovered long haired whippets at The Toronto Sportsman

Show, and brought one home soon after meeting some. Unfortunately, Puzzle soon developed a number of serious health issues, including irritable bowel disease and an eye problem that would eventually lead to his blindness.

Heather told me that she loved the longhaired whippet breed, but Puzzle's health problems were genetic, so she turned to the Internet to find another similar but healthier dog that she could do sports with. Like us, she was enticed into getting a silken windhound after reading about their exceptional good health on the Internet. Kim, the only Canadian breeder, had no puppies available yet, so Heather found a breeder in the United States who matched up with her "heart" dog.

Fable the silken windhound was petite, spirited, loving and easy to train. She excelled in sports and was very fast. Until she broke her leg.

"So did it happen when you were racing her?" I asked, figuring the horrible injury must have happened as a result of some extreme sporting event.

"No. This is actually her second leg break," she said. "It's a long story. Are you sure you want to hear it?"

"Yes!" I replied, dying to know all the details about a dog I would never meet.

As we kept walking and talking, I learned that Fable had broken the same leg twice before she was even two years of age. The first accident happened when she was a year old, while running in a park.

"It wasn't just a crack – the two bones in her foreleg were broken in half," Heather said, matter- of-factly.

"Holy crap. Did she fall in a hole?" I asked.

"No. I thought that at the time, but when I went back to where it happened, I couldn't find anything that could have caused it."

Heather went on to tell me about how the emergency veterinarian referred Fable to the highly regarded Ontario Veterinary College where a Board-Certified orthopedic surgeon rebuilt the bone, using a metal plate to hold it in place, with nine screws attaching it. I winced at the thought. Heather explained that it took about five months for Fable's first leg break to fully heal, and then a second surgery was needed to remove the metal from her leg.

Heather didn't want to give up her dream of participating in dog sports with Fable, so she consulted one of the best dog rehabilitation specialists in Canada - a team veterinarian for the Canadian World Agility Team. This specialist supervised a program that included underwater treadmill, cold laser, and massage.

But despite the intensive and expensive rehabilitation, approximately two months after the hardware removal surgery, Fable broke the same leg again, this time while being walked on a short leash on a sidewalk while wearing a support splint. It happened when she reared up on her back legs after being startled by a bee. She was now in her second round of physiotherapy.

"Wow, that must be expensive," I said, knowing how much human physiotherapy costs, given that most of the car accident victims in my files had to have it.

"Yep. $400 a month and I have to drive an hour each way to Guelph."

"Oh man, that sucks," I said, not knowing what else to say.

"Yep. It really sucks. We're in debt because of it."

"Do you have insurance?"

"Sadly, no. It was too late to get it with Puzzle because he was already sick. With Fable, we assumed she wouldn't need it, given all the good reviews about how healthy silken windhounds are."

We had arrived back at the parking lot, and Puzzle was already sitting behind Heather's van, waiting obediently for a drink of water and a treat. Heather offered both to Maple too, which, once again made me feel like a bad dog mother.

We said our good-byes as we loaded our respective hounds into our respective vehicles, and made vague promises to meet up again.

As soon as we were back on the road, I looked over at Maple and said, "I'm soooo glad you're healthy." Seemingly in response, she stood up and carefully placed one and then the other of her two long skinny front legs awkwardly on my right leg, causing me to press down a little harder on the gas pedal. She stretched her long neck across my line of vision and touched her nose to the driver's side window. Stupidly, and dangerously, I let her stand that way for the rest of the drive, craning my neck to see over her.

By the time I got home, despite all that I had just heard from Heather, I decided not to worry at all that something like that could ever happen to Maple. I told myself that Heather just had rotten luck, that's all. I still believed that Maple was the perfect dog. I still also believed that silken windhounds were the perfect breed. Little did I know that in thinking this way, I had unwittingly beckoned the fickle hand of fate.

8

REVERSAL OF FORTUNE

L IFE WITH OUR PERFECT dog just continued to get better and better. Until it didn't. A few weeks before Maple's second birthday, something happened that made us realize a harsh truth: that perfection is an illusion and that no living thing is immune from unpredictable misfortune.

It was Father's Day and my extended family had all gathered at my parents' house for an afternoon barbeque to celebrate. Even though the calendar said it was still spring, the weather was so warm that it already felt like summer. The trees were fully leafed and the lawn had been freshly cut and smelled amazing.

All of the adults were sitting around a patio table on the upper deck, talking loud enough to be heard over the happy noises the kids were making while playing a lively game of soccer on the lawn below.

As usual, we had Maple with us, and as usual she was snoozing peacefully in the shade on the comfy dog bed that we brought along for her.

I was feeling pretty relaxed as I slipped off my shoes and walked barefoot towards the house to begin bringing the food outside. I had barely gotten myself into the kitchen, and was just taking a plate of deviled eggs out of the fridge when my dad ran in and hollered for me to come outside because something was happening with "your dog."

To help you understand how I was feeling in that moment, I can tell you that my father doesn't run. Ever. He also doesn't yell. To have him doing both was shocking. To have him doing both in relation to Maple, who was now the centre of my life, caused my bones to turn to jelly.

My initial thought was that Maple had bitten one of the kids, and I immediately felt sick to my stomach. Dropping the plate of eggs on the counter, I ran outside.

Before I saw anything, I heard it - a noise that has been seared into my brain for life. There's a name for it in the dog world, or at least in the sighthound world. The "scream of death" sounds uncannily like a woman shrieking. To witness this primal, gut-wrenching cry coming out of a dog is a horrifying experience, yet, what I saw that day horrified me even more than what I heard.

Maple was writhing around on the lawn. Tim was kneeling beside her and everyone else was standing around them in a huddle, looking worried. There was no noise apart from the screaming. I thought Maple had been shot, which didn't make any sense, but what else could explain what was happening?

By the time I got down on the ground, I noticed there wasn't any blood. A broken back was the only thing that I could think of that could explain the noise and her behaviour. My heart, which was in my throat, was beating a million beats per minute, while everything else felt like it was happening in slow motion.

Tim was calmly telling Maple in a matter-of-fact voice that she was going to be okay, but even after her high-pitched screams had softened into a whimper, her eyes remained open so wide that the whites were showing. Her breathing was short and fast.

Tim's steady soothing words eventually consoled Maple to the point where he was able to examine her. He then managed to get her upright, which was how we realized that the injury was to her front right leg. She wasn't able to put any weight on it. In fact, she wasn't even able to stand up on her own without Tim steadying her.

It was at this point that everyone broke their silence and started talking about what happened in the moments before I made it outside. Maple had been seen bolting across the lawn in pursuit of a squirrel, which was not unusual. When she fell down suddenly and started screaming, everyone figured she must have stepped in a hole. In hearing this, I got up from my crouched position beside Maple and began walking around on the lawn to see if I could find a hole, or anything else that could have caused the accident. I found nothing but perfectly manicured grass. It just didn't make any sense.

By the time I got back to the group, Tim had scooped Maple up into his arms, and was carrying her towards his pick-up truck. I found my shoes, grabbed my purse, and hollered good-bye to everyone and then jogged to catch up with them.

I got in the vehicle first and as Tim carefully set Maple into my lap, I asked, "Where are we going?"

"She needs to see a vet."

"I know. But nothing's open; it's Sunday."

"There are emergency vets – google it."

As Tim began driving in the direction of home, I pulled out my phone and awkwardly, with my hands around Maple, used it to find the closest emergency clinic, which ended up being located in a strip mall about five minutes from our house. I had driven by it a million times without even knowing it was there.

The first thing we found out about emergency veterinary treatment is that the service carries a premium. Unlike at our usual vet, there is a "consultation and emergency fee" which had to be paid up front. After the receptionist charged our credit card, we were asked to sit in the waiting room with the other sick animals and their worried owners.

We didn't have to wait long before a technician took us to a small treatment room, where he took Maple's temperature and left us waiting almost half an hour to finally see the vet, who was middle aged, female, and in a hurry. She curtly requested that Maple be put up on the examination table without even introducing herself.

Tim gently placed Maple on the slippery stainless-steel table and held her steady while the unfriendly vet examined her leg. Before we had even finished explaining what happened, she abruptly and somewhat dismissively declared that the leg was not broken. She instructed us to see our regular vet first thing in the morning, and then she left the room. The vet tech escorted us back to the reception desk, where I paid the bill while Tim stood holding Maple in his arms.

As soon as we were back in our vehicle, Tim said, "I can't believe we just paid all that money for nothing."

"It's not for nothing. At least we know her leg isn't broken."

"Why couldn't she tell us what's wrong?"

"Maybe they're too busy with emergencies. Who knows. I just hope she's better by tomorrow and we won't have to take her to our vet."

"That ain't happening," he said.

The following morning, Maple let out a short high-pitched yelp when she tried to get up and once standing, she refused to put any weight on the bad leg. Despite my coaxing, she wouldn't even try to walk.

"How the hell are we going to get her to go to the bathroom?" I asked, as Tim carried her down the stairs. He didn't answer. He just headed straight out the front door and down the outside steps to the front lawn where he set Maple down on three legs.

I followed them outside in my pajamas and was standing on the porch, watching as Tim looked at Maple and sternly gave the order, "Do your business!"

I was fighting back tears as I watched Maple just standing there with her back all roached up, looking pathetically up at Tim. If she could talk, I'm sure she would have said, "I'm hurting Dad, please don't yell at me."

"Well, it looks like we're going to the vet," he said glumly.

Our regular vet was young, friendly and looked sporty with no make-up and her medium length dirty blonde hair pulled back in a loose ponytail. She wore a black long-sleeved t-shirt under her blue scrubs. We had only ever seen her for Maple's vaccinations over a year prior, but I could tell she remembered us, probably since Maple was the first silken windhound she had ever met. Maple was, after all, not a dog that could easily be forgotten.

"Hi, guys, I understand Maple has hurt her front leg. May I take a look?" she asked in a chipper voice as she entered the room. She moved toward Maple, who was standing on a blanket I had brought along with us, still not putting any weight on her right leg.

The young vet lowered herself to a kneeling position on the floor and placed her hands on Maple's back, sliding them slowly forward and then moving them down Maple's long skinny right leg, right to the toes, which she then splayed and examined individually. She held Maple's shoulder with one hand, and bent the sore leg at the knee, and then the wrist, all the while watching Maple for a reaction, which she failed to give. Maple didn't respond in any way, and just continued to stare straight ahead at the wall, looking uncomfortable.

The vet stood up and, much to our disappointment, said, "Well, I'm stumped."

I looked at Tim as he let out a big sigh.

She continued, "I can't tell what's hurt. I'd like to do radiographs - they are $200."

We both nodded in agreement, as she then candidly admitted she was not familiar with sighthound anatomy. "I'll need images of both legs for comparison."

"So, $400?" Tim said.

"Yes," she replied.

We agreed, not feeling like we had much of a choice, and then we were left alone in the examination room to wait. There was only one chair. I sat. Tim leaned against the drab peach-coloured wall. I tried to engage him in conversation, but he wasn't in a talking mood. He was anxious to get to work, and also, I think, concerned about how much our bill was going to be.

When the vet returned to the room, she told us she didn't see any obvious fractures on the x-rays. She explained, and not in a particularly confident way, that we were probably dealing with a soft tissue injury. She sent us home with drugs and instructions to restrict

Maple's activity while indoors and keep her leashed when outside. We were to return in a week if there was no improvement.

Tim was quiet all the way home. When I finally asked him what was wrong, all he said was, "Six hundred dollars. Really?"

"At least she doesn't have a broken leg," I replied, thinking of what Heather had gone through with Fable.

"Then why won't she use it?" he said, "I find it hard to believe that a sprain would cause so much drama. She can't even touch her foot to the ground."

I paused, not knowing exactly what to say, and then blurted out, "Well, hopefully with the medication and some rest, she'll be back to normal in a few days."

I was trying to sound optimistic, even though I didn't feel it.

The following morning, Maple wouldn't eat her breakfast. This was very unusual. I was a bit worried but had a shower and got ready for work anyway. Tim had already left hours earlier. When I was just about ready to walk out the door, I checked in on Maple and found her standing up, hunched over and heaving.

I felt worried. Knowing there was no way I could go to work; I called my assistant and asked her to rearrange my morning appointments. I didn't tell her that I was staying home with a sick dog, and instead said that I wasn't feeling well, which is ironic, since I had never called in sick before in all the years I had worked there. I even faked a sick voice.

Throughout the day, Maple vomited intermittently and by dinnertime she had developed diarrhea, which meant many trips up and down the front steps with me carrying her on account of her leg injury. Later that evening, when I told Tim that I thought we should take her back to the vet, he convinced me to wait until morning, which turned out to be a mistake.

At midnight, Maple became extremely restless. I knew she needed to urgently relieve herself, so I carried her out of the house and steadied her on the grass. On three legs, she wasn't able to fully squat, and this, combined with the long strands of white long human-like hair around her rear end made for a big mess. Throughout the day, I had been wiping her butt off with paper towels as best I could, but this time the liquid looked different. When I got back inside, I was terror struck when I realized in the light, that the liquid coming out of her was blood. I woke Tim up, and with his blessing, but not his company, I rushed Maple back to the emergency vet clinic that we had just been to a few days before.

An old man who was in the waiting room of the clinic saw me through the window as I struggled to carry Maple from the car. He held the door open for me. I thanked him and headed straight to the reception desk, where I turned Maple around so the staff person could see the bright red blood that was all over her formerly beautiful white fur around her backside.

We were seen right away by a kind older male vet with an Indian accent. He wasted no time in giving Maple an injection to stop the nausea and oral medication to treat her severe gastrointestinal symptoms. He ran some bloodwork but found nothing to explain what could be causing the problem. He sent me home, but instructed me to bring her back right away if the diarrhea didn't stop.

My temples pounded as I was driving back to our house. What on earth could be causing this? She had never been sick before. I spent a sleepless night, fighting off a sense of panic, while regularly checking on Maple to make sure she wasn't still throwing up. She wasn't. The medical treatment worked, and I didn't end up having to get up again through the night to take her outside.

In the days that followed, with the gastrointestinal emergency behind us, our focus shifted back to Maple's leg injury. Though she was gradually able to put her leg down on the ground, she still walked with a pronounced limp. We returned to our vet after a week, and she tried to reassure us by reminding us that soft tissue injuries can take a long time to heal. We didn't feel reassured though.

Going forward, Maple's leg would improve if we restricted her activity for a week, but then she would start limping again when we let her off her leash to run, which she wanted very badly to do.

Tim grew impatient. Not good at moderation, he unilaterally decided that we would severely restrict Maple's activities for three months straight in order to "make" her better. He dictated an aggressive recovery regime that did not allow Maple the freedom to do anything other than lay down or walk on a leash. We lifted her in and out of vehicles, on and off of furniture, and carried her up and down any stairs. I bought an ugly utilitarian harness with a handle on top to avoid pull on her neck.

Sticking to Tim's plan was difficult for all of us, but it worked, and after a long three months, we were confident that it was time to slowly return Maple to normal activities, since she had been limp-free for a few weeks.

All was going well, and it felt briefly like Maple's "bad" leg was finally better, but our reprieve was short lived. While Maple was doing "zoomies" at the golf course, all of a sudden, she stopped, held up her leg, and then refused to walk again. It was the same leg, and I was crushed. While this accident wasn't as dramatic as the Father's Day fiasco less than six months earlier, the result was just as severe, leaving Maple unable to put any weight on her right leg again.

Our vet gave us the same instructions and the same medications. We were back to square one and my mood sank considerably in response.

Maple's other symptoms soon returned, and they got even worse: lethargy, loss of balance, tremors, vomiting and bloody diarrhea. The mysterious vague but serious symptoms always manifested in the middle of the night, which necessitated several more trips to the emergency clinic, where she was seen by a different veterinarian every time. The treatment was always the same: anti-nausea medication by injection, liquid medicine to coat the stomach and pills to stop the diarrhea. Though the regimen worked to cure each particular incident, it never fixed the underlying problem.

We were spending a fortune on vet bills, yet none of the vets were able to tell us what was causing our previously healthy young dog to have become so acutely unwell. Deciding it was time to find a vet that was familiar with sighthounds, I contacted a local Greyhound rescue group to see who they used.

The new vet investigated Maple extensively, performing a full general blood screening, specialized blood work and tests for all kinds of conditions, including antigen tests for tick borne diseases as well as antibody panels for various other maladies. A fecal sample was given to test for parasites. She was even tested for Parvo, which is a highly contagious virus in dogs that causes severe gastrointestinal illness, especially in puppies. None of the diagnostics revealed anything. It was her best guess that Maple's still undiagnosed musculoskeletal problem was causing pain, which in turn, was causing the other symptoms. She recommended we take Maple to a canine chiropractor that was located 45 minutes away. For the stomach issues, she recommended a diet change, from raw to kibble.

Our lives, mine in particular, were now fully revolving around the management of Maple's health problems. We started taking her to the chiropractor twice per week. I had never even been to a chiropractor myself. It took some time to find a commercial dog food that agreed with her sensitive stomach. The only brand that worked was an expensive holistic food from California (alkaline based and limited-ingredient). We became dependent on the special food, thinking it was keeping Maple "episode free." When there was none available at any stores for a few weeks due to a problem at the border, it caused me so much anxiety that I began preparing homemade dog food using human grade ingredients, which was time consuming and expensive. We also started purchasing nutritional supplements and canine probiotics from our new vet.

Since we still didn't know what was making Maple sick, I insisted on keeping our house free of any potential toxins: chocolate, raisins, acorns, grapes, corn on the cob, Xylitol, Arnica cream, essential oils, and even scented candles. We monitored Maple's every move to avoid her eating something that might start another cycle of sickness that could only be ended with vet intervention. Walking her on garbage day required me to keep my eyes glued to the ground for any spilled food. We even stopped hosting dinner parties, in case a guest might unknowingly sneak Maple a tidbit of food under the table or drop something that Maple might eat when I wasn't looking.

Embarrassingly, Tim and I became obsessively focused on Maple's bowel movements. We both actively monitored her poop. Whoever was with her would report to the other by text message every time she went to the bathroom. Our messages went from the usual "how is your day going?" to "did she poo?" We even started using terms like "soft serve ice cream" to describe the consistency of Maple's feces. The soft serve variety was always a harbinger of bad things to come.

Maple seemed to get sick just before we had to be somewhere for an event. Worrying about her health disrupted our lives to the point that I didn't feel comfortable being away from the house for any period of time, so I stopped making plans. Even on good days when Maple was feeling okay, I still had a knot in my stomach and a feeling of impending doom. She was such a vulnerable, sensitive girl, and I felt like I was failing her. Being the guardian of a chronically sick dog that I loved so much opened me up to a world of worry that I had never before encountered.

I wasn't getting enough sleep, and my work life was suffering. As a lawyer, I needed my head in the game, and when Maple had bad days, it was difficult for me to concentrate. I was missing so much time from work, and in a job where every minute is measured and billed, I knew exactly how much my absence was costing my firm (and therefore myself since I was a partner and part owner of the business).

Dogs were supposed to be good for you - therapeutic even; but caring for Maple, watching her suffer, and worrying so much and for so long about her health had become an intense burden, turning the previous joy of owning a dog into something else.

9

PAYPAL PUPPY

A YEAR HAD PASSED since Maple's initial injury. She was now three years old and much of my life was revolving around managing her health problems, while also tirelessly searching for solutions.

Since we still had no idea what could be causing any of the strange gastrointestinal problems, out of an abundance of caution we took Maple off the medications she had been prescribed for her orthopedic injury. We also kept her diet restricted to either homemade food or the expensive California kibble. From time to time, things would improve temporarily, but never for long, and even during the calm periods I couldn't relax because I was always wondering and worrying about when the next episode of illness would show up to disrupt our lives.

Her recurring leg issue also continued to plague us, so we remained vigilant about not letting her jump from any height and we avoided letting her run free on rough terrain. We were still lifting her in and out of our vehicles and on or off the furniture. I was exhausted. Tim was frustrated. Maple was withdrawn.

She was already a pretty low-key dog before getting sick, but now Maple just seemed glum. I confessed my feelings to Kim in one of our late-night telephone conversations, admitting that I was really worried about her low mood. "Can a dog be depressed?" I asked, desperate to try anything to make our dog happy again.

Kim paused and then cautiously said, "Have you thought about getting another silken windhound?"

I laughed a bit, and then replied, "Um, no. I'm not doing a great job taking care of the one I already have."

"Well," she said, pausing again, and then gently adding, "I've found that taking care of two dogs, especially two silken windhounds, really isn't much different than looking after one."

We talked some more about what this might look like, and I have to admit that by the end of the conversation, I felt a spark of something ignite inside me. I think it might have been a bit of excitement. Maybe Maple was lonely? Maybe a puppy would cheer her up? Thinking about having another silken windhound around certainly cheered me up. In fact, it made me feel almost giddy.

The next day, I shared the idea with Tim. I knew it sounded crazy; getting a dog for a dog, and I was fully expecting him to refuse to even entertain the idea, but surprisingly he didn't, which only fueled my own desire to proceed with the plan. I'm sure he didn't actually believe that getting another silken windhound would do anything to improve Maple's mood, but I bet he was hoping it would help with mine.

Searching for Maple's new companion became a welcome distraction, although it didn't take long before I ran into the same problem that we did years before. Finding one. There simply weren't any silken windhound puppies available in Canada. I contacted a number of breeders in the United States. I filled out countless Puppy Questionnaires. Nobody would give us one of the rare and sought after puppies. They were all going to "show" or "breeding" homes. We just wanted a pet.

About a month after I started the search, a breeder in Texas announced on social media that he had two litters of silken windhounds "on the ground." I followed a link to the kennel website, where there were loads of pictures of the puppies and their parents. As I scrolled through them, one of the pups in particular really grabbed my attention. She was mostly white with ginger-coloured ears, a light ginger patch around one of her eyes, and another ginger spot on her back. Her registered name was "Kumbaya Raise Your Glass" and her call name was "Pink." The theme of the litter was "Uplifting," which I took to be a sign that this was meant to be our puppy.

I emailed the breeder and he answered quickly, describing the puppy as a pretty girl who "loves to stand and model in a stacked pose or lounge in a regal pose as if she were a princess." He said her parents were known for producing dogs with lots of curves, lots of muscles, dark pigment and dark eyes against white coat. He added that a lot of silkens are slab sided (flat chests) with a cathedral front (no depth of chest), but this puppy's mother had very good "ribspring" and a deep chest which she seemed to have passed on to her pups.

It all sounded very good, but all I cared about was that the puppy was female, mainly white, and that she was available. I wanted a white silken this time because when Maple was only about a year old, the beautiful brown mask on her face developed flecks of grey that seemed to intensify before our eyes. As her face whitened, she started looking like an old dog, even before she was two. Breeders called it "an early graying gene," and Maple certainly had it. In fact, it looked like most silken windhounds did. I figured getting an all-white silken would make this undesirable trait less noticeable.

We were almost instantly approved to buy the petite puppy with the eye patch named Pink. The breeder said we could change her call name to something else, but that her registered name would remain "Raise Your Glass" which he told me was a popular song by the artist Pink from a few years back. I wasn't familiar with the song, and when I pulled it up on YouTube, as soon as it began, I couldn't stop myself from dancing around to the cheerful beat. It was uplifting! Empowering. Dancy. All about celebrating a good time. It was simply perfect.

I paid the deposit through PayPal to reserve the puppy formerly known as Pink, who we were going to call Raisa. A party girl with an elegant name. I was told that we would receive her in a few weeks, as soon as she was old enough to be away from her mother. The entire transaction was done online.

When we announced the good news to our family and friends, everyone had the same response: that we were insane. Having witnessed us (mostly me) losing our minds over the problems we were still experiencing with our first silken windhound, everyone asked, "Why would you get another one?"

I didn't begrudge them for their skepticism. After all, they didn't understand just how special silken windhounds were. They didn't know that these weren't regular dogs. They were unicorns. And besides, our new puppy was coming from a different kennel in a different country. I was absolutely certain that she would be perfectly healthy.

Importing a dog from Texas turned out to be a complicated and expensive undertaking. Beyond figuring out the paperwork, we needed to ensure that the travel crate conformed to regulations set by the International Air Transport Association as well as the airline. There were special dishes required and a travel mat, as well as "Live Animal" stickers, all of which had to be purchased at the breeder's end but paid for by us. We also had to pay for a driver to transport our new puppy several hours from the Kumbaya Ranch to the Dallas Fort-Worth airport.

There were tough decisions that had to be made. Rabies shots were required for puppies over 12 weeks old but not recommended for dogs under six months of age. Raisa would be over 12 weeks, but under six months, so we had to decide whether to prematurely vaccinate her or put a younger age on the paperwork (which was suggested by the breeder). As a lawyer, I hated the idea of falsifying a document, but given all of Maple's health problems, I wasn't taking any chances.

We also had a weather issue. It was mid-September, and there was a heat wave going on in Texas. The airline had a policy that prevented any dogs on flights when the temperatures were over 80 degrees Fahrenheit, so our puppy's departure was delayed for over a week.

Prior to this we had never considered buying a dog sight-unseen and having it shipped by air. I can say quite confidently that we will never do it again. Besides being an administrative nightmare for us, it was no picnic for our new puppy, who was about to be taken from the only home she had ever known, plunked in a crate, driven in a car, shuffled around as cargo at two airports, picked up by strangers and driven to a house in a city with an adult dog. The whole ordeal was estimated to take 14 hours, which I knew was going to cause a whole lot of stress for a tiny creature that had only been on the earth for a mere couple of months.

Remembering how traumatized Maple had been, I felt guilty putting our new puppy through all of this, but I justified it by telling myself that she was going to have the best life ever with us.

Picking up our new puppy was a fiasco. After arriving at the Toronto airport, we paid for parking before walking all the way through Terminal 3 to get to the Delta Airlines arrivals section. We located the flight, and we naively tried to stroll straight into the baggage area to collect our puppy. We were stopped by a husky dark-skinned security guard, who told us sternly that we weren't allowed back there without a ticket. I told him we were picking up our new puppy, and he sent us to an information desk, where a Delta Airlines agent informed us that we were entirely in the wrong place. She provided us with an address, and told us that the cargo facility was a 15-minute drive from the airport. Thank goodness we had left early.

The cargo facility just looked like an industrial compound. We drove by a row of closed warehouse bay doors, and only one was open so we parked in front of it and went inside. The only person we could see was driving a forklift, which just happened to be moving a dog crate. I ran over, waving my arms at the bearded man in reflective gear who was driving. He looked angry. I pointed to the crate with the Live Animals stickers all over it, and he just shook his head and yelled over the noise of the machine that we had to go to the office next door.

We hurried out of the warehouse and into the office, where an airline agent provided us with documentation that we needed to take to yet another office in another building in order to clear customs. Once done, we returned to the original office, handed over the customs clearance paperwork, and finally the forklift driver was summonsed to bring the crate holding the puppy to us.

Tim carried the big crate out of the small office, and as soon as we were in the hallway he set it down. I opened the latch on the crate and in a flurry Raisa burst out, jumping excitedly all over us, kissing our faces. She was so tiny! She danced around the hallway like a sugar plum fairy, madly wagging her long tail and looking like the happiest little creature I had ever seen. We thought she would be timid and frightened from the flight. Boy, were we wrong!

We gave Raisa some of the dog kibble that was taped to the top of the crate and she ravenously gobbled it up. She lapped up the water we brought for her too. I picked her up to carry her to the truck. She was so much smaller than Maple had been at the same age. She had an incredibly dainty build.

Raisa seemed excited to be with us, almost as if she already knew that we were her new family. She had no hesitation being put in Tim's truck and for the hour-long ride home, she laid between us in the vehicle with her long front legs stretched out in front of her, looking much like a little Egyptian sphinx. She didn't seem frightened at all, and in fact, looked like she was enjoying herself.

Once home, Raisa pranced around the house, confidently exploring every room. She moved like a tiny ballerina on four preposterously skinny little stilts. Taking every toy out of Maple's toy box, she settled on a squeaky green lizard as her favourite, carrying it around proudly. Squeak. Squeak. Squeak. She was hilarious.

Kim's dogs were so calm and a bit aloof, even the puppies, so we assumed that all silken windhounds were like that. We weren't expecting Raisa to be as animated, friendly and outgoing; a magical little elf of a dog that always appeared to be smiling. It felt like my favourite childhood stuffed animal had come to life, and I was already hopelessly in love with her.

Unfortunately, Raisa didn't have the same effect on Maple. Minutes after we arrived home, she retreated to a bedroom and refused to come out. The next few days didn't get any better, and in the weeks that followed, she continued to actively avoid the new puppy. Even though Maple was still a young dog, this little spitfire just seemed to annoy her. When we forced Maple to be in the same room as Raisa, she would look at us with eyes that said, "How could you do this to me?"

I should have been more upset about the fact that we now had two silken windhounds that weren't friends; that my plan to cheer Maple up had failed miserably. But I wasn't. Raisa was my medicine; my emotional morphine. Everything about her seemed pure and right, and just being in her presence made me feel happy enough to dance around the kitchen carrying her little 11-pound body in my arms, with the song "Raise Your Glass" by Pink that inspired her name cranked up so loud that the neighbours probably thought I was having a party.

10

MEETING THE GREYHOUND GOD

I T TOOK US OVER an hour to drive to Long Point Provincial Park. We were always looking for soft, flat, open spaces where we could bring Maple for safe off-leash outings, and this place fit the bill because it featured a 40-kilometre-long sandy beach. It was early autumn and since the weather was cool and windy, we knew we would likely be the only ones there and could let the dogs run free.

As we pulled into the empty parking lot, I saw two huge white sand dunes flanking the entrance to the beach. Maple loved sand. At the golf course, she did zoomies in the sand traps, spinning her body in a circle with a look of pure glee on her face. I knew she was going to adore the beach. She had never been on one before.

As soon we reached a safe distance from the road, we unbuckled the dogs' harnesses and let them go. Raisa began bouncing around me in the sand like a little fox. She never wanted to be far from wherever I was. Maple on the other hand, immediately took off, galloping full tilt down the beach. She looked so beautiful running with such effortless elegance. It took my breath away.

I grabbed my phone out of my pocket to capture a video, but it didn't take long before she was far enough away that I began to feel uncomfortable. I was still filming when all of sudden she stopped running. I knew immediately something was wrong. As we ran to her, Maple was standing perfectly still, with the exception of her chest, which was heaving. She was also holding up her right front leg. As soon as I saw it, a sense of dread washed over me. You know the rest of the story by now. Same leg, same injury.

When we got home, I watched the video a few times, but couldn't see anything that might have caused such an injury. I felt deflated, thinking about how all of the happiness that Raisa had brought to our lives was about to be overshadowed by having to return

Maple to the strict rehabilitation routine we knew was necessary to heal her leg. It just wasn't fair. She was much too young to be chronically lame.

In the weeks that followed, Tim and I were both upset but we reacted in different ways. His frustration manifested as anger. Mine as sorrow. Once again, through a telephone call, I leaned on Kim for moral support. Feeling a bit ashamed that we hadn't taken Maple to the vet this time, I probably overexplained how much money we had already spent and how disappointed we were that we still didn't have any answers for any of Maple's mysterious but serious health issues.

"You need someone like Dr. Radcliffe," she said.

"Who's that?"

"He's a racing greyhound vet that spoke at a dog show I was at last year. An orthopedics guy. He repairs performance injuries in sighthounds."

"He sounds perfect!" I squealed.

"Yes. You need someone like him. Someone in canine sports medicine. He's also a really nice man and he even owns several greyhounds himself."

"We need to see him."

"He's in the States somewhere. That's why I didn't tell you about him sooner," she replied.

"Where?"

"West Virginia, I think?"

My heart sank. I had no idea how far away that was, but the fact that it was in a different country seemed like a deal breaker. Nevertheless, I hung up the phone and immediately googled "Dr. Radcliffe/Greyhound/Vet."

Multiple sighthound websites and forums popped up in the results. I read as many as I could and they all contained gushing comments describing Dr. Radcliffe as one of the premiere greyhound vets in the country, and even "the greatest vet in the universe." I couldn't find a bad review.

Later that evening when I told Tim about Dr. Radcliffe, he said, "If he's the expert then he's the person we need to see." He then quickly added, "We can't keep going on like this."

Tim was right. We couldn't keep going on like this. The following day I called Dr. Radcliffe's clinic in Wheeling, West Virginia. A cheerful woman answered the phone and told me I had reached the Town and Country Animal Hospital. When I explained our situation, she wasn't at all fazed that we were travelling all the way from Canada. She told me that sighthound owners come from all over their country and ours to have their dogs seen by Dr. Radcliffe.

I was given an appointment in a month's time, which would give me a chance to get organized for the trip. The dogs needed vaccine certificates and we needed to renew our own passports. Using Google Maps to plan our route, I discovered it was going to take us seven hours to get there, meaning that I needed to find a place to stay that was close to the clinic and allowed dogs. We would need at least one night over, and maybe more if surgery was required.

The evening before we travelled, we modified the back seat of Tim's pick-up truck so that Maple could rest comfortably during the long trip. He cut a piece of plywood and, placing it over the back seats, made the area one level by eliminating the foot space. I put an outdoor lounge cushion on top, some comfy blankets, and even a pillow for Maple to rest her head on. Raisa would ride in the front seat on a dog bed between us.

It was mid-November when we made the journey. We crossed out of Canada at Fort Erie, where the US border patrol officer didn't care that we were travelling with dogs. He didn't even ask to see their paperwork. The only time he said anything about the dogs was after he ordered Tim to open the tinted window so he could look in the back seat of the truck. He looked surprised when he saw Maple calmly looking back at him from the luxury of her back seat bedroom. "Wow, that's one weird looking dog ... big nose."

We travelled through New York State and then Pennsylvania, stopping only once at a rest stop so the dogs could stretch their legs and do their business. Other than observing a shocking number of dead deer along the side of the road (it was hunting season), the rest of the drive was uneventful.

Seven hours after leaving home, we arrived at our destination in the dark. The economy roadside motel in West Virginia was nestled in a valley between mountain ranges and was visible from the interstate highway above. Inside the cramped room, the carpets were dirty and the bedspreads had cigarette burns in them. The dogs didn't seem to mind though. After eating their dinner late, they took their places on the grubby beds, blissfully oblivious to the shabbiness of their surroundings.

In the morning, we loaded our canine passengers back into the truck and began the 15-minute drive to Dr. Radcliffe's clinic. Raisa was bright eyed and full of energy; eager to be back in the truck for another adventure. Maple on the other hand looked depressed, probably because she wasn't allowed to have her breakfast. We were told her stomach needed to be empty just in case surgery was required. My stomach wasn't happy either.

It was doing somersaults thinking about what was to come. While the cost of surgery was a concern, I was even more nervous that we might not get a diagnosis at all, and we would have to return home to the same sad situation. I was pinning all of my hopes on the Greyhound God.

After we left the interstate highway, the terrain changed dramatically from mountain ranges to rolling hills. The winding roads were dotted with farms and quaint houses with huge yards. It felt like we had gone back in time, to a place not unlike the small rural towns where Tim and I both grew up - a time before big box stores and stuccoed McMansions took over our area.

The entrance to the Town and Country Animal Hospital was so understated that we drove right past it. Turning around in the farm driveway next door, we drove back and entered the long curvy gravel driveway that led to the clinic.

The hospital itself was set back quite far from the road and was at the top of a hill. As we snaked along the long lane up to the parking lot, we passed another building called "Camp Radcliffe," which appeared to be a dog boarding facility. Between the two buildings was an enormous fenced dog-walking area, which we were grateful for, since we had arrived much too early for our appointment.

We parked in the empty lot beside the clinic. We leashed up both dogs, and they seemed excited as they walked around the inside of the hilly dog park, smelling all the interesting doggie smells. After about ten minutes, I headed back to the truck and lifted Raisa inside, placing her in Maple's back seat bedroom. "You be a good girl and wait here for us while the doctor sees Maple," I said, kissing the ginger dot on her forehead and then cracking the window to give her some fresh cool West Virginian air while she waited.

Tim had already walked across the parking lot with Maple and he was waiting for me at the entrance to the hospital, which was decorated with cornstalks and chrysanthemums. Maple was sniffing the display intently when I arrived.

"Is it open?" I asked.

"The lights are on," Tim said.

I cupped my hands to peer inside through the heavy glass door. The clinic was closed as our appointment had been scheduled before regular clinic hours to give Dr. Radcliffe time to do an assessment of Maple to determine if she needed surgery. I saw someone behind the desk, tried the door and it was unlocked.

"Here we go," I said, and Maple's ears perked up as I opened the door and held it open for them to walk through.

As soon as Maple made it inside, she froze, and then refused to walk any further. She began trembling and Tim scooped her up into his arms, carrying her to a chair, where he put her on his lap.

I headed to the front desk with my "Maple" file folder full of vet records. While I was filling out a form at the counter, another couple came in with their sighthound. They were from Canada too, and in chatting with them, I learned that they had driven six hours further than us to have Dr. Radcliffe perform surgery on their racing whippet's broken toe.

I returned to the waiting room which was full of empty chairs that were shaped in a horseshoe pattern around the perimeter of the clinic. I sat down beside Tim. Maple was still on his lap, but she seemed calmer now. Looking around, I was surprised at how ordinary the place was. It didn't seem fitting for such an important vet to be operating out of this humble venue.

Moments later, we heard some loud voices and a bit of a commotion as Dr. Radcliffe came hustling into the room. He walked over and shook Tim's hand first, and then mine, as he said, "Call me Jim."

A tall man with a lean build and piercing blue eyes, he was wearing a navy-blue surgical scrub shirt which was tucked into jeans. He had a stethoscope slung around his neck. A colourful scrub cap was covering his hair and he wore wire-rimmed glasses. He looked to be about 60 years old. With a bit of a southern twang, almost but not quite a drawl, he then said, "This must be Maple."

Tim stood up and set Maple down on the floor. Dr. Radcliffe bent down and then addressed her directly as if she were a person. Placing one hand gently under her chin, he looked right into her eyes and said, "What have you done to yourself child?"

Remaining in a crouched position, Dr. Radcliffe directed Tim to walk Maple around the waiting room in a figure eight pattern. He became engrossed in examining Maple's body in motion, intensely observing her movements. He then asked Tim to repeat the pattern in the opposite direction.

Standing up, Dr. Radcliffe walked over to Maple, leaned down and put his hands on her shoulder and gave it a squeeze. She let out a sharp cry.

"Yes, that's it right there," he said. "Now let's go and take a picture."

We had a hard time keeping up with the Greyhound God as he briskly walked out of the waiting room and down the hall to an examination room. Almost immediately, and somewhat magically, a technician showed up and collected Maple to take her for an x-ray.

Dr. Radcliffe then left the room, telling us he would be back soon with the results. It was all happening so fast.

About five minutes later, the technician returned with Maple, who didn't look any worse for the wear. She told us that Dr. Radcliffe was preparing his other Canadian canine patient for surgery. I felt nervous, wondering if he would be doing the same for Maple soon.

As we waited, I marveled at how well equipped and modern the exam room was. There was a flat screen computer, and also an extremely large television screen on the wall beside it. I could already tell that this clinic was technologically much more advanced than any we had been to at home.

About ten minutes later, Dr. Radcliffe came bursting back into the room, simultaneously talking while pulling up digital images of the radiographs of Maple's right leg onto the big screen. I missed the beginning of what he said, and felt a bit confused as he explained that Maple, like all sighthounds, was a rear-wheel drive vehicle, and that her front legs were just the steering mechanism, which "sometimes fails."

He was pointing to the screen, and he saw me squinting my eyes, so he enlarged the portion of the image. I still didn't know what I was looking at.

"That's it right there," he said. "Her scapula is fractured. More precisely, the acromion process."

"So, her shoulder's broken?" I asked.

"Right here, see that?" he said, moving his finger over a faint dark line along the white bone.

"It's partially healed, so at this point, I'm just going to let Mother Nature do her thing. I'm going give her a little bit of help, though."

"No surgery then?" Tim said.

Dr. Radcliffe then turned his body around from the screen and folded his arms across his chest, as if to give us a lecture.

"I only do surgery when it is absolutely necessary. This is my general rule, but it's especially true with sighthounds. Anesthesia which is safe for other dogs can kill a sighthound."

I shook my head in agreement and he continued on, "I take special precautions when performing surgery on them, but even then, sighthounds sometimes die on the operating table."

"So, what do we do now?" I asked.

"Well, if I had seen Maple immediately after the injury, I would have inserted a wire to stabilize the fracture, but since it's already started to heal, I'm thinking we should treat it conservatively."

He then explained that we would be sent home with pain killers, anabolic steroids, anti-inflammatory drugs, and antioxidants. We were to apply hot compresses to her shoulder for 15 minutes twice daily. He explained that "ice is your friend" only for three days after the acute incident. After that, the injury is considered chronic and heat should be used. He explained how we could make our own heat packs by running a towel under hot water and then putting the towel into a Ziploc bag, which could also be heated in the microwave. He showed us exactly where on Maple's shoulder he wanted them applied. He wanted us to take Maple for laser treatments to her shoulder three times a week at our local vet clinic.

Dr. Radcliffe then told us that Maple's activity was to be curtailed to leash walks only (for "elimination purposes") and otherwise she was to be on strict crate rest, until he examined her again in four weeks.

"Speed is her enemy," he said.

He didn't ask us if we would come back to see him, he just matter-of-factly told us that it would be so – that he would see us again in four weeks. I knew from Tim's facial expression that he was thinking the same thing that I was – that a return trip to West Virginia in December might put us into treacherous winter weather. But we weren't about to question the Greyhound God.

Dr. Radcliffe walked us out to the front desk of the clinic, and asked a staff person to make a digital copy of Maple's x-rays for us to take home. It was at that point that I noticed a kitten behind the desk.

Dr. Radcliffe saw me looking at it, and in an animated voice said, "Poor little guy was born with no eyes ... but don't tell him he's blind, because he doesn't know it."

He went on to explain that the clinic staff were finding the kitten a home. It warmed my heart to hear this. I didn't think I could like this man any more than I already did. Dr. Radcliffe wished us a safe drive and said that he would see us in four weeks.

When we got back into the truck, we were greeted by sweet little Raisa, who wagged her tail, kissed my face, and then very gently put her nose to Maple to smell her. As we drove away from the Town and Country Animal Hospital, I thought about how lucky we were to have her. She was still a young puppy, but she had travelled on a very long journey like an angel. She hadn't fussed at all about staying in a motel, or being left alone in the vehicle. With her deep gaze, bright eyes, and a waggy tail, I was becoming much fonder of her than I ever dreamed possible. Before Raisa, I didn't think that I could ever love an animal as much as I loved Maple.

We made it home without making any stops, apart from the Canadian border, where we were questioned intensely due to the volume and nature of the medications we declared. The dour female border official carefully examined all of our documentation, scrutinizing the veterinary records and prescriptions that Dr. Radcliffe had sent us home with. She seemed skeptical that we had driven that far to take our dog to a vet – and who could blame her.

We were getting used to people looking at us like we were crazy. And perhaps we were! But at that point I didn't care, because we finally had an answer for what was making Maple lame – and a supervised plan from an expert to get her better. Things were finally looking up!

11

THIS IS YOUR BRAIN ON DRUGS

W E ARRIVED HOME FROM our American adventure in the dark. I was tired and eager to get inside our house, but Tim told me I had to wait.

Tim loves rules. Insisting we implement Dr. Radcliffe's protocol immediately; he ordered me to stay with the dogs while he went inside to set up the crate first. He wasn't taking any chances – we WOULD be following the dog doctor's orders to the tee.

Once inside, it was my job to get Maple into the crate, which didn't turn out to be a pleasant experience for either of us. Wide-eyed, she u-turned in a way that only a circus contortionist could pull off, with her head coming back out of the crate at the same time as her back end was being pushed in. Now that I knew her shoulder was broken, I was so worried about making it worse. I asked Tim for help. He seemed irritated that I interrupted him from carrying in our suitcases and other supplies from the truck.

After we finished unpacking, I let Maple out of the crate so I could implement another one of Dr. Radcliffe's recommendations. I thought that applying a warm compress to her shoulder would feel good, but getting her to lie down with her bad shoulder facing up was impossible. My heart was torn between my love for her and my fear in causing her pain. Another caregiving duty that I had to relinquish to Tim.

When it was time to go to bed, it was also time to give Maple her medication. Administering the prescribed drugs should have been the easiest job. It turns out that Maple's sense of smell is as sensitive as an airport drug-sniffing dog. She was able to detect the pills in any type of food I tried hiding them in. Once again, it ended up taking two of us to get the job done. As Tim pried Maple's locked jaw open, I jammed the pills into the back of her throat, and then he held her long narrow crocodile mouth closed until she swallowed them. This was going to be a very long four weeks.

Maple was visibly upset. For the remainder of the evening, her eyes followed me suspiciously whenever I walked by the crate, presumably because she now believed that I was trying to harm her. It distressed me to be the cause of her distress. It irritated Tim that I was distressed. He couldn't hide the fact that he was disappointed that I wasn't able to get the necessary dog duties completed on my own. Skeptical about my ability to apply tough love, he announced, "I'm taking Maple to work with me tomorrow."

Just as I was about to protest, he added, "Don't worry. She'll be safe in my office."

I was worried, but truth be told, I was also a bit relieved to let him take over the job of being Maple's primary caregiver, since I was extremely burned out from looking after her so intensely over the past 18 months. I needed to catch up at work, and the new arrangement would also give me more time with Raisa, who hadn't received the attention she deserved due to the intense but necessary re-focusing of our energy on Maple's medical issues.

The following morning, about an hour after Tim left the house, I received a text message from him: "Maple won't eat. Diarrhea."

A man of few words, Tim was not one to raise the alarm prematurely, especially when it came to the dogs. He knew how I would react (or overreact), so usually kept these things to himself.

When they arrived home that evening, Maple looked terrible. She was having a hard time standing upright and was stumbling into things as if she couldn't see. To keep the peace, I agreed to wait until morning to take her to our vet. We moved her crate to our bedroom so we could keep an eye on her overnight.

During the night Maple woke us up at least once an hour by standing up in her crate, moaning and trembling. Since Tim had to get up for work so early, I volunteered to take her outside. Because of her broken shoulder, I carried her down two flights of stairs to get to ground level outside, where she repeatedly released a foul-smelling liquid from her bowels. She was shaking, vomiting up bile, and by morning was excreting blood. It was the sickest I had ever seen her, and she was the sickest dog I had ever seen.

Before I called work to tell my assistant I wouldn't be coming in, I called Dr. Radcliffe. He told me to waste no time in getting emergency treatment - that Maple was having a potentially life-threatening adverse reaction to the drugs. He instructed me to immediately stop all medication, get help, and call him back once her condition was stabilized.

My anxiety level rose even higher on hearing this news, along with an increase in my guilt for not taking her to the emergency vet the night prior. I called my mom and she rushed over to taxi us to the vet in her car. Sitting in the backseat with Maple draped over my lap, I wasn't sure if I was feeling nauseous because of nerves or on account of the intense sickly odour of blood, feces and vomit. I was terrified that she was going to die.

By the time we arrived at the clinic, I was in the middle of a full meltdown. I didn't even close the car door behind me as I rushed into the office, carrying a limp Maple up to the front counter where I begged that she be seen right away.

It was a long, brutal day. I was so glad to have my mom's company. Once the vet was able to get Maple's condition stabilized, we were allowed to take her home. She wasn't shaking or vomiting anymore, but she was still lethargic and refusing to eat. She also still had diarrhea, but it was no longer bloody.

Back at home, I didn't feel that we should force Maple back into her crate after all that she had been through. Tim felt differently.

"Her shoulder won't heal if we don't follow the rules. Dr. Radcliffe said she had to stay in the crate."

"Tim! She's so sick, she's not going to be moving around anyway."

"We can't chance it. Especially now that she can't have any drugs. She's going in the crate."

"No. She's not," I insisted, with tears in my eyes and a lump in my throat. "I'll stay with her."

"Guess it doesn't matter what I say. You're going to do whatever you want anyway," he said and walked away, his face darkened with anger.

I went ahead and set up a healing camp in our formal living room by dragging in a mattress for Maple and I to sleep on. I shut both sets of French doors to close off the room from the rest of the house, and fortified it with blankets, pillows, my phone, iPad, and laptop. I stayed in that room for several days, only leaving to go to the bathroom, grab food and drink, and to let Raisa out in the back yard to do her business.

Despite my round-the-clock attention, Maple didn't rebound from this episode as quickly as she had in the past from similar, if milder episodes. For several days she did nothing but sleep. She continued to refuse food, turning her nose violently away from anything presented to her, as if she was repulsed by the sight of it. I was still worried that she might die, having made the mistake of googling the rare side effects of some of the medications she had taken, which included "death."

When Maple started to gently and gingerly take tiny bits of food out of my hand, I knew that we had rounded the corner. With the emergency behind us, I called Dr.

Radcliffe back. I had a list of questions for him, but he interrupted me by asking, "What's Maple's MDR1 status?"

"She's a carrier," I replied.

He made a drawn out "aahh" sound, as if he suspected as much.

"Which medication do you think she reacted to?" I asked.

"Maple shouldn't be put back on ANY drugs," he said, instructing me to continue with the other treatment (strict crate rest, warm compresses, laser treatments at the vet).

After I hung up the phone, it took a moment before I realized that I now knew exactly what had been making Maple so intermittently sick for so long. It wasn't her diet, pesticides at Tim's golf course, scented candles or acorns. It was the drugs! Well, to be accurate, it wasn't the drugs themselves, but rather it was a gene mutation that caused a reaction to the drugs. And the condition was hereditary, meaning that the defective gene had been passed down from one generation to the next.

I pulled out the package of paperwork that Kim gave us when we brought Maple home. I found the one-page genetic lab report which confirmed that Maple was a "carrier-dog" carrying one copy of a genetic mutation of the MDR1 gene. At the time, Kim assured us that as a carrier, Maple would not be affected by the disorder in any way, and since we weren't breeding her, we didn't need to worry about it. So, we didn't.

I then did what I should have done years ago; I looked up the condition, which is called multi-drug sensitivity. Dogs with a mutation of the MDR1 gene can suffer severe and even fatal reactions to common medications, and are at risk of serious drug toxicities at doses that are safe for other dogs.

What I didn't understand was why Maple was so sensitive to drugs if she was only a carrier? A little more reading allowed me to learn that this condition was a dominant disorder, meaning that Maple only needed to inherit one copy of the mutated gene to be at an increased risk of developing adverse reactions to normal doses of certain drugs.

Had we known that being a carrier for this genetic mutation would make Maple susceptible to serious drug reactions, we certainly would have told her treating vets, but it wasn't even on our radar to do so. It upset me to think about all of the needless suffering that she had endured; not to mention our own stress and worry, not knowing what was wrong with her for so long. And, of course, all the money we spent on veterinary intervention every time she got sick.

When I talked to Dr. Radcliffe on the phone, he told me that he would treat Maple as "affected" from now on, and that he would not be prescribing any more drugs for her, which would make her rehabilitation "difficult but not impossible."

Strangely enough, his statement echoed what was printed at the bottom of the invoice from his clinic: "The difficult we can do right away ... the impossible takes a little longer."

12

YOU SAY YOU WANT A RESOLUTION

THE AIR WAS COLD and the sky was bleak, but lucky for us there was no snow expected for those few days in mid-December when we made our second trip back to West Virginia.

Dr. Radcliffe reviewed the follow up x-rays, and much to our delight, reported that Maple's broken shoulder had almost completely healed. Having become accustomed to bad news, I was both surprised and incredibly relieved to hear this. Our rehabilitation efforts had been successful, even without the drugs. He sent us home with the promise that if we kept up with the protocol for two more weeks, Maple's shoulder would be fully healed.

We had been through a grinder of a year, and I was happy it was coming to an end. When New Year's Eve rolled around a few weeks later, I only had one resolution – to adopt a positive outlook so I could be happy in my life again.

I was determined to get myself out of the funk I had fallen into, so I could start enjoying life with my two dogs like normal people with normal dogs did. Though I suppose our dogs, even when healthy, could never really be described as normal.

Even though they were from the same breed, they had different physical features and wildly different personalities.

Maple looked just like a small borzoi. With her long snout and perfectly folded ears that she always carried close to her head, her demeanor matched her elegant looks. Calm, soft, and quiet, she was a true standoffish sighthound. Reluctant to being touched, any attempt at cuddling her was akin to hugging a sack of elbows. She was too dignified to give kisses or fawn over anyone, including us, although she did have a modest way of showing her love, and I adored her for it.

At six months old, Raisa was much smaller than Maple at the same age. A tiny sprite of a dog, she had exceptionally fine long legs supporting a petite frame which was laced with silky white tinsel fur. She had an expressive animated face, with ears that she could lay flat against her head or prick up and move around like antennae. Her buoyant spirit fit her appearance perfectly. Pure lightness and joy; she was helium at the end of a leash. Effervescence.

While Maple kept to herself, Raisa had a strong desire to be with me all the time. My little white shadow was always by my side, day and night. If I had to leave the house without her, I would find her waiting for me when I got home - a tiny white elf of a dog holding my slipper between her front paws like a child holds onto a teddy bear. It became my habit to drop whatever I was carrying and scoop her right up into my arms, burying my face in her silky fur. Her body would immediately relax in a feline way, making it feel as if she had no bones.

I didn't know that this kind of devotion was something that I wanted from a dog, but once I had it, I couldn't imagine life without it.

It was at about this point in time that Tim started referring to Maple as "his" dog; maybe because he had cared for her so intensely while her fractured shoulder was healing. Before that, Maple was "our" dog, and Raisa was supposed to belong to Maple. Now Raisa, according to Tim, was "my dog."

Everyone could see the intense bond that had already developed between Raisa and I. With her waggy tail, wiggly body, and extreme gregariousness, just looking at her made me smile. Having her around made it easy to keep my positive outlook; meaning that my New Year's resolution was already a success.

Until it wasn't.

In fact, it only took nine days before my New Year's Resolution spectacularly crashed and burned. And it all started with the weather.

The "Polar Vortex" arrived with a series of brutal ice storms and ridiculously cold temperatures, even by Canadian standards. The initial winter storm rained a shellac of ice onto every horizontal surface. The deep freeze that followed cemented it down, making it nearly impossible to get around.

Tim had to use a pick axe to clear a path in our back yard for Raisa to get out to do her business. Maple still refused to use the yard for that purpose, so leash walks in the neighbourhood were necessary to get the job done.

I dreaded taking Maple out into the icy conditions, but since she was still recovering from her broken shoulder she was walking slowly and steadily, which eased my worry a bit. Raisa, on the other hand, was much too rambunctious and far too delicate on those long toothpick legs. There would be no neighbourhood walks for her until the weather broke.

It was the ninth day of January, and I had bundled myself up to take Maple out for her morning walk. Due to the extreme bone-chilling temperatures, we were both wearing winter coats. Only one of us was wearing winter boots however, which is what put the unfortunate series of events into motion.

Most of our well-intentioned neighbours had over applied salt to the sidewalks in front of their houses, probably due to a fear of being sued by personal injury lawyers like myself. As a result, sharp rock salt kept getting wedged between the pads of Maple's paws. Such a sensitive girl, she would take a few steps, stop, and then hold one of her feet up off the ground and refuse to walk until I brushed the salt away with my mitten. A few steps later, we would repeat the process with another foot. It was a grueling procedure getting her to walk far enough from the house for her to be willing to do her business.

About half way through our short walk, Maple sat down, then laid down, and then completely and intentionally capsized herself onto her side in an attempt to get all four of her feet off the freezing salty ground. I had no choice but to pick her up and carry her home.

We were on a slopey cul-de-sac called Ravenscliffe Avenue, and as I was carrying my precious cargo awkwardly down the incline towards home, my feet slipped out from under me, and we both went down hard. My back landed on someone's recycling box, and the weight of Maple falling on my stomach knocked the wind out of me. As I caught my breath, stabs of lightening-like pain shot up my back and into my chest.

I somehow managed to make it home in a half-crawl position, while towing a reluctant Maple behind me on her leash. I didn't know it yet, but would later find out that I had broken both a rib and my tailbone. It hurt to laugh. It hurt to sneeze. It hurt to move. It even hurt to breathe. I couldn't sit because of the tailbone pain and couldn't lie down due to the broken rib. I should have gone to the doctor right away, but I didn't. Because of the weather.

That evening, Tim took Maple out for a walk before bed. While he was gone, Raisa presented me with her favourite squeaky toy. I swear that she knew I was hurting and was trying her best to cheer me up. She stood in front of me with the green lizard in her mouth, squeezing it slowly at first and then faster and faster. When I didn't pick it up and throw it (I was too sore), she decided to make her own fun. A resourceful little hound, she started flinging the rubber reptile high up into the air, grabbing it, and then shaking it violently, and then making it squeak, squeak, SQUEAK before flinging it again. I was laughing at her and cheering her on. Then something terrible happened.

While descending from a leap to catch the airborne lizard, Raisa came down on her back legs and let out the most hideous of screams. I knew instantly what it meant. It was the scream of death, and it pierced my soul.

In that moment, I couldn't think; I could only feel. My adrenalin made my own pain temporarily disappear as I rushed over and picked her up. I phoned Tim and wailed into the phone that he needed to get home fast. By the time he and Maple arrived back, Raisa had stopped screaming but her back leg was just hanging grotesquely.

"We need to take her to the Emergency Vet," I said breathlessly.

"No. I'm not wasting my time with the vets here again. We'll take her straight to West Virginia."

"But she's in extreme pain," I cried.

"She'll be okay. We'll leave first thing in the morning."

A few sleepless hours later, I knew it was too early for Town and Country Animal Hospital to be open, but I called anyway, expecting to leave a message. Surprisingly someone answered (I would later learn that the clinic was staffed around the clock on account of the surgical patients). Dr. Radcliffe wasn't in yet of course, but the staff person was able to reach him by phone and he called me right back. After I explained our situation, Dr. Radcliffe said only one thing.

"Get yourselves on the road right away and I will meet you at the clinic at 8:30 tomorrow morning."

He was going to see us on a Saturday! I was so relieved and grateful that this very important and busy man was going to go to come in on a weekend just to help us. We wasted no time in packing up the truck and loading our canine family into it to begin the long journey back to West Virginia for the third time in two months.

We arrived at the border with our documents in hand, and a blanket over Raisa's back end to hide her broken leg. When the female official asked us the purpose of our trip, Tim said we were on our way to visit friends that lived in West Virginia. We had decided on the story ahead of time, not wanting to risk being delayed or inspected because we had an injured animal on board.

The border official leaned out of her hut and peered into our vehicle. When she spotted the two dogs, she asked, "Are you crazy dog people?"

Tim replied, "yes" without hesitation and in such a serious way that it made me chuckle. But he was serious. And he was right. We were crazy dog people, and he knew that. She allowed us to enter into the United States without any further questions.

The drive was uneventful weather-wise, but was excruciating for me, both physically and mentally. I was holding a broken Raisa on my lap and didn't want to jostle her around at all, choosing her comfort over my own. I couldn't even recline my seat due to the board behind my seat holding up Maple's travel bed. My chest felt squeezed and I was having a hard time breathing, which was probably a result of my injuries, although it certainly seemed like a manifestation of the doom that I was feeling. I just knew that Raisa's leg was broken, which meant that we were dealing with another broken silken windhound. My poor perfect dream puppy was damaged, just like Maple. So much for positive thinking.

It seemed so unfair that this terrible thing happened while I was trying to protect my pup from the exact injury that she ended up experiencing – and just hours after I had been so badly injured myself. She wasn't even six months old yet. We had already been through so much. Maple's fracture wasn't even fully healed yet. I felt cursed.

We made it to our destination, but this time we were lodging across the river in the State of Ohio because a staff person at Dr. Radcliffe's clinic recommended the Red Roof Inn as the best place to stay with dogs. She was right. They were friendly and accommodated us with a room on the ground floor that we were able to drive right up to.

Once inside our freshly renovated room, I was commenting on how much nicer it was than the last place we stayed, when Tim interrupted me by loudly blurting out, "Fuck."

"Everything is soaked," he said, as he pulled a pair of damp jeans out of his suitcase.

Our baggage had travelled in the bed of the pick-up truck because there was no room inside on account of the set up for the dogs. Even though it was hard-cased luggage, the frozen salty road spray had penetrated the soft fabric area where the cases zipped up. It was late, so all we could do was hang the wet clothing around the room and hope it would dry by morning.

I mentally chalked up the luggage fiasco as more evidence proving that I was the subject of a curse. What else could explain all of this bad luck? Even playing the "things could be worse" game in my head wasn't working. I was broken. My puppy was broken. Maple was still broken. And my life was turned upside down again on account of another terrifying dog emergency. Prior to owning silken windhounds, for the most part I had always felt in control of my life. But things were now starting to spin out of control – and I wasn't very good at dealing with these types of feelings. In fact, it would be fair to say that I was unravelling because of them.

Despite my own broken bones, and against protests from Tim, I insisted on sleeping on the floor beside Raisa to keep her safe from moving around or falling off the bed. We should have brought a crate with us, but in our hasty departure, we forgot it. I self-medicated with some prescription painkillers I had left over from a dental surgery, which helped ease my pain, but added to my brain fog.

Poor Raisa had the runs and needed to be taken outside frequently during the night. Every time she needed to go out, Tim had to put on his coat and boots and carry her across an icy parking lot to a small flat area. I watched them out the window, worried that one or both of them would fall. As soon as he set her on the ground, Raisa was able to scoot around okay on three legs, but it made me wince looking at her back leg dangling from her body. She must have been in so much pain.

Early the following morning we backtracked on the interstate highway to get back to West Virginia, exiting onto a turnpike for the rural drive through the hilly roads. Tim was quiet, seemingly concentrating on the road. He was drinking a free coffee from the motel lobby, which was in a white Styrofoam cup. The dogs were quiet too. I stared out the window of the vehicle, and my stomach churned when I recognized a sign that told us we were entering the village of Bethlehem, which meant that we were getting close to the clinic.

Dr. Radcliffe greeted us in the waiting room and didn't waste any time in taking Raisa from Tim's arms into his own to carry her to the back for x-rays. We were sent to wait in the same examination room that we had been in with Maple just a few weeks prior.

Tim paced around the small room, which made me even more nervous. I sat on a plastic chair, staring at the pictures of greyhounds on the wall. Even though it was cool in the room, I was sweating, and wiping my clammy hands on my pants while simultaneously trying to steady my uncontrollable bouncing knees.

When Dr. Radcliffe returned to the room, he delivered the news that I had been dreading but expecting. Raisa's leg was indeed broken. He explained that there was an avulsion fracture to the tibial tuberosity, better known as the knee. Two pieces of the bone had been pulled off and Raisa's kneecap had slid up because the ligament's tension was off due to the broken bone. Surgery was required. My heart sank.

Dr. Radcliffe told us that he planned to use hardware (pins and wire) to stabilize the break. Raisa would be kept at his clinic overnight and if all went well, we would be able to take her home the following day.

I couldn't stop my mind from thinking about what Dr. Radcliffe had previously told us about sighthounds and surgery. I was also concerned that poor Raisa might have a terrible reaction to the drugs that would be needed. She weighed only 23 pounds and was just a skinny wisp of a dog - a delicate little thing about half the size of Maple.

Dr. Radcliffe must have sensed my anxiety, because he went over his surgical protocol in detail, emphasizing the extra precautions he always takes to ensure that his sighthound patients are as safe as possible while they are under anesthesia. He said that Raisa's blood work was being completed as we spoke, and that he would review it before proceeding.

He ushered us out of the room by opening the door, and telling us to go and get something to eat; that he would call us in a few hours when he was finished operating.

As we were passing back through the waiting room, I noticed a Scottish deerhound in the lobby, standing regally beside its seated owner. I had never seen a Scottish deerhound in real life before. I poked Tim and whispered, "A Scotish deerhound!"

I began walking towards it and Tim didn't whisper back when he answered "No," putting his arm around my lower back, and ushering me out the door. Normally a gesture of affection, he commonly used this method to move me along when I wasn't walking as quickly as he wanted me to.

When we got back to the truck, Tim said that he was going to take Maple out to the fenced area to do her business. I took the opportunity to head back into the clinic to see the dog, telling Tim I was going to use the washroom. I deserved a happy distraction.

Back inside the clinic, as I walked by the Scottish deerhound, I stopped and put my hand out for him to sniff.

He bit me!

Then all hell broke loose. The owner was so upset, and rightfully so, since I didn't ask permission to approach her dog. I went into the washroom and put paper towels around my hand, which was spurting blood out of the holes where the hound's teeth had punctured it. One of the staff must have notified Dr. Radcliffe, who was waiting for me in the hallway when I emerged from the washroom. He took me to an examination room where he cleaned the wounds and used steri-tape to close them up and then bandaged my hand, all the while assuring me that "Oliver" was up to date on his shots.

I was so embarrassed.

Needless to say, I was given more than one "I told you so" from Tim when I arrived back at the truck with my hand in a bandage. I didn't even have to tell him what happened. I mentally added this event to the growing list of bad things that were happening to me. More proof that I had been cursed.

We drove back to the motel and parked outside the Denny's Diner next door, leaving Maple in the truck. I was paranoid that if we left her in the motel room, someone might open the door to clean it and inadvertently let her out.

In the restaurant, Tim urged me to order the Grand Slam breakfast, as he was doing. I told him I wasn't sure I could eat. Even though I felt hungry, my stomach was still upset, and I knew it would continue until I knew that Raisa had come through the surgery okay. I told him that I was just going to get some toast, which would be cheaper than wasting money on something that I probably couldn't eat anyways.

As Tim continued to insist that I get a full breakfast, and I continued to insist that it would be a waste of money, an older couple that had been dining at a table next to our booth walked over to us and silently handed Tim a coupon for a "buy-one-get-one-free" meal. They had undoubtedly overheard our conversation, and must have thought that we couldn't afford two full breakfasts. I was mortified.

Several hours passed before we heard back from Dr. Radcliffe. We were back in our motel room when Tim's phone rang. He handed it over for me to answer. I breathlessly said "hello" with my heart pounding.

"Michelle, everything went well."

I exhaled and said, "Thank goodness."

"The heart monitor didn't even flicker while she was under. She's cruising along on morphine now in the recovery room."

Dr. Radcliffe told me that we could call the clinic anytime for an update, adding that we could even visit Raisa if we wanted to, as they had staff working around the clock. He ended the conversation by saying that he would meet us in the morning to give us instructions before we took Raisa home. I think I said thank you about twelve times.

Late in the afternoon, we decided to go and see Raisa. A staff member brought us to the back of the clinic where she was lying in a hospital cage, hooked up to an intravenous line with her tongue hanging out of her mouth. She looked like she was dead. I gasped.

All of her pretty white fur had been shaved off her back leg. There was a large incision that circled around her knee. A semi-circle of perfectly aligned blue stitches stood out against her pale pink skin giving the appearance of a Frankenstein leg, or a stitched-up piece of meat. The technician roused her a bit to show me that she was in fact alive. Miraculously, she attempted a tail wag, even though she was clearly out of it.

We picked up some groceries and ate in our motel room, where we could keep an eye on Maple. I was ridiculously tired and finally slept well for the first time in several nights, now knowing that Raisa was okay.

The following morning Dr. Radcliffe unlocked the door for us to enter the clinic. It wasn't open to the public, being a Sunday. I was so grateful that he had come in just to see us. It felt strange to be in there with nobody else around. There must have been staff looking after the hospitalized dogs in the back, but the reception area was dark and quiet.

Dr. Radcliffe turned on a few lights as he disappeared into the back of the clinic. When he walked Raisa out to us (yes, walked – she was walking) I was so surprised. She looked good! She was hobbling along, mostly on three legs, and as soon as she spotted us, her tail started wagging madly and her head began swaying from side to side with a big grin, as she pulled on the leash to get to us. My chest surged with happiness. If I had a tail, I would have been wagging mine too.

I bent down and kissed her on the top of her head, holding her shoulders to keep her from jumping up. I nestled my face into the soft fur around her neck, noticing that she smelled like antiseptic. I whispered in her ear that she was a good girl.

As soon as I stood up, Raisa squatted and took a pee on the floor – a big long huge pee. As I was apologizing, Dr. Radcliffe handed me her leash, grabbed some paper towels and cleaned the puddle up himself, saying not to worry, that she had been on fluids all night.

Back in the examination room, he showed us the before and after x-rays on the big screen mounted to the wall. He told us that due to Raisa's young age, the bone should heal quickly. He added that we were very lucky that the growth plates weren't affected, so there shouldn't be any long-term damage. I had no idea what growth plates were, but I was over the moon about his positive prognosis.

Dr. Radcliffe then looked away from his screen and gazed over at Raisa. She looked right back at him as if waiting for him to say something. He took a few steps towards her, leaned over and cupped her chin in the palm of his hand and said to us, while still looking at her, "You have a very special dog here."

Before I could agree, he added, "If you're ever in a position that you can't keep her, she can come and live with me and my wife and our greyhounds."

When his gaze returned back to us, the spell was broken. Back in doctor mode, he matter-of- factly informed us that Raisa had been medicated for pain and infection but we would need to re-administer the drugs at eight- and twelve-hour intervals. He handed me a bag containing the medication, along with some typewritten instructions, assuring me she would be okay on the drugs because she didn't carry the genetic mutation that Maple had.

Back in the reception area, our veterinary hero gave me a big hug, shook Tim's hand, and told us to drive safely.

We paid our bill, said our good-byes and began the long drive home. We left West Virginia in a much better mental state than we entered it, thanks to the kindness and expertise of a man that that had proven that the reviews about him online were accurate. Dr. Radcliffe was indeed the best vet in the universe.

13

REJECTION

A
S SOON AS WE arrived home, Tim positioned the big plastic crate near our back door so I wouldn't have far to go to get Raisa outside for bathroom breaks. We knew the drill ... strict cage rest and carry her outside for "elimination purposes only."

On my instructions, Tim had lined her crate with a comfy Sherpa blanket, but as soon as he placed Raisa inside, she became visibly agitated and there was nothing we could do to coax her to lie down. She had been so content during the long drive home, so I knew immediately what was wrong.

"It's because she associates that crate with when she was trapped in it for 14 hours when she was shipped here," I said.

Tim replied, "You're crazy."

Nonetheless, he lifted Raisa out of the crate and put her in my arms. It was late, and instead of arguing about whether I was wrong (or crazy), he returned to the basement to dig out the other crate. Made of metal, our back-up crate had wire bars and was essentially just a big cage. It was also collapsible, and surprisingly heavy. We had never used it before.

Once Tim finished setting up what would be Raisa's home for the next six weeks, he somewhat gruffly took her from my arms and placed her inside. She circled around once and then folded her little white body into a position of comfort. I shot Tim an "I told you so" look.

As I was admiring her cuteness, it all of a sudden dawned on me that her long skinny legs could fit through the gaps between the bars of the cage. I decided to wait until morning to address the issue with Tim, as I could tell that his patience for our patient (and for me) was waning. Being too anxious to leave Raisa alone overnight, I threw a few big dog beds down and slept beside her cage on my own broken bones, which I still did not yet officially know were broken.

We had been given a disposable e-collar (cone) for the ride home so Raisa wouldn't be able to chew out her stitches. It was made of shiny flexible cardboard and was a vibrant shade of peacock blue with white fabric edging and a series of white laces that tied up into bows in order to fasten it around her head. It looked like she was wearing an Easter bonnet, and I chuckled a bit when I put it on her before I tried to get to sleep.

During the night, Raisa started pushing the flimsy cone aside and licking the surgical wound, so the next morning Tim went shopping for a more reliable one. In typical Tim fashion, he returned with three different styles. The inflatable donut device and the soft vinyl collar were both disqualified right out of the gate because the combined length of Raisa's swan neck and crocodile jaw made it possible for her to reach the incision. The big ugly tried-and-true "cone of shame" was the only contraption that was going to keep her teeth safely away from her stitches. Made of hard stiff plastic, it had a much bigger circumference than the others. While it worked well for its intended purpose, the see-through satellite whacked the sides of the cage every time Raisa turned around, and then thunked along the bars in a jarring way until she settled. Another drawback was that it had to be removed so she could eat and drink and it also prevented her from being able to get her nose to the ground to do any smelling when outside.

We had to use zip ties to fasten the cone to her collar so it wouldn't slide off her skinny head. I hated it as much as Raisa did, but Tim reminded me that unless I was willing to have eyes on her all the time, it was necessary.

With the new cone in place and Tim at home to hold down the fort, I finally headed off to the walk-in clinic. It had been four days since I fell, and a disturbing crackling/gurgling sound had developed in my chest area whenever I took a deep breath.

The walk-in clinic sent me straight to the hospital, where they took x-rays which revealed that a jagged end of a broken rib bone was dangerously close to puncturing my lung. I was ordered to completely minimize all activity and take painkillers that would allow me to breathe deeply to avoid any lung complications such as pneumonia.

I returned home with my physical injuries attended to but with my emotional ones still festering. I couldn't stop thinking about the danger that existed because of the bars of Raisa's cage. I finally confessed my concerns to Tim and asked him if we could reinstate the plastic crate.

Tim disagreed. Firmly.

"If she can get her leg out through the bars, then she certainly can get it back in."

I wasn't convinced. As soon as Tim took Maple out for a walk, I headed to the basement and attempted to drag the heavy plastic crate up the stairs. When Tim got home and caught me half way up the basement stairs with the crate, his face turned red and as he looked me straight in the eye and said, "I can't believe how stupid you are."

His words hit me like a punch to the gut. I wasn't used to him speaking so harshly to me. I turned away from him so he wouldn't see the tears welling up in my eyes.

Tim took the plastic crate back downstairs and insisted that I sleep in my own bed. I refused, and continued to camp out on the floor beside Raisa's cage, letting him know that I would stay there for as long as the danger existed.

Tim went back to work the next day, which was a relief to both of us. My perceived paranoia about the cage bars combined with the intensive canine care that Raisa now required meant that I was going to have to be home with her all the time.

I was also nervous about the drugs. Even though Raisa didn't have the mutant drug-re-action gene, Dr. Radcliffe still prescribed a painkiller known to be safe for sighthounds sensitive to drugs. Antibiotics were to be given every eight hours and pain pills every twelve.

Mid-week I had a law association board meeting that I couldn't miss (I was the past-president), so I asked a neighbour to come and sit with Raisa while I was out of the house. I felt anxious the entire time I was away.

For the remainder of the week, I had my assistant drop off files so I could work from home. I didn't really get much work done though – or anything else for that matter.

Very early on Friday morning (five days after we arrived home from West Virginia), Raisa began stirring in her cage, which woke me up. I took off her cone, fed her, allowed her to drink some water and then carried her outside. Back inside, she still wouldn't settle, which was unusual.

I noticed a few bumps near her incision which looked like pale pink mosquito bites, standing out against her shaved white fur. Was I imagining things? I didn't think so, but Raisa remained agitated throughout the day. I kept looking at the bumps, which in my mind were getting bigger, and turning from pale pink to red. I hoped I was just being paranoid, but when Tim arrived home from work, he agreed that something was wrong. Which meant that something was definitely wrong.

I called Dr. Radcliffe and he requested that I email him photos, which I did right away. He called me right back, saying he didn't like what he saw, and asked us to get Raisa's leg x-rayed locally. It was early evening, but luckily, we were able to get to our own veterinarian before the clinic closed for the day.

Dr. Radcliffe used digital x-rays. Our vet did not, so after waiting about half an hour, I was escorted to the back of the clinic – that mysterious area where dogs are taken away from their owners to run tests. It was a large room with multiple exam tables, pieces of equipment, and animal cages. On the wall, giant x-ray films of Raisa's leg were lit up on a light box, and I had to take pictures of them with my iPhone. Minutes after emailing them, my phone rang.

"Her body is reacting to the hardware in her leg," he said, sounding disappointed.

"But why?" I asked.

"Well, these surgical metal implants are made of stainless steel to avoid this type of thing from happening, but sometimes a dog's body will reject any type of foreign material."

"What should we do?"

"You go ahead and apply warm compresses to the knee, and call me back if things get any worse."

We headed home, hoping that we could stave off another emergency.

The following day was a Saturday. It had been exactly one week since Raisa's surgery. While Tim was applying a warm compress to Raisa's shaved knee, he called me over, and what I saw caused my chest to tighten.

A piece of stainless steel was literally starting to poke out of her skin through one of the bumps in her knee. The metal piece was about the circumference of a small nail, and the end that was protruding had a slight bend to it, like a hockey stick.

I called Dr. Radcliffe's office, knowing that he wouldn't be there, but that the receptionist would call him at home. She called me back a few minutes later and said that Raisa required immediate surgery for a revision of the metal implants. It was an emergency due to the fact that the protruding metal was an avenue for infection to enter the bone. I hung up and felt sick to my stomach.

I googled and found an Emergency Specialty Hospital about an hour away from us that had canine orthopedic surgeons on staff, and a comforting statement on the website which read, "When emergencies occur, we're here for you 24/7."

I called the number, assuming that we could get in right away. I was told a referral was needed. I explained that Raisa's surgery had been done in the United States and that Dr. Radcliffe could make the referral. The staff person told me that the referring veterinarian had to be Canadian.

I called our local vet. The receptionist told me she wasn't in the office.

"What do I do now?" I asked, hysteria slipping into the tone of my voice.

She reluctantly agreed to find another vet to make the referral. She also told me that the Emergency Hospital would not accept a referral without the x-ray films, which would have to be picked up before noon, when the clinic closed.

Tim raced there to get the radiographs. We paid $200 the evening prior for one x-ray, and our clinic charged a further $50 to take it off site. To add insult to injury, we were told that the Emergency Hospital would also take before and after x-rays of their own.

When the Emergency Hospital called to confirm they had received the referral, a crabby woman told me to bring Raisa in right away. I thanked her and politely asked what time the surgery would take place. She snapped back coldly that she would be kept at their clinic until Monday morning when she would be assessed. Then a surgeon would be assigned to her case. She wasn't able to tell me exactly when the surgery would happen, repeating snarkily that we were going to have to wait until at least Monday to even talk to a vet.

How could this be? We were in an emergency. This was an emergency hospital. I wondered how it was possible they wouldn't even be assessing Raisa for at least two days?

Deflated, I hung up the phone and filled Tim in on the other end of the conversation that he didn't hear. We had just started talking about what to do when my phone rang.

"Michelle, if you and Tim can get yourselves here, I will do the surgery tomorrow morning."

I blurted out, "But it's a Sunday."

He replied, "Don't you worry about that – you just get that little girl to me and I will look after her ... but do me a favour and get some Neosporin on the wound and keep it completely covered, okay?"

"Yes, and thank you. Thank you so so much."

Before hanging up, Dr. Radcliffe said, "Don't forget the Neosporin - that piece of metal sticking out of her leg is a highway for bacteria straight to the bone."

Dr. Radcliffe had come to our rescue again. It felt like a giant weight had been lifted off my chest. Even though we had another surgery to go through, not to mention a crazy long drive ahead of us and another big financial hit. At least I knew that Raisa's emergency was going to be addressed by someone caring and competent and in a timely fashion. Unlike at home.

It was snowing heavily and was bitterly cold by the time we pulled into the parking lot at the Red Roof Inn in St. Clairsville, Ohio. We brought Raisa's collapsible cage with us this time, so I was finally able to sleep in a bed, which after a week of sleeping on the floor felt like heaven.

The next morning when we met Dr. Radcliffe at his empty clinic, there was no need for x-rays, as he could clearly see what the problem was. As he took Raisa from Tim's arms into his own, he said, "You two go and get yourselves a bite to eat. I will call you when I'm done." It gave me a feeling of déjà vu, but it was our cue to leave so he could get down to the business of fixing our dog. Again.

Back at Denny's, we had the same waitress as the weekend before. She recognized us. "How y'all doing today?" she said, as she filled our coffee cups, somehow remembering that we were both coffee drinkers.

This time we waited in the restaurant for the post-surgery phone call. Due to the super cold weather, I went to the parking lot periodically to check on Maple, but she seemed warm enough, all curled up in a nest of blankets. While these silken windhounds were turning out to be a nightmare health-wise, they sure had great temperaments, especially when travelling.

When Tim's phone finally rang, he handed it to me and as soon as I answered, Dr. Radcliffe started talking. I carried the phone to the little vestibule at the entrance of the restaurant so I could hear him better. I was standing beside a vending machine full of stuffed animals when he told me that one of the pins had migrated out of Raisa's knee. It had been holding a loose bone fragment to the knee. He explained that he removed the pin and put a screw in its place "which should stay put."

He paused and then said, "I'll be honest, I'm still a bit concerned that another one might come out."

I took a deep breath, and said a little silent thank you that she made it through the surgery okay. I thanked him and hung up the phone. I then realized I was shivering. Without a coat, I was standing between the two sets of doors, and every time a customer came in, the cold January air rushed in with them. I returned back to our table and told Tim the news.

We picked Raisa up the following morning and headed home. Dr. Radcliffe wasn't able to be there, but he phoned us while we were driving. In a friendly but firm way, he said, "That little girl has just had another major operation, so you are back to square one with the healing process, okay?"

Before I could say anything, he added, "She is young so the bone should knit back together fairly quickly – but we'll see you in a month's time just to make sure."

We said our good-byes and just before he hung up, he said, "My wife and I have a spot available on our bed between our two greyhounds." He laughed, and then added, "In all seriousness, if y'all decide you can't keep her, for whatever reason, I will drive to Hamilton to pick her up."

I knew he was serious. That wonderful man must have sensed that we were close to our breaking point. I wished the conversation hadn't taken place on the truck's speakerphone though, as I suspected Tim was tempted by his kind offer. If he was though, he knew enough to keep it to himself, as he knew there was no way I would ever give Raisa up, even to what would have been a perfect home.

There was freezing rain in Erie, Pensylvannia and it was snowing in Buffalo, New York, but we forged on through, driving all day and into the evening. When we finally got home, Tim announced that he was going right back out again.

"I'm heading to Home Depot."

"What? Why?"

"I need supplies to make a better crate."

Tim is a problem solver. And his biggest problem at that moment was that his wife was a basket case. He wanted me to sleep in my own bed, heal my own injuries, and get myself back to some semblance of normalcy. He thought that my vigil beside Raisa's crate was stopping this from happening.

Tim is also very handy. He knew exactly how much welded wire mesh to buy and how many two-by-fours he would need to build a safe roomy cage for Raisa.

It was after midnight by the time he finished, and the results were impressive. Using the corner of our family room as two walls for the enclosure, the cage was large enough to fit Raisa's big rectangular dog bed inside, which gave her plenty of room to turn around without bonking her cone. It had a proper door with hinges and a little sliding latch. Best of all, there were no gaps in the wire big enough for her spindly legs to fit through. It was a tiny apartment fit for a canine princess.

Having two-by-fours bolted to the walls of what was once my showpiece of a house would have upset me a few years prior, but due to the emotional survival-mode I was in, the homemade dog cage provided enough comfort to override the fact that it was an eyesore.

My life had changed so much since bringing dogs into it ... but the jury was still out on whether the end result of the fateful decision would turn out to be a net positive or a net negative.

14

BURNOUT

WITH THE WEIGHT OF worry keeping me too paranoid to leave Raisa alone, I stayed home all the time. I was housebound again, tethered to the bedside of my broken dog. Living my life almost entirely within the confines of our family room and kitchen left me lonely, but I didn't feel like I had the energy to see anyone. Even making my way upstairs to take a shower started to feel like a burden.

I checked Raisa's leg too often, even in the middle of the night, just to make sure that no more metal was pushing out of her little knee. My nights were spent sleeping on the floor beside her cage, which caused even more friction in my marriage. I now realize that this was a personal choice and not a necessity, but at the time it absolutely felt necessary because my logical brain had been hijacked by my nervous system which was scaring me into believing that if I wasn't observing her all the time, something (else) bad was likely to happen. Sleeping pills helped me to fall asleep, but they did nothing to stop the nightmares that were waking me up in the middle of the night, soaking my pajamas in sweat.

The fact that I was never getting a break from it all compounded my stress. At least Tim was getting out of the house to go to work every day. Unlike me, he was able to compartmentalize the health issues of the dogs, and still be functional at work. He thought I worried too much. I thought he didn't worry enough. We both began to resent each other. As a result, Tim started spending more time at work, probably to avoid being around me. This left me feeling abandoned, which made things even tenser at home, causing him to be home even less.

In terms of the downward spiral of my life, the final nail in the coffin was leaving the practice of law. Don't get me wrong, there were other big issues that contributed to the decision besides the dogs (which I can't get into because of a non-disclosure agreement that I signed), but at the time, it was the stress I felt over the health issues of the dogs that put me over the edge emotionally. I told myself that I was just stepping back from my job temporarily, believing that by eliminating the intense pressures and responsibilities of practicing law until the dogs were better would lower my stress. Unfortunately, it ended up having the opposite effect.

The financial hit from leaving my job was significant, but it was my self-esteem that took the biggest beating. I worked so hard to become a lawyer, and even though I didn't love my job, I was good at it, and without it I felt like a loser. In less than a year, I had gone from being the President of the Hamilton Law Association to being a stay-at-home healthcare provider to my dogs.

I was suffering from caregiver burnout. I didn't know it though. Probably because I never thought of myself as a caregiver per se, I suppose on account of the fact that I was caring for animals, not people. While I recognized that something was wrong with me, I certainly didn't believe it to be a medical condition. I just chalked it up to being very stressed out in response to a whole pile of bad luck.

With time on my hands, I wrote an email to Raisa's breeder to let him know about the second surgery that had just taken place. What I heard back from him made me feel even worse, and ramped up my anxiety about the future health of both of my dogs.

In a somewhat breezy fashion, the Texas breeder informed me that two of his silken windhounds, both of whom were closely related to Raisa, had suffered broken legs at his kennel. One of the dogs was a young male that "snapped his right front leg" requiring surgery to insert a plate to set the bones. The steel plate became infected and required another surgery for removal and several months of antibiotics to cure the infection. The second dog was a young female who snapped her front right leg at the pastern (wrist). His vet recommended amputation due to the severe nature of the break. He took the dog to another vet who also recommended the leg be amputated. He eventually found a vet who crafted a metal sleeve to support the wrist joint and saved her leg.

The Texas breeder attempted to end his email on a humorous note: "I refer to one of these breaks as a Hawaiian vacation and the other as a Mexican vacation because of the money I spent."

Having just blown a boatload of money to fix the six-month-old puppy he sold us a few months prior; I didn't find this statement at all funny. In fact, his email caused me to reframe my thinking. Maple broke her shoulder. Raisa broke her leg. Heather's silken windhound, Fable, broke the same leg twice. I could no longer chalk all of these horrible events up to isolated incidents of really bad luck. Finding out that three dogs from Raisa's close family had suffered the same fate triggered my inner alarm bells which called my logical brain to spring back into action. I wondered if the problem was hereditary? Was anyone looking into it? What did it mean for my own dogs and their future?

I decided it was time to reach out to Heather. I hadn't been in touch with her since we had hiked together almost two years prior. I sent her an email telling her about Raisa's leg break, and filling her in on all we had been through with Maple. She emailed me right back, inviting me to meet up for a coffee. For months I had been saying no to every other social invitation that came my way, but for some reason I agreed to meet Heather, and I am so glad that I did.

Heather walked into the coffee shop that day carrying an oversized reusable shopping bag with a bunch of plastic items sticking out of the top. She smiled and waved as she approached the tiny little bistro table that I had commandeered for us. The café was packed, so being the first one to arrive, I had staked out a table to ensure we would have a seat. It was so cold outside that the windows of the café were completely fogged up, making the space seem even more crowded that it actually was.

Heather breathlessly said hello, and then dumped her winter coat and the shopping bag onto a chair before heading to the front counter to order. She told me that she would explain what was in the bag when she got back, making me even more curious about the bright-coloured items that were peeking out.

Back at the table, there was no small talk as Heather sat down and immediately started pulling the plastic gizmos out and setting them on the table. Talking quickly, she explained that these were "lifesavers" when Fable was recovering after her leg surgeries.

I must have looked confused, because she laughed and said "they're food puzzles ... they will keep your pup's mind occupied and tire her out while she's recovering in the crate."

Heather's bag of tricks also included a soft but sturdy vinyl cone with Velcro straps, and a black and grey padded harness that had multiple straps and a handle on top, which Heather said would make picking Raisa up much easier on my back.

There was no awkwardness at all between us as we started commiserating about all that we had been through with our broken dogs. Heather went first, recounting how since we had met up, she had been through a lot more heartbreak with Fable. Tears welled up in her eyes when she announced that Fable had broken her front right leg for the third time, which meant yet another orthopedic surgery, and the insertion of another metal plate and more screws to hold the broken leg together. It was painful to hear what followed.

About four weeks after the surgery, x-rays showed that Fable's surgical repair had broken down and the bones were displaced again. There wasn't enough good bone left to hold another plate. On the advice of the surgeon, Heather and her husband agreed to have Fable's right leg and shoulder amputated. After the surgery, Fable refused to eat, wouldn't or couldn't get up, and lost interest in everything. She had to be carried outside to urinate and defecate, and Heather had to clean her up every time she soiled herself. Fable also suffered serious reactions to the prescribed pain medications, making an already bad situation worse.

I felt queasy thinking about a silken windhound with only one front leg. I remembered that poor greyhound we had met years earlier who was missing a back leg, and how slow and awkwardly he prodded along on his formerly graceful frame.

Heather told me that her life had finally calmed down somewhat as Fable was getting used to life on three legs. She felt that their problems were over, now that the "bad leg" was gone. Opening up about how stressful it had been after Fable's surgeries, she told me that she also had a new (human) baby to care for. I congratulated her about the baby, and she confessed that being off on maternity leave had been a blessing, allowing her to be at home with Fable around the clock after her leg was removed.

I told Heather about leaving my job, and also about how my relationship with Tim had become strained since the dogs started having issues. She said she could relate, and shared her own stories about her own job and her own marriage. During the conversation, there were times when we were both crying, which caused patrons of the shop to steal sideways glances at us, as they pretended not to be interested in what was obviously a very deep and extremely personal conversation.

Being a private person, it was out of character for me to cry in front of anyone, especially someone that I was meeting only for the second time. But despite the embarrassment of not being able to control my emotions, it was such a huge relief to be able to talk to someone who understood in such a deep way how intensely the silken windhound health issues had impacted my life. My friends and family didn't understand. How could they? Before it happened to me, I wouldn't have either. Most people wondered how I could be so upset over a dog with a broken leg.

Our conversation eventually turned from our own sad circumstances to the silken windhound breed in general. We both agreed that it had to be more than just a coincidence that all three of our silken windhounds had broken their bones. I told her about the other dogs at the kennel that Raisa came from, and watched her eyes widen.

"We have to do something," she announced.

"What can we do?" I replied.

"We need to notify the silken windhound community about the issue, and get them to look into it," she stated, sounding extremely certain it was the right course of action.

"How do we do that?" I questioned.

"There's a Yahoo list. It's full of mostly breeders and some pet owners."

"How do I get on it?" I asked.

"You'll need to get Kim to invite you. I'm sure as a breeder, she is a member of the group." She then quickly added, "I'll do the post. You have too much on your plate right now, taking care of Raisa."

I looked at my watch and was shocked to see that two hours had passed. Feeling anxious about getting back to Raisa, I apologized to Heather, but said I needed to get going. She started packing all the dog paraphernalia back into the shopping bag as I put on my coat. With a plan in place, we said our goodbyes and promised to meet up again soon.

When I got home, I tenderly took Raisa out of her cage to try out the new harness Heather had given me. Her body wiggled with excitement as I pulled the padded circle of fabric around her neck. She must have thought she was going for a walk. She dog-kissed my face as I folded the sides of the harness up around her super slim body. Surprisingly, I didn't have to tighten or loosen any of the straps and buckles. Fable's harness fit Raisa just like a glove. It felt like a bad omen.

15

HOLDING IT TOGETHER NO MORE

A S SOON AS I joined the Silken Windhound Yahoo Group, I was able to see the polite inquiry that Heather had made on the discussion board about leg breaks. It was just a simple question ... was there a health committee that could look into the issue to find out if there was a concern for the breed at large?

I was surprised by the responses. Several prominent breeders were extremely dismissive, citing bad luck as the sole reason both our dogs had broken their legs. Others suggested that many "pet" owners (like us) were not giving their dogs enough exercise. Some blamed it on the food or even the drinking water. Others thought pesticides and herbicides could be to blame. The most amusing response was from an American breeder, who opined that living in Canada must be at the root of the problem.

I had been hoping for promises of investigation and action from the breed community, but instead all we got back was condescending remarks and seemingly zero interest in even entertaining the possibility that there might be something going on with the breed as a whole. Many even accused Heather of harming the breeds' reputation just by raising the issue.

The crazy thing is, a number of breeders actually admitted experiencing leg breaks at their own kennels, I suppose to illustrate that "freak accidents" do happen. This of course alarmed me even more, given what I had already been told by Raisa's breeder about the two dogs that broke their legs at his place.

Wondering how many others were out there, I nervously typed "leg break" into the forum's search engine. I was taken aback by how many hits came up. I did the same in the silken windhound Facebook group, finding even more. The fact that so many dogs within a small population had broken a leg was alarming in itself, but what really shocked me was the severity of the breaks, the medical complications, and the excessive amount of time and money that owners had spent fixing them. There were dogs that broke both front legs or suffered multiple breaks to the same leg (three times in several dogs), multiple surgeries, delayed healing, infections, and even leg amputations!

I phoned Heather to talk about it.

"How on earth don't they care about this?" I asked.

"I know," she said, adding, "They seem more concerned about the reputation of the breed than they do about the health of the dogs."

"Heather, the sole reason I didn't get an Italian greyhound was because I read that they were prone to leg breaks. How did I not know this about silken windhounds?"

"Because obviously they have kept it quiet."

"What do we do now?" I wondered.

"Well, you're not going to do anything," she replied, "You have Raisa to look after and that is all you need on your plate right now. The last thing you need is negative comments from those people."

"Well, I need to do something," I said. "I think I'm going to start a list so we can keep track of all the dogs who have broken a leg."

"Okay, good plan. As soon as Raisa's leg is healed, we can meet up again and go over the list."

"Sounds good," I said.

She replied, "Hang in there," and hung up.

A few weeks later, in mid-February, we made our fifth journey to West Virginia, this time in a less frenzied way, since thankfully we weren't in an emergency situation.

It had been four weeks since Raisa's second surgery and Dr. Radcliffe was pleased with what he saw. He told us that Raisa's bone was healing nicely and that the x-rays showed perfect alignment in her repaired leg. He also took x-rays of Maple's shoulder, which revealed that her shoulder fracture was almost fully healed.

Back at home, on the advice of Dr. Radcliffe, we bought an "ex-pen" (short for exercise pen), which is basically just a giant moveable cage. I set it up in the family room and equipped it with a dog bed and some toys to give Raisa a bit of supervised freedom a few times a day. When I first placed her inside it, I sat inside it with her. She looked so happy to be out of her crate; a little white deer fawn wearing a padded gramophone over her head.

Our newfound harmony didn't last long. A few weeks later another bump formed on Raisa's leg, which resembled the one that had appeared before the metal poked out of her leg the last time.

With a lump in my throat, I called Dr. Radcliffe's office and asked to speak to him on an urgent basis. I was surprised when a different veterinarian, a female, came on the phone. She told me that Dr. Radcliffe was away on holidays for two weeks. I felt like the ground beneath me had been yanked away. When I didn't say anything, she then curtly asked me what was going on.

"Another piece of the hardware is migrating," she said. It was more news I didn't want to hear, but that the kind of news I had come to expect.

"Can it wait until he gets back?" I asked.

She paused, and then told me what I already knew.

"If the metal breaks through the skin, it will have to be operated on immediately." She then added, "I suppose you can try to stop that from happening, but it will mean that you have to keep her completely, and I mean Com-Pletely, immobilized in her crate."

"We can do that," I said breathlessly.

"I mean you can't even allow her to stand up or walk. Do you understand? You will have to carry her outside and set her down to potty and that's it," she said, not sounding particularly convinced about whether it would work.

"Yes. We can do this. Thank you."

And just like that, my world was turned upside down again. I was back to focusing all of my attention on a bump, on a tiny pencil-thin leg, on a little waif of a dog - watching and waiting for any sign of the metal trying to make its way out of her body.

Raisa really hated being back in her crate full time. I knew this because she would look into my eyes and then look to the door of her cage, willing me to let her out. It just didn't seem fair. She was a still a puppy and had already spent several months of her short life locked in a crate.

In the days that followed, the bump stayed the same size but the colour turned from light pink to deep red. Five days before Dr. Radcliffe was scheduled to return, it started to bleed. I emailed a photo to his clinic, and the same vet I talked to previously phoned me.

"This really shouldn't wait," she said.

"But it's only a few days. Isn't there anything we can do?" I begged.

"If the metal pokes through, and it looks pretty close to doing that, you can't wait any longer. I'll call in a prescription of antibiotics to your vet. It's a liquid solution that we use to prep surgical sites. You'll need to apply it to the bump several times a day, just in case."

"Ok, thank you."

I was literally counting the hours until Dr. Radcliffe would return. I was determined to hold out. I had sacrificed so much already and he had become the only person that I trusted to treat my dogs. I needed that metal to stay in Raisa's leg, but it seemed as if her little body was fighting to push out the foreign material that I was fighting so hard to keep inside her.

Despite the odds and the challenges, we made it. The day before Dr. Radcliffe was scheduled to operate, we drove to West Virginia and arrived just in the nick of time. Soon after we got to our motel, the metal pushed out of Raisa's leg. We slathered it with antibiotic cream, and by morning it was sticking out even further.

Dr. Radcliffe happened to be driving into the clinic parking lot at the same time as we arrived. As he backed his big SUV into the parking spot beside ours, I noticed greyhound stickers on the bumper. He got out of his vehicle and said, in his friendly West Virginian voice, "We have to stop meeting like this."

He then reached down and looked at Raisa's leg and said, "Yep, there it is," and then added "it's a wire this time. "

As we followed our hero into the clinic, he explained that since Raisa was only seven months old and was still rapidly growing, the wire had probably shifted in her leg as she grew. Raisa was put through the usual pre-surgery work-up including x-rays and blood work. We filled out the forms, consenting to all of the "extras" to ensure her safety during the procedure. This was her third orthopedic surgery in two months.

Hours later, Dr. Radcliffe called and told us that the surgery was successful and he asked us to come in and see him.

We were at the front desk when Dr. Radcliffe came out to greet us, still dressed in his surgical gear. Without speaking, he handed me a plastic test-tube container. I opened it and poured the contents out into my hand. I was shocked that the long screw, a nail (which he called a pin) and a piece of wire in a figure-eight pattern had all been able to fit in Raisa's tiny little knee.

"But why is it all out?" I asked.

Dr. Radcliffe explained that he had removed all of the metal implants with the exception of one pin, which was embedded in the bone and "needed to stay put."

He explained that normally the hardware wouldn't be taken out until the bone was fully healed, but in Raisa's case, he felt comfortable in doing so, since the x-rays showed good healing and he was confident that we would carefully follow his post-surgery healing regimen.

We returned home to the canine convalescent routine that was consuming my life, and making me feel as if any day without a medical crisis was a good day. We were back to square one again in the healing timetable, but at least I was on the other side of the emergency, and for that I was thankful.

16

HELP, I'M SHRINKING

I N THE WEEKS THAT followed, as Raisa improved physically, I spiralled emotionally. I was quick to cry and even quicker to anger, which caused the tension between Tim and I to grow. One day, we were in the midst of a heated argument about Raisa's care when he blurted out, "Maybe it's time to start thinking about other options."

"Other options?" I gasped, dreading the answer I knew he was about to give.

"Maybe it's time we start thinking about rehoming Raisa, or ..."

"No. Don't you even say it," I snapped, turning my back so he wouldn't see the tears welling up in my eyes.

Isolated from everything and everyone; most of the time I just felt sad. It wasn't a good way to live, and some days I started to wish that I wasn't living at all. I existed only to make sure that the dogs were okay.

I decided to go and see a doctor, but not for my mental health. My broken rib was still causing me pain when I breathed deeply, so I went to the walk-in clinic at the local Wal-Mart to avoid the delay and hassle of dealing with my own family doctor.

When the doctor walked in, he greeted me kindly, telling me that he was a retired ER doctor who only worked on Mondays. He examined me and ordered repeat x-rays, telling me that he suspected my rib fracture wasn't healing. He prescribed a strong painkiller, which I was thankful for.

"Do you need a note to be off work?" he asked, and then looked surprised when I started to cry and I couldn't stop.

I told him that I was a lawyer and that I wasn't working. He looked very concerned and then asked me a number of other questions, letting me get it all off my chest. He then gently recommended that I see a psychiatrist, and said that he would make the referral. I was shocked into silence.

He then started writing on his pad and told me that he was prescribing some anti-depressant/anti-anxiety medication. When he handed me the little square prescription, I recoiled, and said, "I'm not depressed. I'm just going through a difficult time."

"There's nothing to be ashamed of. You likely have a chemical imbalance in your brain, and this medication will hopefully correct it."

But I was ashamed. So much so that I didn't tell anyone about my new prescription. But I filled it and I started taking it, feeling like a loser, but also instinctively knowing that I needed it.

Later that very same evening, the psychiatrist called me, and asked me to come and see him the following morning. What had the Wal-Mart doctor told him about me? Never in my entire life had I ever had a doctor call me directly, and not at night.

In the morning, I drove to the psychiatrist's office, which was attached to his home. I felt self-conscious as I parked my car in his driveway and walked quickly to the door, hoping that none of the neighbours saw me. There was a sign on the outside of the door with the doctor's name on it and instructions to enter and to sit in the waiting room, which was just an entrance hallway in the house, with some chairs positioned against a wall under a set of stairs.

There was a clipboard sitting on a table holding a "New Patient Form," which I assumed was for me. I sat down and started filling it out. I heard muffled voices coming from behind a closed door. Music was playing in the hallway where I sat, so I couldn't hear the specifics of the conversation, though I could hear a man's voice and a woman's voice.

When the voices got louder, and it seemed like there was movement behind the door, I sat the clipboard on my knees and picked up a Reader's Digest magazine and pretended to be reading it, as a female patient exited the room, smiled at me, and then left the house.

This all felt so weird.

A man yelled, "Come in," in a very enthusiastic voice.

I entered the room carrying the clipboard, and said hello to the elderly grey-bearded man who was sitting behind a very big wooden desk, which backed onto a wall completely filled with books.

The bearded man greeted me with a European accent that I couldn't place, and thanked me as I handed him the clipboard, and asked me to sit down.

He was dressed formally, in black pants, a crisp white dress shirt with a tie, and suspenders. I almost giggled, thinking how much he looked like Sigmund Freud. I couldn't believe I was doing this.

I had a choice of sitting in one of the two chairs which were situated directly in front of his big desk, or in the more comfortable looking chair, which was beside his desk, which is where I chose to sit. I wondered why there wasn't a sofa. There was always a sofa in the movies.

Once I sat down, the Freud doppelgänger introduced himself as Dr. Buie, and told me that he was 89 years old. He also explained that he was a psychoanalyst. He sought my indulgence while he took a few moments to read through my intake form.

I took the opportunity to look around the room. There were built-in bookshelves from floor to ceiling on every wall, holding what must have been hundreds, maybe thousands of books. The shag rug was dark gold in colour and the three mid-century modern chairs were upholstered in an orange corduroy fabric. The room was a time capsule from the 1970's. I noticed various pieces of art around the office. There were some primitive masks leaning against the books on some of the shelves, and there were several sculptures on his desk, one made of soapstone that looked indigenous. There was also a little metal sign that read, "If you let the fear win, you lose."

After Dr. Buie had finished reading my form, he asked me what had led up to me being referred to him. It was such an open-ended question that I had trouble answering it. He helped me out by asking some pointed questions, which allowed me to admit to him that I had been crying a lot and that I really couldn't seem to get a grip on the health problems of my dogs. I told him that caring for the dogs during the intense periods after their injuries and worrying about them during the other times was taking its toll on me.

He looked perplexed.

I kept talking, telling him more specifically about the effect that the dog health issues were having on my life, my marriage and on my profession. How I felt that everything in my life was out of my control.

Before I knew it, the hour was over. Dr. Buie told me that he would like to see me the following morning, and from there, we would start weekly one-hour sessions.

"You want to see me tomorrow?" I repeated back to him, somewhat stunned.

He replied yes, that he wanted to make sure that I was okay. He then said something about "depression," and I am pretty sure that I actually reeled backwards in my chair as I said: "Is that your diagnosis?"

"Okay, if you have a problem with that label, we don't have to use that word," he said, and he told me not to worry about the diagnosis at the moment. He also said that he would treat me for as long as I required it, but that it was going to take some time, because he wanted to start at the beginning.

"The beginning?" I asked.

"Yes, but for now our time is up – I will see you tomorrow at the same time."

I was simultaneously thinking about the fact that he must have thought that there was something very wrong with me if he wanted to see me again so soon, and I was also worried about how much all of this was going to cost me.

On my way out the door, I turned and asked him about payment, and he told me that our Provincial Health Plan, OHIP, would pay his bills. What a huge relief that was. In fact, I am pretty sure that I wouldn't have gone back had I been required to pay for his services myself.

I returned to Dr. Buie the following day and he started the session off by asking me if my parents wanted me. I told him that I didn't know, but I presumed, yes.

What on earth did this have to do with the dogs? I wanted to talk about my feelings about the dogs.

He then asked me what my earliest childhood memory was. I answered, but again, wondered when we would be talking about the real problem.

I felt like a fraud. There wasn't anything wrong with me that required me to see a shrink. This seemed ridiculous. What would people think if they found out? This all had to be some kind of mistake. I wasn't mentally ill. I was just stressed out. And I would be better as soon as the dogs were better - that I was sure of.

Not knowing what else to do, I answered Dr. Buie's questions, resigning myself to the fact that it might take a while before we would get to talk about the dogs, since after our second session we weren't even through discussing my early childhood.

And right there and then, even though I didn't realize it at the time, I started coping instead of just surviving. I had taken what I thought was a desperate step, but really was a brave one, in agreeing to medication and therapy, even though I didn't think that I needed it.

I will always be grateful to that random Wal-Mart doctor who recognized that I was in trouble, and took the time to ask me questions. Instead of taking a wait and see approach, which may have turned out very badly given the course that I was on emotionally, he laid out a roadmap of actions for me to follow, which was something that I was incapable of doing for myself at the time. The fact that that a respected professional took an interest in my wellbeing made me feel that I should too. In fact, the kind act of that anonymous doctor changed the course of my life and quite possibly even saved it.

17

ROAD APPLES

As Raisa was recuperating from surgery number three, the white tulips in our city garden started bursting out of the earth, defiantly declaring a spring victory over the winter that had tried its best to kill me. And with the return to pleasant weather came a new beginning for us as well, and it all started with a car accident ... luckily not one that we were involved in, but one that was serious enough to close the main road between our house and Tim's parents' farm.

We had been forced off the rural highway onto a back country road that neither of us had ever been on before. Crazy narrow, it had a steep gravel hill with a vision-obscuring U-turn on the way down. A sign told us that the road was only seasonally maintained, making it feel like we were up north in cottage country. I was surprised that a place like this existed only half an hour away from our house in the heart of the city. A different sign welcomed us to the Niagara Escarpment - A World Biosphere Reserve.

Reaching the bottom of the zigzagy hill, we went under an ancient stone train bridge before immediately beginning the ascent back up the escarpment on the other side. I yelled "Stop," and Tim put his foot on the brakes hard enough that the truck skidded a bit on the gravel. He gave me a worried look, as I stuck my hand in front of his face and pointed my finger to his side of the road, where, on the only flat piece of land around, was an inlet of gravel. At its edge stood a For Sale sign on a curious property that had no house in sight.

The only building which was visible from the road was a strange looking shed or cabin that had a stucco exterior and what appeared to be a relief of dancing red gingerbread men on the side. All of the windows were on wonky angles and the high-pitched roof had flared eaves, resembling a witch's hat.

Tim pulled his truck into the small parking lot, rolling right up to an old rickety gate, which had a ratty "Beware of Dog" sign on it. Beyond the gate there was a gravel lane that led into a stand of huge evergreen trees and then disappeared.

We got out of the truck to take a look.

"What is this place?" I asked, knowing Tim had no idea either. He shrugged as he took his hands off the top of the gate, which he had been leaning over in order to get a better look. I went back to the truck and jotted down the name of the real estate agent.

When Tim returned to the truck, he said, "Looks like some kind of kid's camp or something."

Back at home, I found the realtor's website. The listing contained images of an enchanting alpine A-Frame house, which the write-up described as sitting on 18 acres of forested land. I showed the listing to Tim, and he said, "Let's go and see it."

I had no intention of even considering a move, yet something compelled me to call the agent anyway. His name was Vince and he urged me, in fact, he almost begged me, to make an appointment to view the property, revealing that it had been on the market for months and his elderly clients were desperate to sell for health reasons. I almost felt like I was doing him a favour by agreeing to come and see it.

A few days later, we returned to the property for the viewing. The rickety gates were open, and as we drove through them, we noticed a shiny black BMW parked off to the side of the gravel lane. When Vince the agent saw us drive up, he emerged from his slick vehicle, and greeted us with a big smile and formal handshakes.

Vince was dressed for the boardroom, not the countryside. He was wearing dark slacks, a white perfectly pressed dress shirt, and fancy leather shoes. We were wearing our dog walking casual clothes and rubber boots on account of the spring mud.

Vince told us he wanted to show us around the acreage first before taking us to the house. We began walking on a network of wide gravel trails, which were more like country roads than paths. Vince gave us each a glossy brochure and told us that the magical piece of property used to operate as a small amusement park in the 1960's. We strolled by a pond with a sign nailed to a tree that said, Lake Haveagoodtime.

We then circled "the mountain" in the middle of the property, which he told us used to house a train ride for kids. Parts of the old tracks were still visible.

When we arrived back at the funny building with the gingerbread men, Vince told us that it was an old hotdog stand. He called it a heritage building, but assured us it didn't come with any official designation that might hamper our ability to do whatever we wanted with it. It was the only park building left standing, although there had been a number of them back in the day. He showed us a photograph of the old ticket-booth, which was shaped like Old Mother Hubbard's shoe. It felt like we had entered a fairy tale.

We trekked back up another long lane to reach the chalet style A-frame house, which was positioned on a plateau half way up the escarpment, snuggled privately into a stand of towering evergreens.

Showing us the property before the house had been a smart move on Vince's part, since the house, though charming, was rather dated and needed a lot of work.

As we entered the house, Vince mentioned that the owners, Bruce and Jean, were home. Jean, who was sitting in the living room, called out in a British accent, letting Vince know that she had made a pot of tea and left cookies for us on the counter to enjoy while we were touring the house.

After the tour, we joined Bruce and Jean in their cozy living room, and they told us how much they loved nature, animals, and living in such a special place. It was beginning to feel more like we were visiting relatives than viewing a property for sale. It was magic. They were magic. And we were sold. But there was a problem. And it was a big one.

We couldn't afford this house. Not with me not working. We were real estate tourists, not real prospective buyers. I booked the appointment to see the property as entertainment, not thinking about the people who lived there. I wasn't ready to leave the city, or convinced that I ever wanted to. I was just being nosey and was looking for a happy distraction, and now I felt terrible for having to let down Bruce and Jean, who clearly thought we were potential buyers for what they described as their little piece of heaven.

A few days later, I received a follow-up call from Vince. I had to break the news to him that we weren't going to put in an offer, and explaining why.

"Just offer whatever you can afford," he said.

And we did, along with the cliché letter, telling Bruce and Jean how much we loved the place, and why we couldn't afford their asking price. I told them about quitting my job as a lawyer and about our dog surgeries. I emphasized that our offer wasn't a reflection of what we thought the property was worth, but it was a price that we could afford based on what we knew our city house could sell for. We thought that it would end there. But it didn't. Bruce and Jean accepted our offer. I was simultaneously excited and terrified.

When we put our own city house on the market, the timing couldn't have been better. Hamilton, once an industrial steel city, had been undergoing a renaissance of sorts and we were lucky enough to be selling in the middle of a real estate boom (which some were calling a bubble). It was a seller's market, and houses in our neighbourhood were selling for a premium. Ours sold within a week for our full asking price.

It wasn't easy to give up that house on Aberdeen Avenue. So much of my identity was wrapped up in owning it. I wouldn't have even considered it if not for the dogs. Through loving them, I discovered that happiness didn't come from owning a status symbol in the form of a fancy city residence in an upscale neighbourhood – it came from being outside in nature, and enjoying the simple company of my husband and my dogs.

Prior to getting a dog, I had daydreamed about walking an elegant dog around my fancy neighbourhood, but once I actually owned the elegant dogs, I found out that they preferred running free to walking on leashes, favouring trails to sidewalks and dirt to concrete. And even though it took me years to realize it, it turns out that I did too.

Turning the dogs loose was the first thing we did when we took possession of our new house; even before we put the key in the door for the first time.

It was a momentous occasion, and not just because of our new residence. It was the first time our "running" dogs had ever run free together. Up until that point, one or the other of them had been injured or in recovery. Dr. Radcliffe told us it was time to "give them their lives back."

I was on a high, and so were the dogs. They were barely out of the car before they started gleefully chasing each around, deeking around trees and rocks. In the open areas, they ran in tandem with balletic grace, feet barely touching the ground. At first, I was mesmerized, but soon my heart was in my throat as I wondered how I was ever going to stop worrying every time they ran?

Within days of moving in, Maple got sick again. At first, we blamed the well water, but we weren't sick, and neither was Raisa. We hadn't changed their diets in any way. We wondered if Maple had eaten something in the woods.

Although it still took a vet to get her symptoms under control, this time, it didn't take us long to figure out what had caused a resurgence of the condition that had plagued her for so long previously. It was that mutant gene again.

Even though we hadn't given Maple any drugs, she had ingested some, unbeknownst to us. There was a horse boarding stable just up the road from our new house, and people rode their horses on the road. On our walks, even though the dogs were on leashes, both of them sometimes managed to grab mouthfuls of fresh horse manure here and there.

I flagged down the owner of the stable when she was riding by on her horse, and she confirmed my suspicion. All of the horses had recently been de-wormed with a drug called

Ivermectin, one of the problem drugs listed for dogs with the MDR1 gene. Raisa didn't have the mutant gene, which is why Maple got sick and Raisa did not.

Maple recovered, leaving me feel extremely lucky that it hadn't been worse; given that other dogs with the mutant gene have died as a result of eating livestock manure. I was also grateful that this latest dog health emergency didn't set us back much financially and surprisingly didn't set me back much emotionally either. It may have been the new house, the drugs, the psychotherapy, or the fact that our dogs hadn't suffered an orthopedic injury for a few months that made me feel more resilient. More likely it was that I knew exactly what we were dealing with this time. Not to say that it didn't stress me out. Because it did. I just wasn't debilitated by it, as I had been in the past when our dogs were sick or injured. Now, going forward, I just had to try to control that little voice in the back of my head, which kept wondering what would be next with our dogs. It seemed like I was tempting fate to not worry at all.

18

THE CLUB HOUSE

ONE EVENING, NOT LONG after the manure fiasco, my cell phone rang just as I was getting ready for bed. I was surprised that someone was calling so late but more surprised when I saw Kim's name come up on Caller ID.

I said hello in a cheery voice, which was met with silence on the other end, and then sniffling.

"Kim, are you okay?"

"Sorry. No ... something terrible has happened to Lily."

Lily was Maple's littermate, the runt of the litter, and was one of the pups that Kim kept to be a part of their family.

Kim took a long deep breath and then told me what happened. Earlier that day, she had been walking her dogs in the woods on her property. She was alone on the path and the dogs were running ahead of her in the forest. She was jolted out of her peaceful routine by a loud high-pitched scream (the scream of death), followed by the discovery of poor little Lily who was crying and holding up a badly broken front leg.

Kim rushed Lily to her local vet where x-rays revealed that both the radius and ulna bones were broken and displaced near the wrist. Her vet consulted an orthopedic surgeon at the world-renowned Ontario Veterinary College, and he recommended that Lily's front leg be amputated, due to the severity and location of the break. Kim's voice was quivering when she said the word amputation.

It didn't take much encouragement from me to convince Kim to take Lily to see Dr. Radcliffe. In fact, I think that is why she called me.

Kim left early the next morning. She was north of us by four hours, so her journey to West Virginia was even longer than ours. We kept in touch by email while she was away, and I was relieved (but not surprised) to hear that Dr. Radcliffe was able to save Lily's leg, repairing it surgically with the insertion of a plate and screws.

Kim called me a few days after arriving home, confessing that she was overwhelmed, and knew I would understand, given I had been in the same position just a few months earlier. She and her husband both worked full time and their two young boys were busy with extra-curricular activities, so she was finding it difficult to schedule Lily's daily medication and care. To make matters worse, Lily was refusing to eat, which required more veterinary treatment locally.

Talking to Kim intensified the fears I had been trying to suppress about what could still happen to my own dogs. As I added Maple's littermate to my list of silken windhounds that had broken a leg, I realized that there was growing evidence to suggest that these injuries weren't just a result of bad luck.

I got in touch with Heather by email to let her know about Kim's dog, and she suggested we meet up again. It had been a few months since I last spoke with her, and she enthusiastically agreed to come to my house the following day.

The first time Heather and I met, we went on a hike and became acquaintances. The second time we became a support group for one another. During our third meeting, we became research partners (soon to be labelled trouble makers by the silken windhound community).

Heather arrived at my door with a package of store-bought brownies, her infant baby, and her long-haired whippet. She looked happy but frazzled.

I grabbed the somewhat squished brownies from the crook of her arm, and set them on the kitchen counter as she sat the car seat down and unclipped Puzzle's leash. I knelt down and peeked in at the sleeping baby. She whispered to me that his name was Toby.

I directed Heather and her entourage to the living room, where she parked her sleeping baby on one side of her and her obedient dog on the other. Before heading back to the kitchen to grab a pot of tea, I handed her my handwritten list of silken windhounds that had broken a leg.

Back in the room, as I was pouring the tea, Heather looked up from the list and said, "Wow, how many are on here?"

Before I could answer, she added, "I wonder how many of them are related?"

I told her that there were 20 – dogs that is, not broken legs. I explained how the number of leg breaks was higher, since several had broken more than one leg or the same leg more than once.

As I handed her a brownie, I said, "I'm not sure how many of the dogs are related. How would we know?"

"Well, we know of at least a few," she said, "Both of your dogs have relatives that have broken their legs."

I nodded, but then explained that Maple wasn't on my list, detailing how I only included dogs that had broken a leg bone. Since Maple's bone break was to her shoulder, she didn't make the list. I told Heather that I wasn't counting shoulders or toes, because to my lawyer's mind, it seemed to make sense to keep the variables down. She agreed.

We briefly discussed how to find out if there were other leg breaks that we hadn't yet heard about. Heather suggested another inquiry to the silken windhound community via the Yahoo group and Facebook groups. I agreed. We knew that not everyone with a silken windhound was on social media, but at least it was a start. Our list would be under representative of the scope of the problem, if anything.

I began talking about osteoporosis in humans, wondering if it could be the cause of the leg breaks. Heather reminded me that we couldn't make any conclusions about why the breaks were happening – that we had to stay neutral and just present the numbers. The science and the medicine had to be left to the experts. She said our job was simply to identify as many silken windhounds that had broken a leg as we could find and collect basic data like the sex of the dog, the way the break happened, and how old they were. It had to be factual, therefore we would only include situations where an owner or breeder had verified the information.

I loved the idea of a report, and asked Heather whether there was some kind of official place that we should be directing our conclusions to?

"Sadly, we have to take them to the breed club."

With a mouth full of brownie, I replied, "But aren't they the same people who dismissed our concerns already?"

"Yep ... but they have access to the silken windhound breeders and owners, and the authority and funds required for research."

It seemed like a no-brainer to me. In my opinion, 20 silken windhounds suffering the same injury should raise enough red flags to warrant some research on behalf of the people who were producing them. Yet, I knew from the earlier online comments that we had an uphill battle ahead of us.

I asked Heather whether there was any higher power or authority in the purebred dog world that we could go to instead, since I wasn't feeling overly optimistic that we would get anywhere with the breed club. She said no.

My lawyer brain needed to understand exactly how and by whom the purebred dog world was regulated, so after Heather left, I undertook some online research.

I began by looking for relevant legislation, and discovered that in Canada, there is an Animal Pedigree Act, which I figured was a good place to start. After reading it, I understood that it was mainly in place to ensure the purebred status of animals in a particular breed, as opposed to the health of the animals. It did, however, point me in the right direction for where to go next. The legislation granted authority for breed associations to be established. The Act permits breed associations to represent either a single breed or multiple breeds of the same species.

Before doing research about purebred dogs and governance, the word "club" threw me off, until I realized that in the dog world, these "associations" were called clubs, and that basically, there were two main types: kennel clubs and breed clubs. Kennel clubs represented multiple breeds, and breed clubs governed a single breed.

Getting back to the Canadian legislation, when it comes to purebred dogs, the main dog association incorporated under the Animal Pedigree Act is the Canadian Kennel Club, or CKC. Most countries have one national kennel club. In the United States, they have the American Kennel Club (AKC). Being in Canada, I assumed that the Canadian Kennel Club would be the organization that we could turn to for help with the leg break issue, since their website stated that their organization speaks out on major issues concerning dog ownership and the health and welfare of dogs across Canada. But I discovered through reading more, that this institution is only concerned with the health and welfare of the breeds of dogs that the CKC recognizes. Silken windhounds were not one of those breeds. In the United States, the AKC did not recognize the breed either.

I was back to square one, meaning that it was indeed the silken windhound breed club that we had to take our concerns to. I read that each individual breed club would have a health committee and a breed health fund to support research into breed-related health problems.

I pulled up the silken windhound breed club website. The International Silken Windhound Society (ISWS) indicated that it served silken windhounds "worldwide" and that the primary goal of the ISWS was to protect and advance purebred silken windhound dogs, to protect the interests of its members, and to educate its members in the areas of breeding, exhibiting, and maintaining the health and purity of the silken windhound breed. It also noted that the club holds health clinics and subsidizes health testing fees for its members.

Heather was right. The breed club was in fact the only place to go to with our concerns. The website also listed the Board of Directors for the club, and as I suspected, it was comprised of silken windhound breeders, some of whom were the very people who had been so dismissive of Heather's query about leg breaks a few months back.

This was bad news. We would be asking the very individuals who were selling what was essentially a product to acknowledge that there may be something fundamentally wrong with it. It seemed like a conflict of interest to me. Nevertheless, we had to do it. What choice did we have, really?

I composed a post to the Yahoo group, asking for feedback from the silken windhound community about leg breaks, letting the group know that Heather and I were collecting information to provide to the breed club. I urged silken windhound owners whose dogs had experienced a leg break to get in touch with me privately. I explained why we were concerned: that there were only a handful of silken windhounds in all of Canada, but there were 9 fractures, 14 surgeries, 2 leg amputations and a death just in the past few years – all in young dogs.

There was a flurry of responses, and once again, the focus was not on the health issue, but instead was about the public way that we had expressed our concerns and the effect it could have on the breed's reputation. We were told that our inquiry should be taken to the "private" members' forum. Neither Heather or I had even heard of a private members forum. When I found it, and tried to post there, I found out that I didn't have access. When we asked for access, we were told that you had to be a member of the breed club.

This was news to us. We assumed, since we both paid to have our dogs registered with the breed club, that we were members. Turns out that our dogs were registered with the club, but we, as their owners, weren't members.

We asked to join the breed club and were informed that we needed to be sponsored by an existing member, and the club would then decide if we could join. Heather asked if we could have access to the private member's list while our applications were being considered. The reply from the registrar was that access before membership would be completely against the rules. Heather did manage to secure a sponsorship from her breeder to become a breed club member, but was told that her application was lost in the mail. I never did get in. Even my application to have Tim become a member went unanswered.

We were back in a conundrum. The governing body (the breed club) was composed of silken windhound breeders, many of whom had already dismissed our concerns about silken windhound leg breaks. Now they were shaming us about making general inquiries about leg breaks anywhere but on a "private" members forum that we had no access to. We were told not to ask about leg breaks on the public silken windhound groups, yet we had no access to the private group. This seemed ridiculous.

Heather and I communicated by phone about the issue and decided not to give up. We would continue posting about the topic on the silken windhound groups that we had access to. And even though we didn't have a plan about where to go with our data once collected, we would forge ahead regardless, and let the eventual numbers speak for themselves. We hoped that in the meantime perhaps the attitudes would change within the breed club toward the leg break issue ... although we weren't holding our breath.

19

OCD

BEFORE I OWNED SILKEN windhounds, the thought of driving all the way to West Virginia to see a vet seemed like a radical idea to me. Little did I know that the grueling trip would have to be repeated a number of times. We had made six trips in eight months, and sadly, our canine cross-border travel wasn't over just yet.

It was just a regular summer day in July and I had been out running errands. When I returned home, I opened the door to Raisa's enthusiastic greeting. Maple was nowhere to be seen, which wasn't uncommon, but when I called for her, she didn't come. I went looking and found her lying on the sofa, which also wasn't unusual.

"Do you wanna go for a walk?" I said in a jaunty high-pitched voice to rouse her.

Maple struggled to get up on her feet, and then refused to jump down from the sofa. I lifted her to the floor and with butterflies in my stomach, watched her try to walk. She began limping severely on the broken shoulder side again. Feeling like someone had kicked me in the gut, I wondered how on earth she could have gotten injured in the house? Was her shoulder broken again? A shiver of dread rippled through my body.

I called Dr. Radcliffe's office and was advised that he was away for two weeks. Of course he was! Feeling doomed again, I made an appointment for when he returned and we started yet another agonizing waiting game. Tim reassembled the built-in crate, and we confined Maple to it, only taking her outside on leash to do her business. Sadly, having been in this situation so many times before, we knew the drill.

My mood sank. I couldn't stop thinking about all that we had done to get Maple better, and here we were again, just a few months later, back in the same boat. I wondered if we had made a mistake by not opting for a surgical repair of her broken shoulder.

I emailed Kim to let her know what was happening. She replied that she understood how I felt, as she was still in the process of dealing with the aftermath of her own broken-legged silken. She told me that she had considered finding nice city homes for all of her dogs, where they could be walked only on leashes for the remainder of their lives.

Then my phone rang, and before I could say anything, Kim blurted out, "I think you need a break and I have a plan."

I didn't say anything and she went on, "How would you feel about me taking both Maple and Raisa here for a while ... and then I will keep Maple indefinitely."

Choking back tears, I thanked her for her offer, but declined, thinking that I must have sounded like I was at the end of my rope again, just like when Dr. Radcliffe offered to take Raisa when she was in the middle of her treatment.

At the end of the month, we made our seventh trip to West Virginia, for the first time under summer conditions.

As I checked in at the Red Roof Inn, the lady at the desk, who was always the lady at the desk, said, "Your mother called about an hour ago, you should call her back, she sounded worried."

I was floored that she recognized me. I hadn't yet given her any identification. We weren't "regulars" at any establishments in our own hometown, yet we were known at a little motel, in a little town, in a country that wasn't our own. My life had become so strange. I knew my mom was worried because I hadn't been in touch to let her know we had arrived safely, as the trip had taken longer than we anticipated (this time on account of a torrential downpour of rain that we had to pull off the highway and wait out).

The following day Dr. Radcliffe saw us right away and as usual wasted no time taking x-rays. We were surprised to hear that there were no broken bones, however it wasn't good news.

Dr. Radcliffe diagnosed Maple with a condition called Osteochondritis Dissecans (OCD) in her shoulder. He explained that OCD is a painful condition, which is why Maple went lame on her front leg. She had pieces of loose cartilage in her shoulder joint, which was diseased and had separated from the underlying bone. The free movement of the cartilage fragments within the joint space was likely the cause of her pain and also was likely causing further damage. Surgery was required.

He told us that he was going to remove the cartilage that had flapped away from Maple's shoulder bone, as well as any loose pieces of bone in the joint. He would then drill holes in the bone to stimulate new growth. It sounded like a pretty major surgery to me.

I asked him what caused the problem in the first place, and he replied that the condition is inherited and runs in families of dogs, unless it is caused by trauma. In Maple's case, it was possible that the earlier trauma to her shoulder had caused this condition.

He told us to go and get a bite to eat and that he would call us when the surgery was over. So off we went to Denny's again, this time with Maple on my mind, worrying that she might perish as a result of being put under anesthetic. I knew that Raisa could tolerate it, but Maple had not yet been anesthetized.

When Dr. Radcliffe called us later that afternoon, he reported that when he got into Maple's shoulder joint, he saw evidence of trauma, and that cleaning it up required him to make a bigger incision than he had planned. Otherwise, the procedure went well. Maple was in recovery and would be kept overnight.

When we picked Maple up the following day, I was grossed out by the gory incision that had been stitched up with 18 stitches that pulled two larges of pieces of pink flesh together from the top of her shoulder blade and all the way down the top of her leg towards her elbow.

Dr. Radcliffe told us that if her condition had been trauma-induced, it would hopefully be the end of Maple's lameness once and for all. If it turned out that it wasn't from trauma, then there was a good chance that the other shoulder "would go," meaning that the condition was hereditary. He warned us that either way, Maple would undoubtedly experience arthritis in this joint in the future, and since she was not able to tolerate anti-inflammatory drugs, any future arthritis treatment was going to be tricky. He recommended stem cell transplantation when the time came.

I felt overwhelmed.

By the time we got home I was feeling defeated, thinking about the number of hours and the thousands of dollars that we had spent fixing our broken dogs. One canine orthopedic surgery is an unexpected financial blow, but we were on our fourth within the span of several months. And the worst part was that we still didn't know whether we were at the end of it all. These were young dogs. Maple had just turned four, and Raisa had just turned one.

The recovery and rehabilitation for Maple after the surgery was the same as if she had broken a bone. It was a relief to know the routine but depressing to know what a tough few months we had ahead of us.

Maple turned out to be a more difficult patient than Raisa had been. It was difficult to get her to potty on command, so I had to let her walk longer than what was recommended to get her to relieve herself. Carrying her around was hard on my back, as she was much bigger and heavier than Raisa. She also cried horribly when confined to her crate, which made me feel so guilty.

I was tired and stressed.

Maple's last dose of medication had to be given at midnight and her first dose at six in the morning. Tim was in bed before the nighttime dose and up and gone early for work before the morning one, so once again, the medication routine, as well as most of the other caregiving duties, fell to me.

Maple was also difficult when it came time to ice the incision site twice daily, which required her to lie still for 20 minutes at a time with an ice pack on her shaved shoulder. It was hard enough to do warm compresses, but she hated the cold ones even more. This was a lot of torture for a super sensitive dog.

As time went on, we were able to give Maple more freedom, but our house remained set up as a dog hospital. We took our bed frame away and laid the mattress directly on the floor. Seat cushions were taken off the sofas, so the dogs could step up on them rather than having to jump. Once again, there were cages everywhere, with an ex-pen set up in one bedroom, a crate in another and the big homemade cage bolted to the family room wall. Our new routine included separating the dogs every time we weren't in the room with them to supervise their activity.

I began to see danger everywhere, and I couldn't seem to control the recurring thoughts that something else terrible was going to happen to the dogs. These repeated thoughts and mental images of potential harm were difficult to ignore, and caused me a great deal of anxiety. I began obsessively and repeatedly checking to make sure that the doors to their respective rooms were closed every time I left the house. I walked around the back yard before letting them out, searching for any holes or other sources of potential danger. If the dogs were with me in the car, I had to get out slowly and carefully, making sure neither dog jumped down before I could lift them out.

Despite knowing that my behaviour was irrational, I couldn't bring myself to stop. I felt certain that neglecting any precautions would inevitably lead to more misfortune. The measures made sense, but the obsessive and ritualistic checking did not. My love for the dogs had overridden the rational part of my brain, meaning that keeping them safe from injury was now the most important thing in my life. I was back to being a full-time canine caregiver. And it wasn't a paid position. In fact, it was a position that I was paying dearly to be in, financially, socially, and most of all, emotionally.

20

TRAINWRECK

EVEN THOUGH HEATHER AND I fully intended on carrying on with our research, it seemed that there was always a canine emergency to deal with that interfered with our progress. It was only a few weeks after Maple's surgery for OCD when I received this crushing email from Heather:

Hi Michelle. I hate to put any more sorrow in your life but I feel I need to let you know that we had to say goodbye to Fable tonight. She broke her other leg hopping off a mattress and there was nothing else we could do for her. To say I am heartbroken doesn't seem strong enough a description. I am so lost right now. Give some extra hugs and kisses to your girls for me and cherish every moment.

Reading this news made my breath catch in my throat, causing me to feel profound sadness and an immediate increase in fear for the safety of my own dogs. When I called Heather to offer my condolences, she told me what happened. She and her husband had removed their bed frame after Fable's leg amputation so she could have access to their bed (one of her favourite places). Their mattress, like ours, was sitting directly on the floor. Fable was simply hopping off it when her leg broke. Heather's husband witnessed it, and said it made a sickening sound. Both he and Heather were grief-stricken when they took Fable to the emergency vet, where they made the agonizing decision to humanely euthanize their "silly little girl."

Heather tearfully explained that they were emotionally and financially drained and didn't want to put Fable through any more suffering, believing that she had suffered too much already in her four short years of life. I think Heather felt like she needed to justify their decision to me – which she didn't.

She sounded so sorrowful when she admitted that just prior to this happening, they had finally started to feel like Fable was adapting to life on three legs and that she could live a fulfilling life. Heather believed that the leg break issue was behind them since the "problem leg" was gone. They felt blindsided by this break to her other leg.

The day after talking to Heather I went for a walk with my own silkens on our new property. It had been three weeks since Maple's surgery and at this stage of her rehabilitation we were required to take her on several slow leash walks daily in order to build her muscles back.

As Maple and I made our way slowly and carefully along the wide gravel path which wound its way through the property, Raisa was happily scampering around us, finally enjoying the carefree pleasure of just being a puppy, after all those months being confined to a crate.

The late afternoon sun was low in the sky and it was reflecting off the moving water of the creek as we walked over a bridge and through a meadow towards the very back of our property which is bordered by a railway track.

After bounding out of the creek, Raisa started to head in the direction of the train tracks. I called her back to me rather frantically, being super paranoid about the train tracks. Raisa had perfect recall, so she immediately turned on a dime and started running back to me.

As she was flying full tilt towards me, she jumped over an old farm fence that was flattened on the ground. When she landed, she fell, rolled and started screaming. It was the scream of death – the sound I still have nightmares about.

I watched the whole thing unfold as if it were happening in slow motion. I knew immediately that Raisa had broken her front leg and a wave of panic hit me like the freight train that I had been worried would hit her.

As I gathered my screaming beloved little waif of a dog into my arms to comfort her, she bit my hand. Hard. I ignored the blood that started to throb out of my punctured skin all the while speaking softly to her with my face pressed right against her ear, repeating over and over that she was going to be okay. I was also soothing myself and trying to slow down the pace of my heart, which was beating itself out of my chest.

Raisa screamed and screamed and screamed. I whispered, and rocked, and cooed.

When she finally stopped screaming and started to whimper, I carried her back to the house. Somehow Maple seemed to know that we were in a crisis and followed us quietly dragging her leash. I was so lucky that she didn't take off and run, which would have jeopardized her own recovery by blowing out the fresh surgical repair on her shoulder that had only taken place a few weeks earlier.

Back at the house I put Raisa into the big attached crate that we had been using for Maple and then I left the room. I couldn't bear to look at her deformed leg.

And then I had a full-blown panic attack, feeling light headed and sick to my stomach. I went back outside for fresh air and called Tim. I was sobbing and breathing hard, but he heard enough to know that he needed to get home. And fast.

I then called Dr. Radcliffe and was shocked when he told me that he couldn't see us until Monday. It was Friday. He said that Raisa really needed to be treated immediately and should be taken somewhere local.

Between sobs, I begged him to see us sooner and without any hesitation; he agreed to see us the following morning, which was a Saturday.

I have no idea what I did until Tim got home from work. When he arrived, he went straight to the family room to see Raisa and examine her leg. I followed him as far as the doorway but still couldn't bring myself to go inside, waiting in the doorway.

Raisa wagged her tail when she saw him. I found this unbelievable, since she must have been in an incredible amount of pain. However, I bet she was relieved to see Tim, sensing as a dog does, that he is the type of person who gets stronger when faced with an emergency, while I am the type of person who falls apart, at least when it comes to emergencies involving my dogs.

Tim walked out of the family room and told me bluntly that Raisa's leg was broken completely in half. Feeling like I was going to faint, I lowered myself to the floor where I rolled into the fetal position and resumed sobbing. To that point, the only thing that had kept me optimistic about the future of our silkens was the fact that they hadn't broken their front legs, which seemed to be the precursor for the tragic endings that had befallen some of the others, like Heather's dog.

Once I regained enough composure, I called Dr. Radcliffe back to tell him how severe the break was. He said Raisa's leg would need to be stabilized by a vet and that she would require strong pain control for the long journey ahead of us. I called our local vet office and was told that the office was closing. No offer of help from them.

I then called the local country clinic that Tim's parents take their animals to, and the vet agreed to keep his clinic open late that evening in order to help us out, which was a very kind and decent thing to do.

On the way to the country clinic, I called Heather, who emotionally but firmly told me that if she were in my shoes, she would have Raisa euthanized if her leg couldn't be saved – that the amputation that she had put Fable through had turned into such a nightmare that she now regretted it. Heather told me that she had come to realize that unlike other breeds that seem to do okay on three legs, these designer dogs were too soft, too sensitive, and simply too fragile to survive it.

While Heather was talking to me, I looked down at the sweet ethereal creature that had melted and molded into my lap, and she looked back up at me and right into my eyes, as if she knew what Heather had said, and was pleading with me to keep her alive. I had a pain in my chest at the thought of losing her.

When we arrived at the local country clinic the vet told us that he would have to anaesthetize Raisa in order to stabilize her leg and sedate her adequately for the long drive. He told us that he would be using the same drugs that they use prior to surgery.

I immediately went back into panic mode, telling him that this breed was sensitive to certain drugs, although I couldn't remember which ones. Try as I might, I couldn't think straight or remember exactly what Dr. Radcliffe had told me in terms of the protocol he used when anesthetizing sighthounds. My head was in a muddle. I was flustered and terrified but the vet assured me that the drugs were safe for sighthounds. He emphasized that Raisa really needed them; that a fractured leg is excruciatingly painful and she would suffer terribly without being knocked out while he was stabilizing the break.

He allowed us to stay in the examination room while he sedated her. Tim held little Raisa in his arms as the injection was given. The vet then left the room and told us that it would take up to 30 minutes for the medication to take effect. A few minutes after he left the room, Raisa started to vomit quite forcefully. I left her in Tim's arms and took off running through the halls of the empty clinic yelling for the vet to come. I thought Raisa was going to die.

The vet came back to our room and assured us that Raisa was having a normal reaction to the strong medication. He politely requested that I go to the waiting room and stay there. He said that I was upsetting Raisa and distracting him from his job. He escorted me there, and told me to sit down and put my head between my legs, because I was hyperventilating.

We left the country clinic with Raisa comfortably asleep, and another several hundred dollars out of our wallets for the sedation and splinting. I was thankful for the purple temporary cast that the country vet had applied to her leg for stability, as it stopped me from having to see the horror of what I knew her leg looked like.

Tim suggested that we wait a few hours and then drive straight to Dr. Radcliffe's clinic instead of driving there right away and staying in a motel overnight, since it would be the middle of the night when we would arrive. We decided to leave our house at midnight, which would give us a few hours to sleep at home before we hit the road.

I wasn't able to leave Raisa alone, since the country vet had warned us that she might vomit again and we had to be careful that she didn't choke since she was heavily sedated. I bedded down on the floor beside her crate in the family room, wishing that I too had been sedated.

The drive to West Virginia was stressful for many reasons, but mostly due to the sombre conversation that we had to have.

The fact that Fable had died a few days earlier was heavy on our minds. Heather and her husband did everything they could for Fable yet her legs just kept breaking. What if the same thing happens to Raisa? Would her leg break again if we had it repaired? Would another one of her legs break? What if the break was too severe to repair - should we let Dr. Radcliffe amputate the leg? Would she then go on to break the remaining one like Fable did?

I felt horrible discussing these life and death scenarios in front of Raisa, who was sleeping peacefully on my lap, still thankfully sedated and sticking her purple clubfoot straight out in front of her. I felt like a traitor for even thinking about how far and for how long we should go on fighting to save her limbs and her life.

Tim reminded me that we had gone so far already in many ways – financially, emotionally, and even geographically. Yet, she had broken another leg again despite all of our efforts. I told him that I felt guilty, like I created some self-fulfilling prophecy for her by advocating so hard about broken legs in the breed.

As the drive wore on, with my tear gauge on empty, I reluctantly agreed with Tim (and Heather) that if Dr. Radcliffe couldn't save Raisa's leg, then we would choose to end her life instead of amputating the leg.

We were on the same page, but barely. Even though I said the words out loud that I would be prepared to let her go instead of having her go on suffering – in my heart I didn't think I could do it - even if she needed to lose a leg. She was only a year old.

We arrived at the clinic Saturday morning with our sad and sedated little patient. As soon as Dr. Radcliffe walked out into the waiting room to see us, I started to cry.

He looked at Tim sympathetically and then hugged me and told me flat out that he would save Raisa's leg.

I gushed gratitude towards him for everything he had done for us and apologized that we had hijacked another one of his weekends.

While Raisa was being prepped for surgery, Dr. Radcliffe met with us to go over the x-rays, which showed a broken radius and ulna near her wrist joint. It was the same type of break that Kim's dog Lily had sustained a few months prior. And Fable. And most of the other silken leg breaks I had heard about.

Dr. Radcliffe showed us the metal implants he was going to place in Raisa's leg - a specialized plate in the shape of a "T" and a bunch of screws. He explained that many vets would amputate a front leg with a break near the wrist joint, because there wasn't enough room for the conventional straight plate to sit over the break with an equal number of screws on either side of it.

Though I was relieved that Raisa's leg could be saved, I was disheartened to hear the rest of the news. Dr. Radcliffe showed us on the x-ray how poor the bone density was in Raisa's leg. The image demonstrated that she had better bone density in her toes than she did in the long bones of her leg. He said that he had encountered the same situation with Kim's dog.

Then he blurted out, "You silken people have to do something about this situation."

It felt like he was scolding me, so I explained that we had tried talking to "the silken people" who refused to acknowledge that there was a problem at all. He just shook his head.

We left the clinic and headed to the Red Roof Inn, which had become a sort of home away from home for us over the past 10 months. Back at the motel room, Tim had to address my concerns about leaving Maple while we went to Denny's for breakfast. Due to the heat of the summer, we couldn't leave her in the vehicle as we usually did. He convinced me that if we put the "do not disturb" sign on the door, nobody would enter. I agreed, but we soon realized that we had another problem.

Maple, being only a few weeks post-surgery herself, wasn't supposed to jump up on or down from anything. Being a sighthound and therefore a creature of comfort, we knew that she would undoubtedly jump up on the bed as soon as we left. We dragged the mattress off the bed frame and put it on the floor where Maple seemed quite content to stay. We should have had a crate with us, but in the frenzy and fogginess of the leg break crisis with Raisa we had forgotten to bring it.

Dr. Radcliffe called while we were at Denny's to tell us that the surgery went well. He also said that in his experience a broken leg like this in a young dog often meant euthanasia given the cost of a surgical repair. He reminded me that we were fortunate to be in a position to be able to afford Raisa's treatment, but wondered about the other silkens that could end up in a terrible situation.

After breakfast we went back to our motel room and slept, which felt so good after driving all night with two injured silkens in the vehicle.

When we arrived back at Dr. Radcliffe's clinic the following morning, Raisa squealed with delight when she saw us. She looked good. Bright and cheerful, her white plume tail was pumping non-stop, yet she also looked impossibly vulnerable hobbling along with her big club foot of a leg. The splint was wrapped in a soft bandage to form a cast that went all the way from her armpit to her toes. The date was written on it in black magic marker. She was the prettiest peg-leg to ever walk the earth.

A technician gave us a primer on caring for the pencil-thin broken leg, which was now full of metal, and would need to stay protected while the bone mended. Her rather large incision needed regular monitoring and the bandages needed to be covered when outside and changed by a vet once a week.

During the long drive home, we had hours to reflect on the new reality we found ourselves in. Up until this point, we had naively been differentiating our dogs from the other silken windhounds that had broken. Those dogs all broke their front legs. Up until now we had been consoling ourselves into believing that the broken bones that our dogs suffered were different, and there wasn't something inherently wrong with their bones.

Now that Raisa's front leg was broken and her poor bone density had been brought to light by Dr. Radcliffe, we couldn't live in denial anymore. It was tough to admit, but we had to acknowledge that our dogs were so fragile that they could break just from running or playing or doing normal dog things. Not to mention that they were still young dogs, and if they lived to the lifespan that was promised, we could have many years of orthopedic surgeries ahead of us, which we knew we couldn't afford either financially or emotionally.

As we cruised along the I-90 with our two post-surgery silken windhounds, we made the difficult decision that for their own safety, and for our own sanity, we needed to "bubble wrap" them. They were delicate, breakable, invaluable treasures that had to be handled with care. Prior to this, Tim thought that I was being overprotective of the dogs. He now acknowledged that drastic modifications to our lifestyle had to be made, and kept in place indefinitely.

We spent the remainder of the trip talking about all the things we would do going forward to keep the dogs as safe as possible. It felt good to have a plan, even though it wouldn't be put in place for a while, until both dogs were fully healed.

In the meantime, I received an email from Raisa's breeder, who said that he knew how much I loved Raisa and that he would replace her "if that is what you want or need me to do." He went on to say that he was so sorry and wished there was a way he could ease our pain.

I replied and told him that we loved Raisa so much and could never replace her – that she was our family. And she was.

21

STRANGE BEDFELLOWS

IT WAS SEPTEMBER, IT was late afternoon, and I was sitting on our deck, nervously waiting for a phone call.

Beside me was Raisa on a poofy velvet-lined dog bed, in the middle of a very small pen. Unlike me she was totally relaxed, laying on her back with a smile on her face; her casted-leg sticking straight up in the air, hilariously pointing to the sky.

A year had passed since we first brought her home, and I was reflecting on all we had been through. In a mere twelve months I had quit my job, sold my dream house, and had moved from the city to the boonies. We hadn't taken any vacations, yet we had been on eight long road trips and funded five major orthopedic surgeries.

When the phone finally rang, I could tell right away from the tone of his voice that it wasn't good news. Earlier that day I had emailed Dr. Radcliffe copies of the most recent x-rays so he could check on the progress of Raisa's leg repair. I was told he would be calling after his surgeries were finished, but I didn't know exactly what time that would be. In a grim voice our trusted vet confessed that the healing wasn't where he wanted to see it. He warned me that the metal may need to remain in Raisa's leg for the rest of her life, which wasn't ideal, though he said he would re-assess the situation in two weeks and told me to hope for the best; something I wasn't very good at doing, given the year I had just been through.

Several weeks later Kim called to let me know that she was heading back to West Virginia to have the metal implants surgically removed from Lily's leg. On a whim, I asked her if she wanted some company, telling her that Raisa was due back there for a checkup, and it would be great to give Tim a break. It would also give us both a break financially by sharing expenses. She enthusiastically said yes.

After I hung up the phone, I had second thoughts. Even though I had spoken to Kim on the telephone many times, we had only met in person once. I worried that it might be awkward travelling together, and staying in such close quarters. What would we talk about for seven hours on the drive?

A few days later, Kim made the four-hour trek from up north to our house, arriving around noon. When I heard her vehicle churning up the gravel on our long driveway, I went outside to greet her, hugging her as she got out of her minivan. I peeked inside and said hello to Lily, who was laying comfortably in a travel crate. Kim had removed a row of seats from the middle of the van, creating a nice big area where two large dog crates and all of our luggage would fit.

I took Kim inside to visit with Maple while I loaded my luggage. Maple was so excited to see her. I then collected Raisa from her cage and carried her over to Kim, introducing her as our "problem child." Kim giggled, said "Awwww" and when she leaned over to say hello, Raisa almost wiggled out of my arms, stretching her long neck towards Kim. I stepped closer so Raisa could give her licks on the nose. We had a long trip ahead of us, so didn't linger at the house any longer than we needed to.

As we began our journey, I was immediately struck by how nice it was to travel with injured dogs safely and comfortably confined in crates instead of on my lap. Now that I was a dog person I was becoming a huge fan of the minivan.

It turned out that we had lots to talk about during the long drive. I filled Kim in on the details of my leg break research, sharing the numerous sorrowful stories of the many others who had been through similar ordeals to ours. Kim was sad and shocked to hear about what happened to Heather's dog – the gruesome tale of the repeated leg breaks, the amputation and then the tragic end of her life.

Later that evening when we arrived at the Red Roof Inn, we were assigned to a room on the second level, which meant we had to haul all our dog paraphernalia and luggage up an outdoor flight of stairs in the dark. It didn't take me long to realize that it was Tim who had done all of the heavy lifting on our previous trips.

Once we were settled in for the night, I realized that Kim and I made a good team in terms of what we had brought along with us on the trip. Being someone who attended dog shows and events, she came equipped with two collapsible soft sided dog crates for the motel room. I was all about the people comforts. Being a seasoned motel guest, I brought us pre-made meals, a bottle of wine, real dishes and even wine glasses. I knew from our previous trips that there was a microwave and a mini fridge in the room, and that we wouldn't feel like going out for food once we had arrived.

While our meals were warming, Kim and I took turns using the tiny washroom to put on our pajamas. Then we ate dinner while sitting on beds, since there wasn't anywhere else in the room to sit.

As we were eating our lasagna and drinking our red wine, I looked over at Kim and noticed that she and I were both dressed in flannel pajamas, in matching motel beds, with our respective hounds on the floor beside us in their matching crates. I thought about how surreal this all was; being in another country with my dog's breeder – but not the breeder of the dog I had with me. I really wanted to take a picture, but I could tell that Kim was super nervous about Lily's surgery in the morning, and I didn't want to make light of the situation.

The following day we loaded our silkens back into Kim's van and arrived at the Town and Country Animal Hospital early to check Lily in for surgery. The staff immediately took our dogs to the back for x-rays while Kim and I were escorted to an examination room to wait for Dr. Radcliffe. We waited longer than usual and when he entered the room, I could tell right away by his demeanor that something was wrong.

Dr. Radcliffe didn't waste any time on small talk, which was unusual. He opened up images of Lily's x-rays on the big monitor, then turned to Kim and told her that Lily's bone hadn't healed, so the surgery couldn't go ahead due to the likelihood of her bones breaking again if the plate and screws were removed.

We were both stunned. This was such a blow after driving so far.

Dr. Radcliffe then turned his attention to Raisa's x-ray, as he switched the screen from the image of one skinny leg with a plate and screws above the wrist, to the image of another skinny leg with a plate and screws above the wrist.

It was uncanny that both of our silken windhounds had broken the exact same bones in the exact same place in the exact same leg only three months apart.

Raisa's x-ray revealed excess bone growing over the plate, which was causing a lump on her leg; something I had noticed but didn't want to think about. Dr. Radcliffe told me that the main challenge was going to be getting the leg bones healed, and if the bump caused any problems in the future, we would cross that bridge when we came to it.

Seeing Dr. Radcliffe in the past had always made me feel so much better about our situation. His sighthound expertise combined with his take-charge enthusiasm and kind nature had always given me the impression that he could fix anything that went wrong with our dogs. This visit felt different.

When we asked what more we could be doing to help with the bone healing and to prevent future breaks, he answered morosely in his West Virginian accent, "Take these girls home and spoil them and pray."

It gave me a terrible feeling in my stomach to hear this.

The long drive home was steeped in a sombre silence, punctuated only by discussions about the recent terrible news from Dr. Radcliffe. Kim was beside herself that Lily's bone wasn't healed, especially given all she had done to rehabilitate the leg over the past six months. She just couldn't get her head around the fact that there were no answers for how to fix our dogs and move forward in any kind of normal way. She confessed to me that she was terrified of more leg breaks at her home kennel, since three out of four of her dogs were so closely related to one another.

I told Kim about the decision that Tim and I had made to keep our silken windhounds permanently restrained and restricted; a decision which I now felt even more confident about. She admitted that she would have a difficult time doing the same with Lily, given their lifestyle. They had four dogs, two kids, a huge rural property and a cottage. She would need to think more about it.

A few days later, my phone rang and it was Kim.

"I thought you should know that we've decided to let Lily run loose again."

I was surprised, but didn't say anything, and she continued to explain herself.

"We've decided as a family we're going to let Lily live her life to the fullest, knowing what the outcome could be." She paused and then continued on, "If she breaks her leg again, we are going to let her go."

Kim was choked up but told me again that she felt strongly that it was more important to give Lily a better quality of life, even if it turned out to be a shorter one.

"I understand." I said, adding, "I support you and even though we have chosen different paths, we both have good reasons."

"Yes, and I fully respect the decision you guys have made too."

I knew that others were judging me for "bubble-wrapping" my dogs, but Kim understood that we made a choice to lessen their quality of life in exchange for lowering the risk of an early death due to another leg break. I recognized that Kim valued Lily's freedom to run and participate fully in their family activities knowing there was an increased risk of another leg break that would mean the end of her life. Neither of these decisions was objectively right or wrong, but they were the right decisions for each of us in our own situations. Making decisions for these fragile living beings that could not verbalize their own wishes was agonizing. I wondered what our dogs would have chosen for themselves if given the chance?

Before we ended the phone call, Kim told me she was giving up breeding silken windhounds. She had taken down her beautiful website – the one which had attracted me to the breed years earlier. She also said that she wasn't capable or interested in being involved in trying to fight for recognition of the problem of leg breaks in the breed, since conflict wasn't in her nature. I appreciated her self-awareness and her honesty.

It was around this time that I sent Raisa's breeder an email to let him know what was going on. This was his reply:

Hi Michelle, it's great to hear from you. I suspected you might be down in the dumps over all that has happened with your dogs. Thanks for sharing with me the experience you and Kim had during your last visit with Dr. Radcliffe. It had to have been a heart-wrenching trip for the both of you. There are no words to say to speed up the healing or go back in time to avoid any possible genetic issues. I am truly sorry for all that you are going through. Let me know how I can help you in any way...if it can be any consolation for all that you are going through, I would like to offer you and Tim a pup at no charge.

It was such a kind gesture, especially given that our situation didn't meet the criteria for a free puppy pursuant to the contract we had signed with him, which stipulated Raisa would have to be euthanized or returned on the basis of a genetic defect for the breeder to provide a replacement at no charge or refund the purchase price.

I politely answered, telling him that it would not be fair to get a pup at this time; that we were still working hard at keeping Raisa subdued and it would be next to impossible with a pup around; that we needed to concentrate on keeping her risk as low as possible for another leg break.

What I didn't say, and which was the truth, was that there was no way in hell we would ever get another silken windhound again after all that we had been through...not even a free one.

22

CANINE COLUMBO

P RIOR TO LAUNCHING THE dogs into their new lifestyle of curtailed freedoms and near-constant monitoring, we spent a considerable amount of time converting our house and land surrounding it into a fortress of safety.

The dogs now needed (or more precisely, I needed them to have) a safe area to go outside when unsupervised, so the ever-handy Tim used some chain link fencing to build a small rectangular dog run. Every day I inspected the ground of the enclosure for holes or other potential hazards. Gates were latched and double latched. We still hiked on our own property, but only with the dog tethered to extendable leashes when out on the trails.

Inside the house we placed utilitarian area rugs at the bottom of staircases and in all canine landing spots adjacent to furniture. Tim cut the legs off our formerly elegant four poster bedframe and we removed the box spring, permanently lowering the height to a safe level of eighteen inches. Going forward, I planned to lock the dogs up in separate bedrooms when we had guests over to avoid someone inadvertently letting them loose on the property.

While Maple and Raisa appeared to be taking all of the changes in stride, I was still on edge, somehow seeing danger everywhere and never truly feeling as if they were completely safe. My training as a personal injury lawyer was undoubtedly at the root of this paranoia. Assessing risk and imagining every possible worst-case scenario was a skill which had served me well in a professional setting, but was now causing me to be chronically stressed out.

I think the biggest cause of my worry stemmed from not knowing why their bones were breaking in the first place. How could I protect them from future breaks if I didn't know why it was happening? Bone fractures were normally caused by a fairly serious trauma, yet our dogs experienced them while just running and playing. None of our vets, including our own renowned sighthound expert, had any explanation for it. Even the results of the necropsy (autopsy) that was performed on Heather's dog Fable didn't shed any light on the situation. That report contained the grisly description of how poor Fable's rib bones were "abnormally pliable, unusually flexible and broke easily manually." I was horrified when I read it. There were other skeletal anomalies listed, but nothing that explained the reason for the fragility itself.

"You just have to just accept it," Tim said, adding, "They're basically disabled."

"But why? It can't be happening just because their legs are long and skinny and they run fast. Look at deer – they have the same body shape, but their legs don't break when they run and jump."

"How do you know?"

"Well, I guess I don't know for sure, but if it was a thing, I'm sure we would know about it."

"You need to just let it go."

"I can't. I need to understand why it's happening, but the breed club is still blowing us off."

"What do you need them for?"

"They have all the access to the dogs and the funding to pay for research and analysis - hiring a geneticist or whatever. Heather says they're the ones that have to figure it out."

"Michelle, at some point, there's going to be a magic number of silken windhounds with broken legs that will be too big for them to blame on bad luck."

"That's it!" I exclaimed. "I need to find them."

"Who?"

"All the silken windhounds that have ever broken a leg!"

"And then what?" he said

"Hopefully it will convince them. But if they still don't do anything, maybe the puppy buying public will shame them into it."

The very next day my new (unpaid) job as a silken windhound leg break detective began. I started by going back to the Yahoo group forum and reading every discussion right back to the beginning of when the group was formed, something that turned out to be wildly interesting, and also quite productive. I also scoured through every social media site that was devoted to the breed. General search engines also proved helpful, as did plugging in key words on crowd sourcing websites, since people often asked for donations to help pay for the expensive surgical repairs required to fix their dogs when their legs broke.

All of this digging yielded quite a few leads, but in order to add a dog to my official list, I forced myself to confirm the information with either the owner or the breeder of the broken dog. Contacting these people became another job in itself, and one I didn't enjoy nearly as much as anonymously poking around online. Sending out private messages and emails, I explained who I was and what I was looking for. Some breeders ignored my requests, but most pet owners were more than willing to provide me with information. In fact, many even agreed to speak with me by telephone.

Quite a few of the owners I contacted offered up copies of veterinary records, radiographs, and photographs of their dog, which I greatly appreciated, although an insane amount of paperwork started piling up around my home office. When the numerous little mountains of paper became unmanageable, not to mention unsightly, I decided to employ a strategy I used when lawyering to combat the documentary chaos.

When Tim arrived home from work that day, he must have felt a sense of déjà vu as he set eyes on his wife, sitting in the middle of a circle of multiple piles of paper, a giant binder, and a hole punch.

"What the hell are you doing?"

I smiled triumphantly as I stood up and carefully tip toed out of the minefield of paper piles that encircled me. "I'm making a trial binder."

"For what?"

"My research."

"Why?"

"To win."

"Win what?"

I glared at him, wondering how he could even be asking me these questions when he knew damn well what I had been spending all my time on over the past few weeks. He met my scowl with one raised eyebrow, which in Tim language meant mild disapproval, but I didn't care. There was no doubt in my mind that briefing all of the leg break data would make me more productive. It excited me to think about transforming the random piles of paper into an organized binder with an index and tabs. I knew from experience that this would make it easy to locate things quickly, and easy to carry with me when I met up with Heather, which I was still doing regularly.

Heather, who was completely on board with my mission to find all the broken silken windhounds, didn't have the time or the energy to take part in the day-to-day collection of data. She had her new human baby and her two jobs occupying all of her time. And besides, she didn't even have a silken windhound anymore. I on the other hand still had two, and the hope of finding a fix, or at least the reason behind their fragility, fueled my sense of urgency to complete my new ambitious undertaking.

As I put the finishing touches on my Leg Break Brief, I couldn't help but smile. I had done it. I had organized the chaos. The wild beast of paperwork was no longer hampering my productivity. With nothing standing in my way, I was sure that I would soon find the rest of the broken silken windhounds that were undoubtedly out there.

The first binder (which I labelled Volume 1) contained information for 31 dogs that were confirmed to have broken at least one leg. The index doubled as a four-columned chart setting out the registered name, sex, age at time of the break, and circumstances surrounding the injury. Each broken dog had its own tab, where I filed all the information and paperwork that I collected on it.

Summarizing the documents to complete my Leg Break Brief didn't just organize me, it also validated my suspicion that it was more than just a coincidence that Heather, Kim and I all had dogs of the same breed that had broken their legs. I knew I was only supposed to be confirming numbers, yet the patterns that emerged were impossible to ignore. For instance, almost all of the breaks were to the front legs in the area between the wrist and the elbow (radius and ulna bones). This had to mean something. There was also a pattern with regard to the severity of the breaks. These weren't just hairline fractures; they were complete breaks through the circumference of the bones, usually with both bones broken completely in half. Most required surgical repair, usually with insertion of a plate and screws.

There were other trends that supported my newfound belief that freak accidents were a symptom and definitely not the cause of the problem. How the dogs were breaking their bones also told a story. Most of them didn't occur under traumatic situations. Like with our own dogs, most of the breaks resulted while the silkens were just running or jumping from a height that wouldn't normally cause a dog's leg to break.

Something else that really stood out to me was the fact that a surprising number of the dogs had broken more than one leg or broke the same leg more than once - too many to be chalked up as a weird coincidence. Also, many of the dogs suffered complications during treatment for their broken legs, often with delayed or poor healing.

Finding out that other dogs and owners had gone through similar horrible circumstances made me feel a bit better; which then made me feel a bit guilty. Misery loves company, but it was also a big relief to finally realize that the universe probably didn't have it out for me after all.

23

ROADBLOCKS

THE OUTSIDE WORLD DISSOLVED around me as I poured myself into chasing leg breaks, but when a huge freak snowstorm hit our area in November, the abrupt change of weather jolted me out of my reverie.

How had so much time passed without me noticing? The days and weeks usually seemed painstakingly long when rehabilitating one of dogs after surgery, but three months of looking after Raisa after her front leg break had whizzed right by. The month of November also marked the one-year anniversary of our first trip to see Dr. Radcliffe, an event I now used to measure time. We were currently one year A.R. (After Radcliffe).

It was much too early for such extreme winter weather. It wasn't even officially winter yet, but an hour away from us, six feet of snow had fallen in just a matter of days in Buffalo, New York. Stretches of highway across New York State had been closed, meaning that if we had an emergency situation with one of the dogs, we wouldn't be able to get to the Town and Country Animal Hospital. Knowing this made anxious. Dr. Radcliffe had become my veterinary security blanket, and having no access to him left me feeling extremely vulnerable. As a result, I somewhat ironically began using my search for silken windhound leg breaks to distract me enough to take the edge off worrying about my own dogs breaking their legs.

During the weeks that followed, thankfully, there were no orthopedic emergencies. By the time the Christmas season arrived we were comfortably settled into our new normal with Maple and Raisa, who seemingly were comfortably settled too. My non-paid job was keeping me busy and along with feeling festive, we were also feeling cautiously optimistic that our canine management strategies were indeed working.

On Christmas Eve, our short streak of good luck came to an end. This time it was Maple's turn to be injured. There was no scream of death. In fact, we don't even know how it happened. She was just suddenly and unexplainably lame; and this time on her "good" leg. Of course it had to happen about an hour before we were about to walk out the door to attend Tim's family Christmas celebration.

"Nooooo," I wailed. "How can this be happening again? It's not fair!"

It wasn't fair. It wasn't. We had done everything in our power and then some to prevent another orthopedic injury, yet here we were again.

Tim examined Maple calmly and carefully, and then declared, "Her leg isn't broken. I think it's her shoulder again."

I didn't answer him. There was no need. We both knew what had to be done and where we needed to go. But it was Christmas Eve, so there was absolutely nothing we could do in that moment. Seeking help locally had ceased to be an option for us months ago, so that wasn't even up for discussion.

"I'll put the crate back up and we can put her in there," Tim said, trying to avoid the meltdown he saw brewing within me.

"Christmas is ruined," I stated without emotion, even though my chest felt tight and my eyes were welling up with tears.

"No. We know what we need to do. You call Dr. Radcliffe while I get the crate ready."

As I dialed the Town & Country Animal Hospital, I knew I wouldn't be able to reach Dr. Radcliffe, but hoped I could at least talk to someone that could get through to him. My heart sank when I listened to the recording: *"In order to give our employees some time with their families over the holidays, we will be closed from December 24th to January 2nd. We will be here December 26th thru December 30th from 10am to 1pm in the front office for medication and food pick up only."*

That evening, I was barely able to talk to anyone. I was just too glum. The smell of roast turkey, mashed potatoes and steamed vegetables that filled the small house didn't even tempt me to eat much. The following day, I was even more sullen at my own family party. I just couldn't snap myself out it. I was consumed by stress. Again.

On Boxing Day, I was the first caller through to the Town and Country Animal Hospital. The always-friendly staff person who answered the phone told me Dr. Radcliffe was not scheduled to be back until January third. My desperate tone must have made an impression though, because later that day I received a call from him.

"Michelle, get yourselves here as soon as you can in the New Year."

As I was gushing appreciation, he added, "I'm pretty sure this one's going to need a surgical repair."

I think he already knew what the problem was. I think I did too.

Another New Year's Eve had come and gone, and for the first time in my adult life I didn't bother making a resolution. Why would I, given how the past year had made such a mockery of my previous one. As everyone else went back to work after the holidays, Tim and I made yet another grueling trip to the USA with our dogs.

On the day we left, and as we assembled our crew into the truck, everyone's breath was visible in puffs and the tips of my fingers felt frozen, even in gloves. While driving, I looked out the window and marvelled at the sun which was shining brightly against a deep blue sky. I certainly didn't take this weather for granted. There aren't many places as hazardous in the winter as the 180-mile stretch along Interstate 90 between Buffalo and Cleveland. The epicenter of the danger is Erie, Pennsylvania, a place which we always have to travel through, and it marks the half way point of our journey.

Shortly after arriving at the clinic, Dr. Radcliffe came out and greeted us in the lobby. He was wearing jeans and a brown hospital scrub shirt that had pictures of cartoon dogs all over it. He wore a stethoscope around his neck and his shortly cropped grey hair was covered by a blue surgical scrub cap. Shaking his head sympathetically, he had a look on his face that said "here we go again."

Wasting no time, he took Maple's leash from my hand and as he led our limping dog down the hall, we heard him saying, "Okay, Maple, let's go and get a picture."

Just before disappearing from view, Dr. Radcliffe abruptly turned back to us and shouted down the empty hall, "Did you bring Raisa?"

I nodded yes, and he added, "Well, you might as well go and get her too."

After returning from the truck with a very wiggly little Raisa, she was taken by a vet tech for x-rays while we were taken to an exam room to wait. About five minutes later, she was returned to us, but Maple wasn't. We knew what that meant.

When Dr. Radcliffe entered the room, he immediately broke the news that Maple had osteochondritis dissecans (OCD) in her left shoulder. This wasn't a big surprise. In a way, it was even a bit of a relief, knowing now that it was indeed an inherited condition that caused both of her shoulders to go, which meant it wasn't a failure of our safety management strategies around the house that led to her injuries.

Poor Maple. She lost the genetic lottery. The umbilical hernia, the drug reactions, and now this. I figured that Maple's mother Bacardi must have passed the condition onto her, since Kim often had Bacardi confined to a crate due to lameness. When I mentioned this to Dr. Radcliffe, he didn't look surprised. He also didn't want to discuss it. Not being one to dwell on the "what ifs" or "whys," he just wanted to get on with fixing the problem at hand.

Pulling up an x-ray of Maple's shoulder onto the big screen, Dr. Radcliffe explained the surgical procedure he was about to perform, which included cleaning out the sclerotic (dead) bone and degenerative cartilage on the head of the humerus bone. He would then use a tool called a curette to scrape away all of the abnormal bone and cartilage from the joint. After that he would use a small pin to make drill holes to help encourage blood to flow to the area to heal the bone and cartilage. I was learning quite a bit about veterinary orthopedics and was becoming proficient at reading canine x-rays through Dr. Radcliffe's excellent tutorials.

We barely had time to digest the information about Maple's impending surgery before Dr. Radcliffe minimized the image and pulled up Raisa's x-rays onto the screen. Pointing to the hardware, he said it was still looking good. He then rubbed his chin with one hand as he used the other to show us that the bones were still healing, but slowly; and not enough that the plate and screws could safely be removed from her little leg. He told us that the implants would probably have to stay in there for her lifetime; unless an infection developed. It was the same prognosis as Kim's dog Lily.

We were then sent away so Dr. Radcliffe could get on with the work of fixing Maple's defective shoulder.

"Are we going to Denny's?" I said, as soon as I sat down in the truck.

"I wouldn't mind checking out Cabela's," Tim replied, and then added, "You'll like it there – there's lots of animal stuff."

"What about Raisa?"

"She can come too."

Raisa's tail started beating furiously when she heard her name. She didn't care what we were doing. As long as she was a part of it, she was happy. I was too.

When we walked into Cabela's, I realized that Tim was right, there was lots of animal stuff. Just not the kind I was expecting. Raisa looked excited, and was sniffing the air above her head as we began to browse the huge store that felt more like a theme park. I was simultaneously mesmerized and horrified as I entered a room called "Whitetail World," a museum-style display of taxidermized deer standing on rocks among fake but realistic looking trees. Even more disturbing was the variety of equipment on offer to kill them with. Deer stands, hunting blinds, scopes and rifles. There were even deer delicacies like corn and other treats to lure them to their death.

We had no problem putting in time in the store while we waited for the phone to ring, which happened while we were checking out the indoor trout stream. Dr. Radcliffe let me know, first and foremost, that Maple had survived the surgery. He then reported that it was the exact same lesion as the other shoulder. This time though, there was a fragment of bone that he was unable to remove, because it was sitting on her radial nerve, and her heart rate spiked whenever he got close to it. He flushed out the rest of the joint but left that piece of bone alone. He felt that her lameness should be gone now that the sclerotic bone in the joint had been cleaned out, and said that hopefully that last piece of bone wouldn't cause an issue.

"Will she need another surgery?" I asked, and winced, dreading the answer.

"Well Michelle, she's all out of shoulders," he replied in his charming West Virginian accent.

The following day when we arrived at the clinic to collect Maple, we were told that Dr. Radcliffe wanted to speak to us. We waited nervously for him in the examination room and when he entered, he had a serious look on his face. He walked over to the sink, washed his hands and then turned around to address us, leaning back with both hands behind him against the sink. He took a deep breath and said, "I want to talk to you about stem cell therapy."

We both just stared at him, having no idea what he was talking about.

"For the arthritis," he added.

"She has arthritis too?" I squealed.

"No, no. Not yet. But she will. And since we can't give her any drugs, this might be the answer."

"Now?"

"No. She won't need it for a few years, but you need to start thinking about it because I will have to harvest the cells at some point."

"Is that a surgery too?"

"Yes. But for the time being, you just need to concentrate on getting her all healed up," he said, adding, "We will cross that bridge when we come to it."

My feelings had roller-coastered from being deflated about the arthritis prognosis to profound relief that it could be dealt with later. I felt a bit dizzy from information overload. There was a faint knock at the door and before anyone could answer, a technician carried Maple in. Tim stepped forward and she placed a very droopy dog into his arms. I got up and cupped her head in my hands and kissed her nose.

She looked terrible – sad and drowsy. The way Tim was holding her made it easy to see her shoulder, which looked awful. She was shaved from her neck to her elbow, exposing her lavender blue skin, which intensified to a deep burgundy colour surrounding the blue stitches that held her flesh together. It was the biggest incision yet of all the dog surgeries we had been through in the past 12 months; which at this point, sadly, was six.

It was snowing when we left the clinic, but it was the polite variety, all light and fluffy. Within an hour of driving, the scenery started to disappear into a soft white haze. The snow began to fall sideways as the weather rapidly turned aggressive. Dangerous.

Tim, who had been quietly concentrating on the road, finally cursed, "Fuck me, I can't even tell where the road is anymore."

"This sucks," I replied, not really knowing what else to say. It did suck.

For a year we had been winning at the game of weather roulette, but now it was time to pay the piper. Being Canadian, I was used to treacherous winter conditions, but this was unlike anything I had ever seen before. Four lanes of traffic had been reduced to just two grooves in the road, and I could tell that Tim was struggling to keep our tires within them. He activated the truck's hazard lights, presumably to make sure nobody ran into us from behind. It made an urgent clicking sound, which reverberated through the vehicle, making me feel even more on edge. Every few miles we passed a vehicle in the ditch. Looking like ghosts in the storm, a few were upside down. I wondered what happened to their occupants?

As we entered Pennsylvania, we pulled up behind a line of cars which was barely moving. As we slowly crept forward, we noticed all the vehicles were exiting off the highway. When we got close enough, we saw a bunch of State Troopers dressed in fluorescent winter coats patrolling a blockade made of police cruisers. In front of them was a large portable sign with illumined text stating that the Interstate was closed due to extreme winter weather conditions.

After being forced off the highway, Tim pulled the truck into a parking lot of what appeared to be an abandoned gas station. Raisa stood up, thinking we had arrived at our destination. Maple was still conked out in the back of the truck, looking scarily as if she were dead. I roused her and she briefly opened her eyes.

Turning my attention back to Tim, I said, "What now?" as Raisa climbed into my lap, enthusiastically kissing my face.

"We need to find a place to stay," Tim said as he pulled Raisa back onto her dog bed between us, gently forcing her to lie back down.

"Where are we?"

"I have no idea."

We sat in silence for a few seconds and then Tim said, "Screw it, let's keep going."

"How?"

"We'll take the backroads and head in the direction of home. There is no way we're going to find anywhere to stay around here."

We made it as far as a town called Springville in New York State before we were stopped by police putting up barricades. We were now really stuck ... in a raging blizzard ... in the dark. With two dogs, one of whom was just out of major surgery, and was not looking good.

We drove slowly around looking for somewhere to stay, but the motels all had no vacancy signs lit up, presumably because of the other travellers who had arrived before us and had already checked in.

Tim pulled into the parking lot of a Microtel Inn. It was more of a hotel than a motel, and as I looked over to the formal entrance, I asked, "Why don't you pull up under the overhang."

"The dogs. They'll see them."

"Maybe they allow dogs?"

"Not the way our luck is going."

"True. I doubt they even have any rooms."

I put on my parka, and when I opened the door a bunch of snow blew in onto my seat. I pulled my hood over my hair and held it in place as I hopped out of the truck and ran through the parking lot. Fighting the wind and blinded by snow, I headed in the direction of the front doors of the hotel, passing an older man who wasn't moving as fast as I was. Rudely, I didn't wait to hold the door open for him, instead racing right to the desk. I felt like I was a contestant on some kind of game show.

There was only one uniformed agent working behind the counter. An older lady, she smiled and said "Brrrrr" as I stomped the snow off my boots on the heavy black mat that had been placed over the hotel carpet in front of the counter. More snow fell off as I lowered my hood.

"Are there any rooms?" I asked, breathless.

"You're in luck – it's literally our last room," she said, loud enough that the man now waiting behind me could hear. He still waited as I checked ourselves in, which I thought was strange.

Normally I would have asked the price of the room, and then consulted with Tim, but given that it was a bit of a do or die situation, I wasn't going to miss out on the last room. I didn't want to sleep in the truck. As the agent was slowly taking down the information from my driver's license, I picked up a brochure from the countertop and saw the "no pets" policy.

My mind started to race. How on earth were we going to sneak the dogs in? There was only one main door into the facility, and we would have to walk right past the front desk to get to our room.

The agent handed me our room card, informing me that it was on the first floor. She pointed to a set of glass doors and instructed me to go through them and turn left at the elevators.

I thanked her, walked past the poor guy behind me whose room we got, and headed straight for the hallway. It was long and carpeted, and best of all, there was an Emergency Exit door at the end of it.

I located our room, which was about half way down the hall, opened it and jammed one of my mittens between the door and the doorway so it wouldn't lock.

Returning back through the lobby, I smiled at the desk lady, who was still talking to the older gentleman. I pulled my hood back up and went outside to let Tim know where he could meet me to sneak the dogs in.

I tried to look nonchalant as I re-entered the hotel, smiling again at the front desk lady, and the older man who were both undoubtedly wondering what the hell I was doing.

When I got back to the emergency exit door, I pushed the crash bar and the door barely budged. I had to lean back and throw my shoulder into it over and over, opening it inches at a time. The snow was about three feet deep on the outside, and the door felt like it weighed an extra 400 pounds.

Once I had a big enough opening, Tim passed Maple through to me. Good thing we had skinny dogs.

I carried Maple quickly to the room, gently kicking the door open with my foot. When I got inside, I didn't know what to do with her. She wasn't supposed to be moving around at all and we didn't have a crate with us. I stuck her in the washroom.

Jamming my mitten back into the motel room doorway on the way back out, I hurried down the hall to collect Raisa. I was terrified that a hotel guest, or God forbid a staff person would see me and kick us out for having dogs.

Once the mission had been accomplished, we had to figure out what to do about food. Maple wasn't supposed to take her medication on an empty stomach. We hadn't eaten anything since breakfast. I went to the front desk and the friendly desk lady informed me that all of the restaurants in town had closed early due to the blizzard. I reported back to Tim that there was a vending machine in the lobby. Tim, being a three-square-meals kind of guy, didn't want to eat Doritos for dinner. He told me that he remembered seeing a gas station that was open on our way in, and he went out on foot to investigate.

When he returned, he looked like the Abominable Snow Man. He triumphantly plopped down his bounty onto the small desk. It was a crummy but much appreciated pizza, and a package of cheese to feed the dogs. Not an ideal meal for any of us, but still much better than chips and chocolate bars.

When we woke up the following morning, it was still snowing. By turning on the television, we found out that the main highways were still closed but that some of the back roads had been opened. Tim declared that there was no use staying put. We needed to get Maple home.

We loaded the truck first, and then snuck the dogs back outside through the emergency exit. The driving was extremely slow due to the conditions, but at least we were moving in the right direction. Not long after we left the hotel, John Denver's song came on the radio, *"Country roads - take me home - to the place I belong - West Virginia, mountain mamma – take me home."* We had to laugh. We just wanted the country roads to take us home FROM West Virginia.

It took us a ridiculously long time, but we eventually made it back to Canada. Upon arriving home, neither Tim nor I dared to speak the words "let's hope this is the last time we have to make that trip" for fear of jinxing ourselves, even though in our heart of hearts we knew that we would be back; and that Dr. Radcliffe was going to be a part of our lives for as long as our lives included silken windhounds.

24

HAVEN'T GOT A LEG TO STAND ON

MAPLE WAS A MISERABLE patient. Even though I was now feeling fairly confident about meeting all of her post-surgical needs, I still had no idea how to make her comfortable while confined to a crate. Unlike Raisa, there was no cheering her up with food games and cuddles. In fact, Mournful Maple barely even raised her head, and when she did, her forlorn look perfectly captured the misery and injustice of her situation.

To make matters worse, we had to give her painful injections. Because she was unable to tolerate the usual drugs for pain and swelling, Dr. Radcliffe prescribed Maple an injectable drug which is normally used to treat joint diseases. He showed us how to insert the large needle directly into the muscle of Maple's shoulder. She needed this done once a week for a month. The procedure was pure torture for Maple (and for me), but doing it ourselves saved us time and money, and most importantly it saved Maple from more vet visits, which she detested even more than being in the crate.

In a mere twelve months Tim and I had become accomplished canine health-care providers. We were now proficient at monitoring incisions, dressing wounds, removing stitches and administering medication. We were ambulance drivers, paramedics, occupational therapists, physiotherapists, and nurses to our canine patients; activities that I never contemplated would be part of loving and living with dogs; especially dogs that were touted as being exceptionally healthy.

The day after we returned home from the States, Tim went back to work. Looking after Maple alone rendered me more or less completely housebound again, but this time I didn't sulk around feeling sorry for myself. This time, there was no time for self-pity, because I had important and meaningful work to get back to.

Using a fold-up plastic table, I created a little work station in the same room as Maple's crate so I could resume my leg break research, while still keeping a close eye on her. I covered the table with a pretty vintage table cloth, and assembled all my loose paperwork on top, along with my ever-growing binder of confirmed leg breaks and my computer.

I placed one of Raisa's poofy dog beds directly beside my chair, because she just wouldn't stand for being any further away from me than that. Since her latest leg break, she was glued even tighter to my side. When I focused any attention on Maple, she circled my legs like a cat. I am uncertain whether she was jealous or if she was just trying to cheer me up, but either way, her unwavering affection felt like a ray of sunshine and her infectious energy helped keep my mood from darkening in that dangerous way I had become prone to whenever my dogs were hurt.

Prior to Maple's latest surgery, I had collected a fair number of leads on the leg break front. Now it was time to employ some old-fashioned detective techniques to turn them into real data. To that end, I spent a good part of my days contacting "witnesses," asking questions, sharing stories and taking copious notes.

The sad tales of the owners were all too familiar, each one triggering my own feelings about my own dogs. In fact, some were even worse than ours, sounding eerily similar to what Heather had gone through with Fable. Stories with tragic endings that I hated thinking about because they made me feel terrified about what the future could hold for my own dogs.

The story that haunted me the most concerned another Canadian dog. Her name was Delaney. I read an old Facebook post that was asking for good wishes and prayers after "an unfortunate accident" that caused Delaney's leg to break. I sent a private message to the dog's owner, and she agreed to speak to me by telephone about what happened.

Roma, a retired nurse, told me that even though a few years had passed since the accident, she remembered the details as if it were yesterday. Her recollections were vivid and visceral.

She described Delaney as sweet, small-boned, and fragile ... the perfect dog, "an old soul - really special." Delaney loved her daily walks off leash on a maintained green space on a hydro easement. On the day in question, a German shepherd dog charged at Delaney near the access point to the easement area. Delaney initially ran away, but then stopped, and the German shepherd "was on her."

Delaney sustained a broken leg, consisting of a compound fracture of her radius and ulna bones (at the wrist). The bones of her front leg were poking out through the skin. She underwent surgery, and a plate and screws were inserted to stabilize the breaks. The leg was then covered with a splint and vet wrap. Shortly after the repair, Delaney developed pressure sores that Roma attributed to the splint being been put on too tightly. Then, despite daily wound care, the metal hardware started to poke out through Delaney's skin, and Delaney was put on antibiotics.

A month later, the vet told Roma that the hardware had to come out. She underwent a second surgery to remove the plate and screws, and then was put back in her splint.

The very next day, poor little Delaney sustained yet another compound fracture to the same leg. By this time, Roma had already spent $6000 and now Delaney needed to be sent to a canine orthopedic specialist in another city.

Roma told me that as a retiree on a fixed income, she couldn't afford another surgical repair. After some research and advice from her vet, she agreed to have Delaney's leg amputated. She was told that Delaney would be okay since she had already gotten used to living on three legs since the first accident.

Delaney underwent a third surgery in two months to have her front leg amputated. After the surgery, Delaney was in a great deal of pain that Roma and her vet were unable to control. She wouldn't eat and she wouldn't settle. Roma took her back to her vet, and Delaney was put on a lidocaine drip with morphine. She took a turn for the worse after she was released home. In a panic, Roma rushed Delaney back to the vet where it was determined that she was bleeding into her belly. On the vet's advice, and to end her suffering, Roma made the gut-wrenching decision to euthanize her beloved dog.

"I felt we betrayed this sweet dog," she said, and then admitted to me that what transpired with Delaney traumatized her so much that even now, years later, she was still grieving more than she has ever grieved the loss of any human in her life. As a result of this ordeal, Roma decided never to get another dog. "I still miss my girl every day and while my memory fails me on just about everything else, every detail of her attack and subsequent suffering are permanently etched on my brain."

Another similar story started with a fundraiser on the GoFundMe website. It was titled "Sylvan Has Vet Bills." The narrative stated that a sweet, shy, beautiful silken windhound had recently taken a freak fall and now had expensive vet bills. There was a picture of a beautiful white-faced silken windhound with its front leg bandaged in a hot pink soft cast – an image I was all too familiar with.

Sylvan's owner recounted the sad details that necessitated the plea for funding, clarifying that this leg break was not Sylvan's first. In fact, the current broken leg was her

ONLY front leg, as the other one had already been amputated after a "bad break." She said that Sylvan broke her remaining front leg coming down some stairs and simply missed her landing at the bottom and her leg snapped under her. It cost $4000 to repair the leg surgically. Sadly, six weeks later, a very sad decision had to be made, and poor Sylvan was euthanized after the repaired leg had swollen up like a balloon.

Both of these harrowing stories were distressing in themselves, but there was something even more shocking about them. Through my discussions with the owners of these two broken and now deceased dogs, I came to realize that both Delaney and Sylvan came from the same kennel as Heather's dog Fable!

With my mind racing with the implications of this revelation, I phoned Heather, who, up until this point had been shutting me down whenever I brought up the subject of familial connections between dogs that had broken their legs. I just knew this finding would change her mind.

When she answered the phone, I breathlessly said, "You're not going to believe this."

"What?" she said, sounding a bit excited.

"I found two more dogs with broken legs that came from the same kennel as Fable." Silence.

"And they both had a leg amputated."

"Uh huh."

"And they both died!"

"Just because they came from the same kennel, doesn't necessarily mean they are closely related," she said.

Her underwhelming response took me by surprise.

"Don't you think it's beyond coincidence that three dogs from the same kennel are dead after having their legs amputated from leg breaks?" I challenged.

"Yes, of course it is. And I believe it is completely relevant, but we can't start making conclusions before enough data has even been collected. We agreed to just catalogue the basic information, remember?"

"How can we ignore it," I pleaded. "This is crazy!"

"We have to," she replied, adding, "Our job ... our only job, is to find the number of dogs that have broken. Period. We are no better than them if we start jumping to conclusions about what is or isn't relevant."

I mumbled "I know, I know, you're right," even though I didn't really agree with her.

She could sense my resistance.

"Listen Michelle, don't get yourself sidetracked. Chasing pedigrees is a futile distraction. Trust me on this one."

I said nothing, and then she added, "They will just say that the dogs were fed the same diet, drank the same water, or some other explanation that will be bullshit but that we can't refute, because we aren't qualified to."

"Sure, I understand."

I hung up after reluctantly promising Heather that I would stay focused on just collecting the basic information. After all, she knew much more than I did about dog breeding and genetics, so I needed to defer to her. I was just a lowly "pet" owner. What the hell did I know anyway?

25

A TRIP DOWN THE RABBIT HOLE

T HE MORE I TRIED to resist exploring the issue of related dogs breaking their legs, the more tempting it became. I couldn't stop thinking about those relatives at Raisa's kennel that had broken and also about Maple's littermate Lily. And finding out that three dogs from Fable's kennel ended up being euthanized after a leg amputation made me even more sure that these connections were more than just freaky coincidences.

The leg breaks seemed to run in families, that I was sure of, but did this mean that there was a genetic cause to them? I needed to know. My inner voice was ringing alarm bells that I just couldn't ignore, and before long, my thoughts became completely consumed with the topic.

Against Heather's advice, I decided to explore the topic anyway ... just a little bit. I figured it wouldn't really be that much more work. After all, it was just a matter of adding another column to my chart. I was already collecting information on each dog anyway, so noting any familial relationships shouldn't really be a big deal. Besides, I was certain that the breed club would be more inclined to pursue the matter if I provided them with evidence of a potential hereditary cause.

Initially, I was able to keep myself focused mainly on searching for broken dogs, but every time I added another family relationship into that extra column of my chart, it drew me back into being obsessed about the connections. I knew the key to unlocking the mystery of the broken legs would be revealed if only I could figure out how all the broken dogs were related. Months earlier, Dr. Radcliffe had suggested that I trace the pedigrees of all the broken dogs to see if they shared a common ancestor. This seemed like a pretty straightforward task -- until I started to actually do it.

So far, I only knew about related dogs if an owner or breeder bothered to mention it. When I tried to find the pedigrees, I ran into problems immediately. Many pet owners I interviewed didn't even know the registered name of their dog. Only a few breeders had full pedigrees of their breeding stock listed on their websites. Others only went back a few generations. A surprising number of them didn't even have any pedigrees listed at all. In fact, some breeders didn't even have websites.

After chasing my proverbial tail for weeks, and almost giving up, I made a discovery that changed everything.

I had been on the breed club's website many times before, but for some reason I never paid any attention to the "Database" tab. When I opened it for the first time, I literally gasped when I saw a link to something called "The Pedigree Database."

It felt like I had won the lottery. The pedigree database was an online registry of bloodlines for the entire breed! I couldn't believe my luck.

When Tim arrived home from work that day, I immediately announced, "I found the pedigree database!"

To which he replied, "Huh?"

"It's the family trees for all the silken windhounds in the world ... and it's online, so I can look up all the dogs that have broken and figure out how many of them are related."

"Great," he said, trying unsuccessfully to sound enthusiastic as he opened the fridge and searched for a snack.

"It's their studbook, and its public, and I can't even believe I didn't know about it until now!" I said to his back.

He turned around with a block of cheese in his hand and laughed. "Studbook? What about the Bitch Book?"

"The pedigree database IS the stud book. Female dogs are in there too. They all are. And the pedigrees go all the way back to the original dogs that were used to create the whole breed."

"What does it say about our dogs?"

"I don't know, I haven't looked them up yet."

"Will it confirm we were sold lemons?"

"No. And don't say that, they aren't lemons. The database won't say anything about their health, it's just a record of the names of the puppies born to parents that are already in the registry. It means they're purebred."

"Go crazy," he replied, not knowing that he actually foreshadowed what was about to happen.

The following day I woke up with one thing on my mind. The Pedigree Database. I didn't even wait until I had my morning coffee in hand before searching Maple and Raisa's pedigrees

I pulled up Maple's first. Then Raisa's. Then I compared them. Back and forth, back and forth, I looked at each relative, going back five generations. My heart started racing as I realized they were related. In fact, they were fairly closely related, with common ancestors showing up in just a few generations. How on earth could this be? After all, they came from different kennels, in different countries!

I used the other functions in the database to search breeding information and reverse pedigrees for all of their relatives, discovering that both Maple and Raisa were also closely related to a number of other silken windhounds that had broken legs (beyond the ones I already knew about from their breeders).

This was brilliant! It felt like I was putting pieces of a giant genetic puzzle together. Reviewing the pedigrees and figuring out how the various dogs were related to one another became as gripping as a Netflix series, and I soon became hooked on the pedigree database as if it were sugar.

My new obsession began to suck up all of my time. It also sucked up all of my mobile data. On account of being located in the middle of a forest, our new house had loads of privacy but no high-speed Internet access. I had been using the hotspot on my iPhone to connect to the Internet on my computer, which had been working reasonably well for checking email, but became much too expensive now that I was downloading so many pedigrees.

Once Maple no longer needed my undivided attention, I started driving half an hour to the closest McDonalds to take advantage of the free Wi-Fi, creating a new daily routine that involved sipping coffee, eating fast food and searching pedigrees on my iPad. I took screen shots of the pedigrees of each broken dog, its parents and its siblings, and emailed them to myself. It didn't take long before I was as addicted to Bacon McDoubles as I was to the Pedigree Database - both afflictions I still suffer from to this day.

Back at home, I printed off all the pedigrees and related information, and sorted them into piles based on the broken dog they were associated with. There were so many pieces of paper! I soon realized that in order to study and compare it all, I needed more space than my current set-up in Maple's recovery room would allow for.

Our loft bedroom is the biggest room in our quirky A-Frame house, so it was there, on the floor, where I spread out all the family trees of the affected dogs I had printed off. I was initially overwhelmed by the labyrinth of registered names, but once I zeroed in on the ancestors in common, the tangled web of bloodlines started to reveal some major clusters of relatedness between broken dogs. I created diagrams for myself that joined together the pedigrees of each of these clusters.

Eventually, I found a cluster of relatedness for every one of the broken dogs in my study. By going back further in their ancestry, I was able to find even more distant relatives in common between the clusters. Whenever this happened, I would scotch tape their family tree diagrams together. I ultimately ended up with one giant unwieldy document linking most of the individual family trees. It was so big that I had to use packing tape on the back to hold it all together. I highlighted the names of the broken dogs in orange and used yellow to draw the lines that connected them. It looked kind of crazy, with my messy writing and too much tape, but I liked looking at it. It reminded me of the way I used to study in my various university dorm rooms over the years.

Every evening, after I finished my canine ancestry work, I would fold up the giant collage of family trees and put it on the dresser. When it got too big to fold, I taped it up on the wall. Our bedroom was beginning to feel like one of the war rooms in a crime detective show.

Tim didn't share my exhilaration for our new bedroom decor. In fact, I think he was becoming a bit concerned about my excessive preoccupation with silken windhound bloodlines. Lying in bed each night, I would excitedly tell him about the canine familial connections I had discovered that day, and he would answer with statements like, "You haven't even traced your own family tree ... I don't get it. Why are you so interested in a bunch of dogs you've never met?"

After a few days of patiently listening to me rattle on about Maple's great aunt in Holland, he finally said, "Please no more."

I started phoning my mom, who was always very supportive. I knew she would like to hear my revelations from the day, and at first, she did, but eventually, even she started to sound a bit overwhelmed by my enthusiasm.

Reflecting on it, I'm unsure if it was beneficial for my mental health to dive so deeply into this pursuit. However, considering it distracted me from my own difficult situation with my dogs, I believe it was a positive thing in retrospect. It also filled the gaping hole which had been left in my life when I stopped lawyering. My new "job" in canine ancestry had given my life a sense of purpose again, and the work I was doing felt oddly similar to my old life ... collecting evidence to build a case.

Late one evening, after Tim had already gone to bed, I pulled the bedside table lamp onto the floor beside me, where I was carefully working on linking up pedigrees. As I was drawing a few more yellow lines between broken dogs, I finally made a groundbreaking discovery that connected every broken silken windhound to just a few common ancestors! I literally threw my hands up over my head and very quietly let out a long "yesssssss."

Naively thinking I had cracked the case, the following morning I phoned one of the prominent breeders that I had been in discussions with about getting a puppy a few years earlier. When I shared my exciting news, unphased, she casually quipped back that ALL silken windhounds were closely related.

"Those dogs you found are behind the entire breed," she nonchalantly said.

Her revelation hit me like a gut punch. I didn't want to believe her. And she must have sensed this, because she instructed me to look at the pedigrees of some of the silken windhounds that hadn't broken their legs.

As soon as I hung up the phone I did just that, and sadly, it was true - the same dogs that appeared in the background of all the dogs that had broken legs also appeared in the backgrounds of a whole pile of dogs that had not.

I was stumped. Now I had even more questions, the most pressing of which was why on earth the whole breed was so closely related?

When I asked Heather, she laughed and said, "I told you not to go there."

She then joked that her silken windhound's family tree looked more like a log.

But why? In desperation, I posted to the official Facebook page of the Silken Windhound Society to question the issue, and was answered by the president of the breed club in five words: "Welcome to a new breed."

26

MONKEY BUSINESS

I WAS IN A conundrum of my own making. Studying pedigrees had revealed so many family relationships between dogs; which confirmed my gut instinct that some dogs were inheriting a propensity for leg breaks. But discovering that all silken windhounds, not just the broken ones, were closely related just confused me. What did it all mean? I had no idea.

I had been so sure that by studying pedigrees, I would unearth a smoking gun – that single common ancestor responsible for passing down a problematic gene. But the entire breed being so closely related made this impossible to do. Hell, maybe the issue wasn't even genetic after all? My passion for searching silken bloodlines was fading fast. Maybe Heather was right. Maybe I had been on a wild goose chase after all?

Weary of wasting more time, I decided to put the pedigree research on hold, promising myself that I would tackle the perplexing contradictions at a later date, after I had a chance to learn a little more about canine genetics. In the meantime, I would go back to where I started: merely finding all the silken windhounds that had ever broken a leg. At least there was no confusion in that. A broken leg was a broken leg. It didn't have to mean anything. It just needed to be counted.

While the task itself was simple, the impact of jumping back into it was not. Locating more dogs meant that I had to go back to posting on the various breed forums again, a practice which was much less peaceful than privately analyzing data in my bedroom. To say that I wasn't welcomed back to the online community with open arms would be an understatement. In fact, every single post I made provoked heated debates between myself and those who seemed hellbent on belittling the significance of my findings. An avalanche of anger came mainly from the breeders, all of whom declared with certainty that silken windhound leg breaks were caused by freak accidents and nothing more.

It didn't take long before it wasn't just my data that was being called into question. Comments like, "Be upset about your dogs but don't drag a whole breed down" started to dominate the discussions. I was branded a trouble-maker that was trying to harm the breed. The president of the breed club even started making remarks like, "Some people prefer their own emotional narrative over actual data."

Having my research skills (and my character) criticized ignited my combative nature, pushing me back into litigator mode. Armed with my ever-growing empirical data, I began using inflammatory language to broadcast every new leg break I heard about, along with some strong commentary about the urgency that something needed to be done.

Unapologetically defiant, I became extremely confrontational, which turned out to be the dead wrong approach. I treated every online conversation about leg breaks as a battle to be won, but my adversarial demeanor completely backfired on me, transforming what should have been a benign health issue into a taboo subject, and thus significantly hindering my ability to collect data going forward.

A well-known breeder posted a reply to one of my online inquiries with this statement: "I have had a bitch with a traumatic fracture that was plated and I absolutely will not release any information about it to anyone."

The president of the breed club announced on Facebook (in relation to one of my inquiries about leg breaks) that, "No one is under any obligation to report to a group not doing a scientifically based study" – basically encouraging people not to talk to me. She also called me a troll. Pet owners, understandably, became reluctant to share any information with me, or be associated with me in any way.

I didn't give up though. Despite the stigma that had been attached to both me and the subject-matter, some owners still reached out to me privately. Others, who refused to talk to me, surprisingly still posted online when their dog broke a leg. To garner sympathy (and sometimes money), these posts often included photographs and vet records. I took screen shots and catalogued all of it, and continued to update the community regularly, despite the pushback.

Eventually, my persistence paid off. I was beyond thrilled when the president of the breed club announced that the organization was going to conduct a study on broken bones. She shared a link to a questionnaire organized on the software platform called

SurveyMonkey. It purported to be an "official" survey by the health committee (I suppose in contrast to my "unofficial" survey).

I was so excited. I felt like I had finally won – that the breed club was open to admitting that there might be a problem. I just knew that once they actually verified the numbers, they would have no choice but to allocate some funding to get to the bottom of it. All my hard work had paid off.

I filled the survey out for both of my dogs and shared the link on my Facebook page, urging all silken windhound owners to do the same. I sent the link to Kim and Heather and asked them to include as many details about their dogs' leg breaks as possible, sharing my belief that this would hopefully lead to further research and maybe even the discovery of a cure for our own dogs.

Weeks passed by, and then months, with no news about the SurveyMonkey or its results. I began to lose hope. Nobody from the breed club ever followed up with myself or Heather regarding the data we had collected or the details about our own dogs and what we went through.

Participation in the survey wasn't anonymous, and I began to wonder how many breeders didn't disclose a broken leg at their kennel, for fear that their breeding program would be stigmatized. I also wondered whether the SurveyMonkey reached all of the pet owners who did not belong to the breed club or the online groups? As far as I could tell, no outside experts were consulted in order to develop the survey or to interpret the results.

No report ever materialized. In fact, it took ages before any results from the Survey-Monkey were ever shared, and when they were, it was underwhelming, to say the least.

There was an announcement on the Silken Windhound Facebook page that a presentation had been made at an annual meeting by the volunteer who ran the SurveyMonkey. The short summary of her presentation indicated that 40 broken bones had been reported (not just legs). I already knew about significantly more. The club reportedly collected information for over 900 dogs, yet there were only 157 "complete" surveys filled out. I found this a bit strange, until I read a post by the breed founder who stated that she filled it out for 400 to 500 dogs, commenting, "I am not exactly sure how many."

The breed club and its members began offering the results of the SurveyMonkey as proof that leg breaks weren't a problem in the breed. This left me feeling like the only reason the organization did the survey in the first place was to refute and de-legitimize the data I had collected. In other words, to shut me up.

One prominent breeder posted a short essay on social media called "The Myth of Broken Bones in Silken Windhounds," and he used the SurveyMonkey results as evidence to dispel any rumours about "the supposed fragility in the breed." He stated that someone (presumably me) was exploiting the tragedies of car accidents, livestock attacks, and other such traumatic injuries that are "so wildly outside of the scope of a reasonable definition of fragile to make it absurd."

In retrospect, I suppose that what I should have done at that point was to keep my findings to myself and just go about quietly collecting more data. Instead, and with personally disastrous results, I stayed active on social media, where even the simple mention of a broken leg unleashed a shitstorm of controversy.

Even on my own Facebook page, whenever I mentioned broken legs, I was subjected to a torrent of hostility. One day, I commented about being upset whenever I walked by the location on my property where Raisa broke her front leg. A breeder commented that my dogs were living in lockdown in solitary confinement and that I was their prison guard. She told me to stop blaming the breed for my "lot in life."

I responded that I didn't say anything about the breed, only about my own situation, and that I was hurt that she and others whom I considered friends were judging and insulting my choices with respect to my dogs. A bunch of online bickering and nasty comments followed.

A different breeder chimed in, referencing the SurveyMonkey results as proof that there was nothing wrong with the breed (implying that there was something wrong with how I raised my dogs). Someone else chimed in and said I should consider re-homing Maple and Raisa. Another suggested that repairing Raisa's leg through surgery had weakened the area around the breaks, which "would only lend itself to a re-break." A different breeder announced that I didn't exercise my dogs enough. Another called me "an unbelievable liar." Others stated that my claim of broken legs was highly suspect, and that I was just spreading lies.

Arguing online was a terrible thing for me to do – a lesson I learned the hard way. Being not just contradicted, but insulted in such a personal and aggressive way made me feel like I was being attacked in person. The cruelty in their comments left me emotionally battered and mentally drained. I knew it was counter-productive and downright harmful to my psychological health to be engaging in this online battle, yet I kept going, under the misguided belief that I could somehow defend my reputation and convince the group that my findings were valid.

Then something extreme but not altogether unexpected happened. As a result of that exchange on my own Facebook page, most silken windhound breeders and owners un-friended or blocked me. Then I was kicked off every social network dealing with silken windhounds.

I had stirred the hornets' nest and got stung. I was now a pariah. An outcast. Even those who had once been supportive turned their backs on me. It felt so horribly unfair to be cut off from the entire community just because I demanded that a health issue be taken seriously by the group that was supposed to care. For the first time in my life, I had been completely marginalized from a group, and I was surprised how much it hurt, given that it was a group that had been so negative and even hurtful towards me. I suppose maybe there was some kind of primal instinct kicking in, making me feel vulnerable from being excommunicated. Being on the outside also made me extremely anxious because I was unable to see what was going on in the silken windhound world - a world that had become central to my day-to-day life for so long.

Luckily, a sympathetic pet owner on Facebook started secretly sending me screen captures of the posts that the breeders and breed club representatives continued to make about leg breaks and about me. I was super excited about it at first, but being an online spectator to discussions about me turned out to be an extremely upsetting experience – especially given that I couldn't respond and defend myself.

The volunteer that conducted the SurveyMonkey posted that there was "a crazy person on the loose ... with a personal witch hunt against the breed."

The Registrar for the club responded, "It's Michelle Stark – glad I now know. Lying bitch."

Another breeder wrote: "*I read her lamentations of her near PTSD caused by the injuries her silkens sustained. I would like to know why, if she is so disturbed by their ill health, she would keep them ... I wish I knew of a way to shut her down but nothing comes to mind right now. If I can be of any service to you all, all you need to do is let me know.*"

The president of the breed club suggested that I had a version of Munchausen Syndrome by Proxy, which is a psychiatric condition whereby a caregiver makes up or causes an illness or injury in a person under his or her care (such as a child, an elderly adult, or a person who has a disability). Another breeder chimed in: "Otherwise known as look at me syndrome common in toddlers and small Far East dictators."

The president stated that my "attention seeking behaviour" had little to do with what was going on with my current situation. In a post to the Facebook breed group, while discussing some of the causes of leg breaks, she said, "it could be abuse." She didn't mention me by name, but the implication was there, and I was mortified.

Emotions aside, what transpired online had practical consequences too. Being discredited by the very community that I had hoped to enlighten with my research left me once again without a clear path forward. With no access to the places where silken windhound owners gathered online to discuss breed health, I was left wondering whether there was any reason to keep going?

For a few days I mulled it over, coming very close to throwing in the towel, but every time I looked into the faces of my sweet, vulnerable, fragile dogs, I felt like I was disappointing them. And let's face it, there was also an element of wanting to win against the people who had injured my ego so badly.

Deciding there was no way I was going to stop collecting data, I also had to admit that there was no option to continue doing it in the way I had been, even if I wanted to. I saw only one viable path forward, but it posed an ethical dilemma.

Infiltrating the various breed groups and forums using a fake online profile was easier than I thought it would be. Donning a cloak of anonymity, I slipped undetected into almost all of the virtual silken windhound groups, becoming a silent observer. It felt somewhat deceptive to be operating this way, but I justified my actions by reminding myself that if my identity wasn't concealed, I would have no access to the data I needed to continue with my work. I eased my conscience by promising myself that when the composition of the organization changed, I would engage with it again, but until then, my virtual alter ego would discreetly lurk about online, covertly collecting valuable data for my study.

27

THE COMFORT ROOM

BEING BEHIND THE SCENES in the silken windhound world ended up suiting me just fine. It was actually quite peaceful not trying to convince the silken people that they were wrong about me. And as time passed, other than some rather undramatic and fairly typical canine health problems, our lives with Maple and Raisa became fairly stable.

Manageable isn't a word I previously would have used to describe an ideal relationship with a pet, but given all that we had been through, I was okay with it now. In fact, the lack of dog drama on any given day never went unnoticed or unappreciated.

A few months turned into a few years, and while there were many moments of joy, in the background of those moments there was always some lingering sadness about the "normal" lives we never got to live with our dogs because of the limitations that were necessary to keep them safe in their fragility (and me safe from my anxiety about it).

My leg break research eventually faded comfortably into the background of my day-to-day life, never fully disappearing, but also never taking centre stage as it once had. It would flare up from time to time whenever I heard about another leg break. But after a few days of frenzied outrage while I gathered the details and updated my chart, the binders would go back up on the shelf, and I would go back to my busy life. I never lost interest in vigilantly monitoring the various social media sites, but I still had zero desire to subject myself to any breed club backlash.

The void left by my leg break advocacy had created room for other new passions to develop and flourish. I was finally able to devote myself in a serious way to growing my legal writing business. Tim and I also took up some agricultural pursuits on our country property. We started a business selling maple syrup, honey, cut flowers and seasonal produce. We even got another dog!

Our new pup was a big friendly far-from-purebred dog who grew up with free run of our huge property. We loved having a "normal" dog so much, that less than a year later, we brought home another one from the same farm. There were no contracts to sign, or interviews conducted. We just drove over, picked out our puppy, handed over a trivial amount of cash and drove home. Winter and Starla (aka the "big dogs") spent their days outside, working alongside us. At night, they happily came inside and lounged around with Maple and Raisa (the house dogs). Life was good. Until one random January morning.

It was a day that started out just like any other. I was sitting at my computer working on a writing assignment when my otherwise peaceful morning was shattered by the scream of death. It came from the direction of the bedrooms and I knew immediately it was one of the silken windhounds.

Without thought, I instinctively ran up the stairs to see who was in trouble. Pushing open one of the partially closed bedroom doors, my heart stopped when I saw Raisa standing beside the low bed with her front leg hanging at a grotesque angle. For a moment, there were no thoughts, just feelings – the strongest of which was terror.

I picked her up and stroked her head rocked her and whispered in her ear: "It's okay, it's okay, you're going to be okay."

I carried her slender white body to the bathroom and closed the door behind me so the other dogs couldn't get in. The big dogs had charged up the stairs behind me and I didn't want them near her. I had no idea where Maple was, but figured she was still sleeping somewhere, unfazed by the commotion.

Raisa's death-defying screams petered out and then the whimpering started. Both ripped at my heart in equal measure.

When I examined her leg, her eyes widened, and she started panting heavily. The whimpering intensified to crying. What I saw made me realize that she must have been in excruciating pain.

Her front right leg was clearly broken…in half.

I felt physically sick. Lightheaded. Most of all, I instinctively knew that if I didn't stand up and immediately move around, I was going to faint.

I carried Raisa to the spare bedroom, carefully placing her down on her side on a dog bed. Then I went to look for my phone, closing the bedroom door behind me so none of the other dogs could get in.

I found my phone in my home office downstairs. From there, I called Tim at work. I walked around the room in circles, waiting for him to answer.

"Hello?"

"It's Raisa," I stammered. "She's broken her leg."

"What? How?"

Half-crying, I answered, "I don't know."

"Okay, I'm coming home. Call Dr. Radcliffe."

I hung up without saying good-bye.

I didn't call Dr. Radcliffe though. I called my mom. I needed to hear her say that everything would be okay. I also needed to know that she could stay at our house and look after the other dogs so we could take off for West Virginia right away.

My third call was to Dr. Radcliffe. I was dreading this call, being nervous that he might be away, or unavailable. It had been so long since we had been to see him. The receptionist told me that "Dr. Jim" was out of the office at the greyhound racing compound. I explained who I was and what we needed. She informed me that he was double and triple booked, so she was unable to give us an appointment until we spoke to him directly. She promised that as soon as she reached him, she would pass along our information.

I needed to keep moving. I should have been by Raisa's side to give her comfort, but the trauma of the situation left me unable to even look at her. I loved her so deeply that my overwhelming distress took precedence over my instincts to give her solace. I called the local country vet that stabilized her for the journey the last time she broke. He wasn't in the clinic and there was no other vet in the office that could set the leg. I was told to go to an Emergency Clinic.

Then I called the Red Roof Inn, making reservations for two nights. I got out our passports and paperwork for Raisa that we would need at the border.

Then I did something very strange. I cleaned the house. Something I hate doing. I told myself it was because my mom was coming to stay, but really it was because I knew that if I stopped distracting myself, I would go into full panic mode. I even washed the kitchen floor. Every time I slowed down, my stomach would churn, and I could feel my heart racing. Nausea would overwhelm me, making it difficult for me to breathe.

Tim collected my mom on his way home from work. When they arrived, he went immediately to look at Raisa. My mom and I followed him. My mom went to the doorway of the room and peered in. I stayed back, not wanting to look. Tim admitted to me later that he had hoped that I was wrong and that her leg wasn't in fact broken.

When Tim came out of the room, I heard him whisper to my mother, "It's really bad."

She replied in a whisper, "You're going to have some decisions to make."

They didn't think I could hear them.

Tim then walked over to me and said calmly, "We have to get the leg set so we can travel."

"I tried – the country vet isn't there."

"We'll have to do it ourselves then," he said. "Go and get the first aid kit. Do we have any cardboard?"

"What for?" I could still barely breathe.

"I'm going to have to make a splint."

We gave Raisa some pain medication that we had left over from a prior surgery. Tim made a splint from cardboard and a tensor bandage, and did the best he could at wrapping up her tiny deformed leg. As he was working on it, he mumbled something to himself that I didn't hear.

"What did you say?"

"Nothing."

"No – what did you say?"

Afraid of upsetting me even more, he admitted that he was afraid that more damage had been done than just the broken bones. He said he was worried about the muscles, blood vessels and nerves, given how bad the break was.

"Michelle, we can't wait. This is really bad."

"What should we do then – I can't make Dr. Radcliffe call us back?"

Tim was a take charge kind of guy. Waiting for a phone call was not something he was prepared to do.

"By the time we get her seen here, we could be part way to West Virginia. We need to be there. Let's just go."

"What if he can't see us? Or what if he wants us to get her leg stabilized before we go?"

"If he wants us to, we can stop along the way and have her leg splinted at an emergency clinic near wherever we are when he calls. If he can't fix it, I'm sure someone in his office can."

After Tim loaded the truck with our luggage, I got in the passenger seat and put a small fleece dog bed over my lap and he laid Raisa down on top of me. When we arrived at the border, the officer was all business until we told her the reason for our trip. Her demeanor softened when she looked at Raisa through her booth window and she said something sweet in a baby voice to her.

Raisa didn't even lift her head, but when she looked up at the officer who was speaking "dog" to her, she wagged her tail, despite the pain that she was in. We didn't have to show any of our veterinary paperwork.

The drive was uneventful at first. We were lucky as there had been unusually mild weather for January, however by the time we reached Pennsylvania, it started to rain so heavily that we couldn't see anything, including the lines on the road. The cars in front of us put on their hazard lights, and we followed suit. The temperature dropped and it started hailing. The shoulders of the road turned white.

To make matters worse, it became clear to us, because the car started to smell rotten, that Raisa's stomach was upset, probably from the pain, but potentially due to the painkiller that I had given her.

We exited off the highway and stopped at a McDonald's parking lot, where Tim held Raisa up while she emptied her bowels of foul-smelling runny diarrhea. It was all over the plumes of fur on her tail and on the backs of her legs. I went into the McDonald's and got some toilet paper and returned to clean it off. It didn't work and I couldn't get the sticky stinky liquid off her long fur.

I went back to the truck and got a tea towel that I had packed for the motel room, and took it back into McDonald's, where I wet it with warm water. I then went back and forth between Tim and Raisa and the McDonald bathroom several times, washing the towel out and wetting it again, and then cleaning up Raisa while Tim held her steady.

As I was going back outside on one of the trips, an employee sweeping the floor by the bathroom said: "Did you forget your food, Miss?"

We were in hell. The driving conditions were shitty and the car smelled shitty. It felt like we would never get there.

Dr. Radcliffe eventually called us while we were driving. He said to bring Raisa to his clinic first thing in the morning and he would meet us there and see her before it opened. He said to give her more pain medication and keep her as still as possible.

When we arrived at the Red Roof Inn that evening, Tim took Raisa to a grassy area as she still had an upset stomach. I went into the room and pulled one of the double bed mattresses off the frame and wedged it on the floor between the bed and the window. I put her dog bed on it and made a fortress of pillows around it.

When Tim arrived back in the room, Raisa's back end was covered with liquid excrement. He took her straight to the bathroom and gestured for me to follow.

He placed her in the tub, holding her up on her hind legs with her bum under the tap while I cleaned her off. To that point my heart had been aching, but I think it broke in half as Raisa's eyes locked with mine as I watched this scene unfold in front of me. She was standing pathetically in the bathtub, being supported by Tim, who was also standing in the shower with her. Her splinted broken leg was hanging hideously beside her, with her wrist turned over the wrong way. It appeared as if her broken right leg was much longer than her left one.

We went to bed almost immediately. I set my phone alarm for two in the morning, so I could give Raisa another pain pill. It was one of the longest nights of my life. We had been given a room on ground level, which I had asked for, but I had been warned when booking most rooms had been rented out to construction workers that were putting in a pipeline nearby. Their diesel trucks "beep beep beeped" as their owners backed them into the parking spots outside our room all night long. I could also hear the cars whizzing by on the highway, which wasn't all that far from the motel.

What I wanted to do was take a sleeping pill myself, but I didn't dare, given I was lying on the floor with Raisa, making sure she didn't move around and hurt her leg even more. I couldn't let myself be in a deep sleep.

It turned out that I wasn't going to get any sleep at all, because Raisa was awake all night, gently whining and panting. I kept my body circled around her, stroking her ears, kissing her nose, and telling her that I loved her and that Dr. Radcliffe would fix her. I calmed her with the words that I myself wanted to believe, but I didn't know if her leg could be fixed. It was the same leg that had already been broken, and it still had the plate in it from the previous repair. At that point if you had given me the choice, I would have broken my own arm to take her pain away.

We opened the curtains in the morning to a grey day. There was snow coming down slowly but steadily. As I carried Raisa to the truck, she molded her body so tightly against mine that it felt as though she might at any moment flow right into me. I cradled her in my arms on my lap as we drove to the clinic. As we made our way there, I looked out the windows of the truck, watching the warm yellow lights turning on in the houses that were perched partially up the sides of the mountain ranges which towered over us on both sides of the road. The regular people were starting their regular days. I noticed the smoke rising out of the chimneys and thought that there must be a lot more wood burning stoves and fireplaces in West Virginia than there are in Ontario.

I felt jealous of the ordinary folks who weren't in a crisis like I was. I would have given anything at that moment to be getting up on a regular ordinary Wednesday morning at my own house with everything as it was before this happened. I longed to be drinking my morning coffee while reading my emails, and checking in on Facebook to see what had happened while I was sleeping. Instead, I was in another country with a broken family member and a nervous stomach.

When we arrived early to the clinic, the receptionist asked us to weigh Raisa by putting her on the digital scale, which was on our side of the front desk. Tim had to hold Raisa steady on the scale, and while he was doing so, she looked into my eyes. I could tell she felt safe and reassured because we were both by her side. Raisa and I didn't need words to communicate how we were feeling.

Our little white waif weighed in at 35 pounds. We took a seat in the lobby and Tim put Raisa on his lap while we waited for Dr. Radcliffe. We watched a trainer bring in three majestic looking greyhounds from the local racetrack. They trotted beside their keeper with loose leashes and wore basket muzzles over their pointy snouts. She took them immediately to the scales and weighed each one, yelling out the weights to the staff behind the desk. She gruffly yelled out 83, 81, and 83 (which gives you an idea of just how petite silken windhounds were by comparison).

A vet technician, Abby, who we knew from previous visits came out and greeted us. She escorted us to an examination room, and Dr. Radcliffe, who seemingly came out of nowhere, followed us into the room, leaning down and addressing Raisa first, "What did you do child?"

As I started to answer for her, our scrub-clad hero scooped her up off the floor and carried her out of the room, saying he was taking her for an x-ray.

While we waited, my stomach was making all kinds of crazy noises, partially because it was nervous and partially because I hadn't been able to eat anything since the traumatic event had occurred over twenty-four hours prior.

When Dr. Radcliffe returned to the room, Raisa was not with him. Before saying anything, he pulled up images of her x-rays onto the big flat screen on the wall. As the first image appeared, he turned to us and said in his charming West Virginia accent, "Well, it's broken...but you knew that already."

I gasped when I saw the broken bones on the screen. The injury was even worse than I had imagined. The two bones in Raisa's long slim foreleg were broken again, but this time closer to the elbow than the wrist. The fractured ends were completely separated, and gruesomely positioned beside each other. It was horrific.

As Dr. Radcliffe was talking about it being a tricky area, I blurted out, "But can you fix it?"

He turned to me and said, "Yes, but I don't have the plate I need."

He then looked at Tim and said, "It will be sent by courier. I should have it by 10 tomorrow morning."

He told us that he was concerned that he might have to take out the plate and screws that were already in there, but he wouldn't know until he "got in there."

"Now, I'm going to go and stabilize that leg. She's already been given hydromorphone, so she's not in pain anymore."

Fairly soon after, a technician brought Raisa back to us with her leg wrapped heavily but neatly from the armpit down. While we waited again for Dr. Radcliffe to come to the room, Tim looked over at Raisa who I was holding on my lap.

"I hope we're making the right decision."

I started to cry.

When Dr. Radcliffe returned to the room, I blurted out "Are you sure we should fix this? We want to do what's best for her."

He looked surprised, as he moved across the room and hugged me and said, "This is fixable – we aren't having THAT conversation, you can relax mom."

Dr. Radcliffe let us say good-bye to Raisa and asked us what her normal diet was, as he was going to get her some food. He told us that we could come and visit her at any time we liked or call in for an update, and that he would talk to us again in the morning prior to the surgery, which he planned to do as soon as he received the hardware for her leg.

"But it's your day off tomorrow," I said (which I had been told by his receptionist).

"This girl needs to be fixed and that isn't for you to worry about."

I hugged him and then we left. We drove to our favourite breakfast spot, Denny's, and ordered the "Everyday Value Slam." I thought I would feel better and was looking forward to eating, but before our coffee even arrived, Tim looked across the table at me and said, "We're making the wrong choice."

I felt like I had been punched in the stomach.

"Why didn't you speak up about this when we were with Dr. Radcliffe? You didn't say anything!"

He stared at me and replied, "This isn't going to get better, there is something very wrong."

I said nothing and he added, "We're now where Heather was with Fable."

I still said nothing and he went on to say, "We're probably just prolonging the inevitable."

Through gentle hiccups of tears, I said, "I'm not ready to say good-bye to her. Even if the repair doesn't work; my heart can't take not trying."

Then I started sobbing. All the stress from the past day that had been pent up came rushing out, and any composure I had left was shattered like broken glass.

Tim looked surprised, "Why are you crying? We are fixing her!"

"Because you want to put her to sleep instead of the surgery."

"Noooo, that's not what I meant. I'm just frustrated and worried. She is our family. Of course, we'll will fix her. It just sucks that we are here in this situation again. I hate it."

I inhaled deeply and smelled freshly brewed coffee and bacon cooking. My breathing returned to normal and I stopped crying.

While we had been talking, loudly because it was so emotional, the customers in the booths directly around us had all cleared out. Our waitress didn't return to the table for a while, which was unusual. I saw her looking over at us nervously, presumably hoping to come by when I wasn't crying. I think the people in the restaurant must have thought that we were breaking up or something.

I was in low spirits all day. That feeling of familiar dread had set back in. It didn't help that the weather was cold and dreary and we only had a small motel room to hang out in. I spent the day ruminating about what had happened, what was going to happen and worrying about the future. I couldn't stop thinking about the logistics of what on earth could have caused such a break to Raisa's leg. She was just hanging out in the bedroom, as she usually did during the day. I contemplated whether a bump from the big dogs earlier in the day on our walk could have caused it. She was on her long leash, but sometimes they bumped into her when running by. If that was the case, it meant that I was somehow responsible for not supervising carefully enough and for bringing danger into our house by getting other dogs.

The likely alternative was that she broke it hopping off the bed, which was only 18 inches off the ground. If this were the case, then it meant that Raisa's bone density was so compromised that she could break that easily again in the future. It was a lose-lose situation, as it often is with these dogs.

The following day we drove 20 minutes back through the mountains to the clinic and waited once again for Dr. Radcliffe to arrive. He came out to greet us in the waiting room, telling us to "come on back," but he didn't take us to an exam room this time. This time, he walked us back to the surgical area, where there were stainless steel tables and a wall that had a whole bunch of muzzles hanging on it. Against one wall was a row of cages. He knelt down and I saw that Raisa was lying in a cage at ground level. She squealed with delight when she saw us. I bent down to see her, and Dr. Radcliffe said, "Go ahead and take her out, and you can have a visit with her while we're waiting on the plate – we tracked it with the courier and it should arrive by ten."

He unclipped the mechanism on the cage door and I awkwardly lifted Raisa out by scooping her long skinny body up into my arms, being careful not to jostle her right leg, which was all wrapped up. Her bandaged leg was about the size and shape of the wide end of a baseball bat.

As Dr. Radcliffe ushered us out of the surgical area, with Raisa in my arms, I had to manoeuvre carefully and partially sideways through doorways so I wouldn't ding her clubfoot. He led us to a room that felt like a living room. We had never been in this room before and didn't even know it existed. It had a sofa, a comfy big chair and a giant dog bed on the floor. A space heater was keeping the room cozy and warm. I sat down on the wool rug and hugged Raisa.

There was a second door in the room that went directly outside to the parking lot and the window in the door was covered in a privacy film. As we fawned over Raisa, I looked around and noticed the bereavement brochures, boxes of Kleenex and "Rainbow Bridge" themed artwork on the walls.

"We're in the room where they put dogs to sleep!" I exclaimed to Tim, who was sitting on the loveseat.

"Who cares, it's comfortable in here," he replied.

At exactly 10 o'clock Dr. Radcliffe came in and told us that he was going to sedate Raisa while she was with us, as she would be more comfortable that way. He put several needles full of fluid into her flank, while she was cradled in Tim's arms, and then he left, after warning us that she would soon become groggy.

About five minutes later, Dr, Radcliffe returned and took a limp but still conscious Raisa out of Tim's arms and carried her off to be prepped for surgery. The plate had arrived, and it was "show time."

We left the clinic and drove to the closest town, walking aimlessly around and then spent some time sitting in a McDonalds. After a few hours had passed, we returned to the clinic, where Dr. Radcliffe took us back into the comfort room again to talk to us. We sat on the loveseat and while he was still standing in the doorway he said, "Well, in typical windhound fashion, once I got in there, things were more complicated than I initially thought."

My heart sank. It turned out that there was another fracture in the radius bone above the break, which made it necessary for him to use a different plate than the one he had ordered. Nevertheless, he said that the radius bone had lined up great, and that he was happy with the results.

"How on earth could such a severe injury have occurred when she was just hanging out in a bedroom alone?" I asked.

He just shrugged.

"The big dogs may have bumped her when we were on a walk. Maybe it was fractured then and then broke outright when she hopped off the bed?"

"No," he said flatly.

"Could this have happened to any other breed of dog like this?"

"Also, no," he said.

Dr. Radcliffe then took us back to the surgery area, where Raisa was in the same cage as before. She was lying with an intravenous drip attached to her leg. Her tongue was hanging out of her mouth. Dr. Radcliffe roused her and she wagged her tail a tiny bit, but then fell right back to sleep. She looked out of it, but comfortable.

We weren't able to take Raisa home until the following day. Due to the delay in getting the hardware, this trip had required three nights over, instead of the usual two.

Before we left, Dr. Radcliffe had his staff give us a tutorial on how to change the bandaging that formed the soft cast over the incision on Raisa's leg. There was a bag of supplies for re-bandaging ready for us to take home.

In the hallway, as Dr. Radcliffe gave me a hug and wished us a safe journey, he slipped a sticky note into the palm of my hand.

"Call me anytime. Even if it's midnight."

It was his home phone number. Tears welled up in my eyes.

He then added (as he always did), "If you can't keep her, just call me and I will drive to Hamilton and pick her up."

The intense range of emotions I always experienced in this man's company made it feel as if our bond had been forged over a lifetime. It was almost inconceivable to me that we had only known him for a few years. The dedication of this remarkable human went so far beyond his professional obligations, which left me with a profound debt of gratitude, both to him and to the universe for putting him into our lives when we needed him.

28

GROUNDHOG DAY

Back at home, Tim headed straight to the garage, where he needed to move a whole bunch of junk out of the way to get to the various disassembled parts of Raisa's recovery cage. When he came inside carrying several of the cage parts, he headed straight up the stairs.

"Where are you going?" I asked, as I followed him with Raisa in my arms.

"I'm putting it up in the bedroom."

"Why?"

"Because I don't want you sleeping on the floor again."

"But I then I'll have to carry her up and down the stairs umpteen times a day," I whined.

"Better that than sleeping on the floor," he said in a tone that I knew from experience formed the end of the discussion.

Raisa and I hung out on the bed while Tim brought the rest of the cage upstairs. As he drilled the boards into the wall, I stroked her iridescent fur. She gazed up at me, soaking in the attention. I wondered if she knew what was about to happen. That old familiar sense of dread was starting to creep back up into my throat as I thought about how this would be the place where she would spend all of her days and nights for the next six weeks or more. It was also the place where I would be spending most of my time too.

The following day, I lugged the plastic table upstairs and set up a writing station next to Raisa's cage. It also became the place where I would take most of my meals. For several days, I only left that room to carry her downstairs for drinks of water, to have some food, or go outside for a potty break.

Repeating these rituals of canine care merged our souls together even tighter. Looking after her to the exclusion of all else was a testament to love in its purest form, but that kind of devotion also came with a price. My world shrank again, to the size of the small radius that surrounded my patient. But I didn't care, because her world was even smaller. She deserved so much better than this, and it made me both sad and furious that she was back in such pitiful circumstances. There was an agony I felt when I realized that my own dog had become yet another statistic in my research. Raisa was now listed among the other dogs that had suffered three leg breaks. Most of those dogs' lives had ended tragically, and knowing about this grim statistic began to push me back into a dark place.

In the weeks that followed, a strange mirroring of events took place, incomprehensibly similar to those that had taken place years before.

In mid-January we were hit with another "polar vortex," and along with it, a series of blizzards. The snow storms themselves weren't a problem, since I didn't need to go anywhere, but spending weeks on end inside one room of the house started to get to me. When the sun finally came out, I decided that I couldn't be contained any longer. I made sure that Raisa was settled in her crate and I headed to the basement, with the big dogs at my heels. Maple was snoozing peacefully in the family room, and had no interest in joining us. I had no idea how the big dogs knew we were going somewhere, but they always did. I pulled their harnesses off the coat hanger, and snapped their leashes on. They were jumping up at the back door, they were so eager to get outside, despite the freezing temps.

The three of us trekked down our long driveway and then through our gates and out onto the road. I was glad to have them pull me up the steep hill, but just as we crested it, a black squirrel dashed out in front of us, and both dogs took off hard in pursuit, towing me behind them. At first, I was able to keep up but they were too fast for me, so I tried to dig the heels of my boots in to stop them. They dragged me standing and as soon as they pulled me over an icy patch, I fell down. I didn't let go of the leashes until it was too late, and my body was smashed against one of the metal road markers, the impact all too familiar as pain exploded throughout my body.

A trip to the hospital confirmed what I already knew – broken ribs. My dog was broken; my own bones were broken and my psychological well-being was going down the toilet. Was it a dream? How could this be happening to me again? And how was I going to care for Raisa, when I was hurt again myself?

Weeks of terrible weather followed – snow, ice, freezing rain, a reprieve for a day or two and then the cycle would start up again. In February, Tim had to travel to the USA for a conference and I was left caring for Raisa alone. Carrying her around with broken ribs was a challenge, but carrying her outside was the worst. When she squatted, her three legs slid out in all different directions because of the ice. At one point, she banged her chin, splitting the skin. Then I noticed that the wrist on her "good" leg was starting to bend in a weird way when she was hobbling along. It looked like a banana. Was it flexing too much? Was it going to break too? Or was I just being paranoid?

We had been checking in with Dr. Radcliffe weekly about Raisa's progress, and after about three weeks he told us that he was concerned that she wasn't putting any weight on the repaired leg. He asked us to get some x-rays done locally and send them electronically so he could see what was going on.

I phoned around until I found a local clinic that used digital radiographs. They couldn't get us in until the following week. It was hell waiting, and then the appointment was cancelled due to an ice storm. I made an appointment for the following day, and it got cancelled again because of the weather. The crazy Groundhog Day scenario that was unfolding was making me feel cursed again. I made a third appointment, and luckily, the weather calmed down enough that the clinic was open, and we were able to get there.

Within seconds of us walking into the new clinic, the staff were all fawning over Raisa, telling us that she looked like some kind of magical unicorn. Raisa relished the attention. She was magical, both in looks and in personality. In her elfin way, she looked at people right in the eyes, and this, combined with her full body wiggle was irresistible. I could barely smile though. Or make small talk. I had a lump in my throat.

I knew something was wrong even before we had the x-ray done, and so did Tim. We had been through these situations enough times to know that Raisa was normally using her repaired leg within a few days of surgery. We were four weeks out, and her bandaged leg just hung limply as she manoeuvered herself on three legs, which also made me nervous, knowing that her other front leg might not be strong enough to bear the extra weight.

When the vet asked us to come to the back of the clinic and look at the x-rays, I just knew that it was going to be bad news. And it was. The bones, which had been all lined up so nicely after surgery, were terribly askew, and still very broken. The plate was out of alignment and was situated at a weird angle. It looked horrific and I had to turn away.

I tried to keep listening to the vet, but I wasn't able to hold back the tears. I needed to get out of there, and as the vet was insisting that Raisa needed heavier pain medication, I turned and carried my girl in my arms back out through the lobby, leaving Tim with the vet in front of the computer screen showing the x-ray of her deformed leg.

When I passed by the front desk, one of the staff members started offering up ideas for increasing bone density, including CBD oil. I knew she was just trying to help, but I didn't have the emotional capacity to engage with her enough to explain that this problem was way beyond any kind of natural remedy. But how could she know the magnitude of the situation ... that Raisa's leg hadn't healed, and that this might be the end.

I went outside, leaving the clinic feeling breathless and nauseous, with my broken dog in my arms and my heart heavy in my chest. The truck was locked so I had to wait for Tim to pay the bill and come outside. I didn't mind though because the cool air felt good on my flushed face.

By the time we got home, the clinic had already emailed the images to Dr. Radcliffe and copied me on a letter which stated, "Raisa is non-weight bearing on her right front. Grossly, it appears mal-aligned. Two radiographs are attached indicating non-union."

I called Dr. Radcliffe's office and he simply asked when we could get there, offering no comments about the x-rays themselves. It was Friday. I booked the appointment for Monday morning and we made arrangements to travel on Sunday, hoping the weather would cooperate enough for us to make it there and then back home again.

That weekend was excruciating for me. I had bouts of crying, feeling dizzy and just feeling really really sad. I realized that Tim and I have wildly different ways of dealing with intense emotion. He was of the view that we shouldn't even talk about what would happen until Dr. Radcliffe was able to see her. I on the other hand wanted to talk about it. Needed to talk about it. Why had the implants failed? Was the density not good? Was the plate too small? What would he do? I also needed to talk through the hardest topic of all: Should we fix her? Is it fair to her? Is it fair to us? Is it fair not to? All of these questions and emotions swirled around and around my head in a loop. But they stayed there because it was a place that Tim just wouldn't go.

29

PRECIOUS & FRAGILE THINGS

RAISA'S EARS PERKED UP as Tim carried her out of the house and gently put her on my lap, where I was sitting in the passenger seat of the truck. Despite the awkwardness of her soft casted leg, she swiftly made herself comfortable on the plush dog bed – so comfortable in fact that she wiggled herself onto her back in a "scratch my belly" position, letting us know that she was not just content but was jubilant. She looked adorable in the little pink kid's tee shirt that we put on her so that she wouldn't lick the tightly-wound cocoon of gauze and bandages on her broken leg, which was now sticking straight up in the air in what we called the "stop in the name of love" position.

Little Raisa didn't know where we were going or why. All she knew was that we were on an adventure and she was elated to be out of the crate that had been her whole world for the past five weeks. Our little whimsical pixie stayed there on her plaid plush cushion for the seven-hour drive, with a happy open-mouthed dog smile on her face the entire time. She was oblivious to the fact that the driving conditions were terrible.

The freezing rain began when we reached Pennsylvania. As we drove along the slick icy roads, there were cars in the ditch on both sides, seemingly every mile. One vehicle was turned on its roof, and there were two fire trucks at the roadside with a crew who appeared to be trying to free someone inside. At home, we would never have gone out in conditions like this – dangerous, life-threatening conditions. But we had to. We had to keep our appointment with the only man who could put our little broken girl back together.

There were only a handful of radio stations that could be heard with any clarity as we travelled through the mountain ranges. Eventually, there were only two: one playing a religious service and the other alternative music. I chose the music, and when a song came on by Depeche Mode called "Precious," the lyrics tore at me so much that I could literally feel my chest get heavy as I looked at Raisa while listening carefully to the words. They perfectly described the sense of fragility I was feeling, as well as the wish that I could take the pain and suffering for her. It felt like the song was written for us. But I wasn't singing. I was quietly crying.

We arrived in West Virginia, where we were staying at a farmhouse beside Dr. Radcliffe's clinic that was owned by the clinic. On the telephone, he told us that he had recently bought the house from an elderly neighbour and fixed it up for his out-of-town clients.

It was dark when we arrived. Tim got out of the vehicle first and went into the house and turned on some lights. I then carried Raisa in. Her tail began pumping when I set her down on the living room floor, and she explored as far as she could reach on the circumference of her leash with her nose to the ground, hobbling along on three legs.

It was freezing in the house, and when Tim went to investigate, he found out the furnace wasn't working. It was too late to call anyone, so he said he would fix it after he took Raisa outside.

While Tim took Raisa outside to do her business, I got our bedroom ready, pulling the mattress off the bed and putting it on the floor between the bed frame and the wall, which made a little sleeping cubby. Tim brought Raisa inside and carried her upstairs to me, and then went to unpack our belongings. I decided to go straight to bed since it was late. And cold. Tim went to the basement to fix the furnace.

When I put Raisa down on the mattress, which was covered in our own blankets that I brought from home, she waited for me to lie down and then curled up beside me just like she had done every other night of her life since we brought her home five years prior. She never seemed to care where she was sleeping, as long as she was beside me. She fell asleep quickly, but I just lay there in the dark, willing my brain to shut off so that I could get some rest. I stroked her white silky fur, which ended up relaxing me enough that I eventually fell asleep.

The next morning began as every morning had started for the past five years, with a cold pointy nose in my face, and an enthusiastic little pink tongue cleaning the sleep out of my eyes. I croaked "ahhh, morning kisses" as I always did, but this time, I did it half-heartedly, worrying about the day ahead. I wondered how far we might need to go for her, and what it would mean for her life and for ours? It was an incredibly heavy way to start the day.

I carried Raisa downstairs but was too nervous to eat any breakfast, so Tim and I just sat and drank our coffee while Raisa hung out beside us on the floor of the dining room of the farmhouse, nestled on top of the giant tangerine-coloured comforter that I brought with us, which I had molded into a soft bed for her.

She was such an easygoing dog – just happy to be wherever we were. I loved her so much.

When we arrived at the clinic, Raisa was uncharacteristically scared. She was usually nervous, but this time she was terrified. We had to weigh her, something that she was very used to, but she didn't want to be put down to step on the scale, and she tried to crawl up Tim's legs to get back into his arms when he set her down.

A woman dressed in pajamas came running into the clinic with her dog in a blanket. I listened to the conversation at the desk. Her dog was having a seizure, and the staff took the dog right back to be cared for. She started to have what I recognized as a panic attack and then the strangest thing happened – she looked at Raisa, whose eyes met her eyes. The woman stopped crying and said, "That is such a beautiful dog."

I started to talk to the lady, who calmed right down. She told me that her dog, a pug, was fifteen years old, and was suffering from diabetes. She was retired, and her kids were grown and lived elsewhere so her dog was her whole life. In that moment I realized that Tim and I weren't unique in feeling so strongly about our dogs – we didn't love our dogs more because we were childless. Everyone loved their dog, and everyone's dog meant something different to them, and for different reasons.

I felt a tightening of my throat as I talked to the lady about her dog and what he meant to her. The people pleaser in me felt obligated to keep her distracted, but at the same time I was being pulled to Raisa, where my attention should have been, but wasn't.

Dr. Radcliffe came out and took us into an examination room. He was talking as he walked, telling us that he had a plan. The screws from the last repair had not held, so he was going to put a long rod on the underside of Raisa's forearm this time, all the way from her wrist to her elbow. He warned us that she would have some impairment of function, but that her leg would be saved. I didn't even care about whether she would be able to move with her usual light-footed grace again; all I cared about was saving her leg and thus saving her life.

I asked Dr. Radcliffe through my tears if he had ever put more than one plate in a dog's leg before this, and he shook his head back and forth and with his eyes closed, he said, "No."

I started to cry harder then, knowing that Tim was about to make the speech that we had planned and rehearsed ahead of time.

He stuttered as he started to speak. It was normally me who did all the talking at appointments when it came to the dogs.

"We have decided that if you can't fix the leg, we don't want you to wake her up."

Dr. Radcliffe nodded.

Tim continued, "We don't want you to amputate her leg."

Dr. Radcliffe's eyes were also tearing up when he answered, "You are making the right decision – I wouldn't amputate a leg on one of my greyhounds."

Tim explained to him about the other silken windhounds we knew about because of my research that had gone through amputations and died from complications or because the other front leg had broken. That Raisa had already broken a back leg, and her front leg twice, so what were the odds that another leg wouldn't go if she only had three?

"We just couldn't do that to her," he said.

Dr. Radcliffe left the room, asking us to stay close, and a technician came in and whizzed Raisa off to prepare her for surgery. I didn't even get to say good-bye to her because it all happened so quickly.

We walked back to the farmhouse and tried to keep ourselves busy, but I couldn't do anything but worry.

As the hours passed, even though we didn't admit it out loud to each other, we both figured that it was good news, since if it was unfixable, we would have heard right away. Of course, he would fix her – he was the Greyhound God. He was Raisa's saviour. It was going to be a tough go, but we would all get through this. Because she was our girl.

When the phone rang, Tim answered, and I leaned close to him and heard Dr. Radcliffe say, "Tim. There's no bone here."

He was calling from the operating room. Raisa was still alive on the table, but Dr. Radcliffe had not been able to fix her leg. As I heard Tim tell Dr. Radcliffe to let her go, I grabbed the phone from him and blurted out, "Is there anything else you can do?"

There was a long pause when all I could hear was the beeping of the surgical equipment in the background, and for a long moment Dr. Radcliffe said nothing.

He then sighed and said, "Amputation is really the only option at this point."

I was ready to agree – for I would have done anything to keep my Raisa alive in that moment, despite what we had agreed to ahead of time. She was my girl and she needed to be saved. Doing "the right" thing now seemed impossible to me.

Tim gently took the phone out of my hands and told Dr. Radcliffe, no, please let her go.

I started to sob. Tim covered the phone with his hand and said to me, "It's not a kindness to bring her back if she can't have a good life."

I grabbed the phone back, and again asked Dr. Radcliffe if there was any other option? I wasn't thinking rationally, but was making this new decision on pure adrenalin and emotion.

Dr. Radcliffe answered my question indirectly by asking if we wanted to see her to say good-bye, adding that he didn't want to wake her up.

I said no, through my tears, and told him I wanted to remember Raisa the way she was when I last saw her, and we would wait a bit and then come over.

I passed the phone back to Tim, and then the room closed in on me. I fell to the ground, physically forced down by the shock of it all. Tim picked me up and hugged me as I sobbed into his chest, broken by the weight of the news.

As we made our way back to the clinic, the world seemed to lose its sense of reality. My brain and my heart were both struggling to make sense of what was happening.

As soon we arrived, Dr. Radcliffe came out from the back and led us to the comfort room again. There was no comfort in this room or anywhere in the world for me at that moment. Looking defeated, he silently handed Raisa's collar to Tim.

Dr. Radcliffe gave me a hug and we both cried. And with my arms around him, I realized that he wasn't the larger-than-life invincible man that I thought him to be. He was just a human. And he was sad too.

I cried that I didn't even say good-bye to her, and he told me that he had prayed over her and gave her a kiss for me.

And then as I watched my hero turn to hug my crying husband, I thought about how hard it must be to be a man in a situation like this. They were both fixers. And while Tim could fix anything mechanical, like the furnace in the farmhouse next door, he couldn't fix my broken heart. And while Dr. Radcliffe could fix every other broken bone, he just couldn't fix Raisa's fragile brittle leg anymore.

Dr. Radcliffe pointed to that door in the comfort room that went right to the parking lot, and told us to just go – that he would arrange for Raisa's body to be cremated and he would send us her ashes and all the paperwork.

We had shared some of our most intimate and life-altering moments with this man. We had made 14 trips to West Virginia for our silken windhounds. He had performed eight surgeries on them. Even though he didn't save Raisa's leg this time, Dr. Radcliffe was still my hero.

When we got back to the farmhouse, for the first time in my life, I couldn't do anything. I just sat in a chair and cried while Tim packed everything up and somehow got me into the truck.

We drove for seven hours with long periods of silence broken up only by my sobs and Tim's sniffling. I used to wonder how much it would cost me to go to the ends of the earth for the dog that I loved. Now I knew the answer. The price was my heart, which was now feeling completely carved out. I have never in my life felt the way I felt that day. The emotional pain was so intense that it physically hurt. I knew that having a dog would inevitably lead to this kind of loss, but I didn't expect it to happen under those circumstances, and certainly not on that day.

When we got home, I walked into my house and felt ambivalence for my other dogs, because they weren't Raisa. All I wanted was Raisa back. It felt like a bad dream. She just couldn't be gone. I didn't sleep in my own bed because that room still had her crate in it, and it hurt me too much to look at it. I took her blanket out of the crate and brought it with me to the spare bedroom instead.

The next day was just as excruciating. Maybe even more so because now that I was finally able to talk about it, I couldn't stop saying out loud to Tim all the thoughts that had been going through my mind.

Did we make a mistake? Did we do right by her? Would Raisa have chosen the decision that we made? Could she have been happy on three legs or would her life have been misery? Was it fair to keep putting her through so many bouts of what amounts to torture on Dr. Radcliffe's table in order to fix her? Was it a matter of what we could afford to do, versus the best thing to do? Did I selfishly want to keep her alive because I wanted her here? Was I selfish for taking her life at such a young age when there were still options left?

I started convincing myself that maybe, just maybe, she could have survived on three legs and still had a good life. Maybe she would have been different than the other silken windhounds that perished after a leg amputation. She was special. She had such a good attitude. I became sure it was wrong to have extinguished such a vibrant life in its prime. And I felt guilty as hell.

Doing the things that needed doing that day felt wrong. I remember thinking to myself, "This is insane. Raisa has just died. Why the hell are you doing the laundry?"

But I needed to do the laundry. And lots of other stuff needed doing too, so over the course of that first day, I emptied the dishwasher, put our travel stuff away and took the other dogs for walks, all the while pushing back tears, and doing my best to just stay upright.

I didn't want to see anyone or talk to anyone except Tim; anyone that is, with the exception of Heather, who dropped everything to meet me at the closest coffee shop as soon as I sent her a message about the sad news.

There is a Tim Hortons located at a truck stop at Peter's Corners; the intersection of two rural highways near our house. I had never been inside the place before, but Heather found it online and agreed to drive there and meet me. She was waiting for me in the parking lot, where she gave me a big hug as soon as I got out of my vehicle. She then led me inside, opening the door for me, and sitting me in a booth. She pulled a box of Kleenex out of her bag and put it in front of me, and then went to the counter, not even asking what I wanted.

When Heather returned to the table, without saying a word, she set a giant brown cardboard cup of steaming chamomile tea in front of me. Then she sat down and just let me cry. Neither of us talked for a few minutes. She then broke the silence by saying, "This is going to be difficult for you to hear; but you need to hear it."

Heather re-told the sad story about what happened after Fable's leg was taken off. This time, she provided me with even more grim details.

"Michelle, I had to force feed her because she refused to eat. For six weeks, I had to pry open her mouth and jam food in, and then hold her mouth closed to make her swallow it."

She paused to take a drink of her hot chocolate.

"After the amputation, Fable refused to even stand up. She peed and pooed while lying there in her crate. It was disgusting and pathetic, and the saddest thing I have ever seen. I cried every time I washed her. Every single time."

"Michelle, you have to understand that after we let them take her leg off, Fable, who used to be so happy, had no life left in her eyes. I can't tell you how many times I looked at her and thought, 'What have I done to you?'"

I nodded, and wiped the tears welling up in my eyes with a rough beige paper napkin. Heather pulled one of the Kleenex out of the box and handed it to me, as she continued on with her speech.

"You would be still be grieving right now. You would be suffering right along with Raisa about the loss of her leg. And you would cry every time you looked at her and I promise that you would feel soooo guilty – even more guilty than you're feeling right now."

She set her hot chocolate down, and stared into my eyes with such intensity and then said matter-of-factly, "Raisa's other front leg would have broken too. That, I have no doubt about."

A few years ago, when Heather had loaned me Fable's harness after Raisa's first leg break, I was so surprised that it fit without having to make any adjustments. Raisa had slipped as easily into that harness as she had into the sad fate of its owner. Heather had realized this long before now, which is probably why she had been so ready to step up and help me get through the excruciating first night at home without my Raisa.

With the tough love portion of Heather's directive over, her demeanor abruptly changed. Softened. And from that point on, we interacted in a more conversational way. We didn't discuss the events surrounding Raisa's death, instead commiserating with each other about all we had both been through as a result of bonding so deeply with our fragile dogs. About the maternal instincts that were triggered in us when our dogs were hurt. About how they became so dependent on us as we carried them around and gave them our constant attention. We agreed that both Fable and Raisa (and Maple too) through no fault of their own, became pure need when they were broken. Normal dogs would have done normal dog things during their lives. Our dogs couldn't, and as a result, we became their worlds. And they became ours. These powerful connections might have looked heartwarming from the outside, but our relationships with our silken windhounds weren't natural.

I admitted to Heather that even though I knew that loving Raisa had devastated me, it was because of her that I now truly understood unconditional love. I had it for her, and she had it for me. Never in my life had I ever had such certainty that another being loved me as deeply, maybe even more deeply than I loved them.

She responded, "The pain you are feeling is the price you paid for the privilege of being able to love her so deeply and to be loved back in the same way."

As Heather and I parted that night, I returned to my grief, but with less guilt, and for that, I will be forever thankful. I suppose that I will always still wonder if Raisa could have been the exception, but when my mind starts to go there, I think about poor Fable and also about Dr. Radcliffe telling me that we cannot go wrong when love is the foundation of the decision to do right by them, even when the outcome is heartbreaking for us.

30

DOUBLE EDGED SWORDS

I N THE DAYS THAT followed Raisa's death, I grieved deeply, walking around with my head in a fog as I adjusted to my new reality, all the while trying to stay afloat in the wake of a world without her in it. For at least a week, I woke up every morning and lost her all over again when I suddenly remembered that she was gone.

The house felt so empty without her; even with three other dogs in it. I felt empty too. But I felt something else too – something that made me uncomfortable. My heart was heavy, but strangely, everything else felt a bit lighter. The result, I suppose, of being suddenly and completely released from the overwhelming responsibility of taking care of and worrying about another being so intensely. It was a bittersweet paradox to be longing for the very thing that had also been my life's biggest burden. All of these strong contradictory feelings made the whole situation even more unsettling. Unlike when a human loved one dies, none of the common rituals are there to fall back on. There wasn't going to be a funeral, a eulogy, or any other ceremony to acknowledge that Raisa had ever existed, and that bothered me.

In an effort to honour her life, I wrote an obituary of sorts on my own personal Facebook page, which garnered lots of kind messages of condolences. It also ended up adding a tremendous amount of grief to my grieving.

Someone from my friend list must have shared my post with the larger silken windhound group, inviting an onslaught of cruel comments, which I was able to read on account of my fake profile.

"She's bitter and tries to stir up trouble about this…maybe nothing better to do with her time."

"One person with two dogs with broken legs speaks more to an issue in the home than with the breed ... something is wrong in that household."

"Blaming the whole breed or stirring up things will not get your dog back or fix anything ... I have a dog with a chronic issue and I don't blame the whole breed for that."

"I understand this poor woman's grief, but science and society refute her claims."

"She gets on her stage and expounds anti-silken stories every chance she gets. Don't listen."

"Logic and reason escape us when we're grieving."

"I am sorry for her losses but don't have sympathy for hurt or pain that they bring out of vengeance born of something that was clearly an accident."

"I feel deep down, she doesn't want to be found at fault and will go to any lengths to prove it...take her off all things Silken! She has lost the right to remain... Something needs to be done. Take her off your friends list, and all Facebook pages and groups, and remove her from any Yahoo groups...Keep trying little girl, you won't get anywhere!!!"

A prominent breeder and member of the Health Committee called me a "very sad and disturbed lady."

The breed founder even chimed in:

I don't know why she does not just move on. My recommendation is that anybody being contacted not just unfriend her, but actively report her to the website for spam and a scam. This sort of thing has got to stop. I no longer have sympathy with the lady, she is just simply nasty.

The person who conducted the survey monkey on leg breaks for the breed club, called me "the breed bone break conspiracy theorist" on her own page. Someone added that I was crazy and then another person wrote this: "...Why can't we slap an injunction against her slandering our breed...that is slander and since she's publishing it it's slander per se. Can't we stop her legally?"

These comments went beyond incivility. They were hateful. How on earth was I the villain in all of this? My dog had just died as a result of the exact health issue that I had been raising awareness about for years. I knew I wasn't crazy. If Raisa had been the only silken windhound with multiple leg breaks; I wouldn't have wasted my time and energy devoting my life to researching the problem. But there were over a hundred of them that I now knew about with broken legs! And there were probably lots more.

I hated being hated. It made me think about how horrible it must be for children and other vulnerable people to be bullied online. I was an adult. I was educated. I had a support system. And their comments still upset me terribly. I knew better than anyone that words do matter. And at a time where I was craving kindness and sympathy, I keenly felt the cruelty of these posts in a deep way.

Dundas is a charming little town close to where Tim and I live – one of those old-fashioned places that still has street parking and lots of small vibrant independently owned shops; a grocer, a butcher, a bakery and even a cheese shop. Our favourite restaurant is housed in an old building that has sat at the corner of the two main streets since 1840. It's called The Thirsty Cactus, and we go there weekly for burrito night.

While sitting in our cozy booth waiting for our food, I was sharing my feelings about the latest horrible things that had been said about me online. As I recounted the worst of the negative posts, I went from being angry to being teary.

Tim doesn't use any social media. He thinks it's a waste of his time; which is probably why when he stared at me (as he is prone to do right before making the type of declaration that will hurt my feelings), I cringed.

"Enough is enough," he said. Then he paused. I wasn't entirely sure if he was going to say anything else.

The country music playing in the background all of a sudden sounded louder to me as I sat there deciding whether to say anything back which might just start an argument.

He took a sip of his beer, and without averting his gaze said, "You aren't ever going to get anywhere with these people. It's time to give up trying to convince them."

I nodded in agreement (even though I didn't actually agree with him).

He went on, "Never wrestle with pigs – you get dirty and the pigs like it."

I giggled. He loved that saying. Then he said, "You need to quit social media. Cold turkey."

Tim is such a cold turkey kind of guy. You know those people who just announce that they will quit smoking, lose weight or stop eating meat, and then, bam, they just do it? Well, that is Tim.

We had been through this conversation so many times. He already knew my position: that Facebook was really the only place I could find more data on leg breaks.

Tim was still staring at me intensely when he stated, "Write a book."

"What?" I heard him but still answered him as if I hadn't.

He said it again, "Write a book." It came out more as an order than a suggestion.

"I can't write a book – I have no credentials that qualify me as an expert on dogs," I replied. "And besides, I haven't solved anything. If I had discovered the reason for the leg breaks, then there would be a story."

"You have a story," he said.

Then he added, "What have you got to lose?"

He was right. Nothing I had done to date had gotten me any closer to helping silken windhounds stop breaking their bones.

"Silken windhounds keep breaking though," I said, and as I opened my mouth to continue, he cut me off.

"And they're going to keep breaking, regardless of whether you keep counting them. You have enough data already – Jesus, if over 100 dogs of the same breed with broken legs aren't enough, then I don't know what is. There are only a couple thousand of them on the planet."

I felt like I was being lectured as he continued on with his address, "Besides, nobody is going to care about your statistics. Our story is the crazy part."

"But what about all my research and data?"

"Put it in there. Or, do a book about our story and make a report separately with all the boring stuff. Publish it on a website or something – then all your dog nerd people can geek out on it."

He paused and then added, "And then you can finally get on with your life. Put it all behind you. And us."

"It's not boring," I said, feeling hurt. I felt weirdly possessive over all the research I had done.

The truth was, I did want to write something. A book seemed like an enormous undertaking, but that's not what scared me. I knew I could write about the data I had collected, and expose what I had discovered. That kind of writing I was used to: objective, factual and persuasive. It was our story that I was hesitant about. I felt extremely uneasy even thinking about revealing anything about my own personal life in such a public way. It was completely contrary to how I had been trained as a lawyer. In fact, the very thought of describing the raw unfiltered emotions I had been experiencing over the past few years on account of my dogs really scared the crap out of me.

But a funny thing happened that evening at the Thirsty Cactus. The more we talked about it, the more I warmed up to the idea of sharing our story. And as we finished our burritos, I also finished making excuses for why I couldn't write a book about all we had been through. It was time to stop counting leg breaks and start recounting our experiences. It was time to tell our sad tales. The good. The bad. The ugly.

31

BODIES & BORDERS

THE DEAD OF WINTER was the perfect time to begin writing a book. My new morning routine now included sitting down at my computer, drinking an extra-large mug of black coffee, and putting our story into words.

Prior to tethering myself to my computer screen for the day, I always took the dogs on a hike around the property. The big dogs ran free, and I kept Maple on her expandable leash, which still gave her lots of room to sniff all the interesting smells. Walking the wide trail that looped around the perimeter took about half an hour. It was an ideal way to prime my mind for a day of writing.

On one particular morning, while walking in the wintry woods, deep in thought about something (probably my book), my phone rang. Fumbling, I tried to get it out of my pocket without dropping my mittens into the snow, and my heart sank when I saw the caller ID. It was Dr. Radcliffe's office.

On the other end of the line was Abby, one of the capable and friendly vet techs that we got to know in our years of repeated visits. She was calling to gently and politely let me know that they had received Raisa's ashes back from the pet crematorium and that she would be sending them by courier the following day.

I was happy for the heads up so I could get myself into the right frame of mind to receive them, and I told her so.

The following day, I received another call from Abby, also while I was walking in the woods.

"We have a problem," she declared.

"Oh no, what's going on?"

"Well, I'm sitting here with Raisa on my desk because our courier won't take her."

"Why?"

"They are prohibited from transporting remains to your address. I think it might have something to do with the border."

My stomach lurched. "Oh no. Now what?"

"Well, don't you worry, we'll get your girl to you one way or another. I'm gonna call around. I just wanted to let you know what was going on."

I wanted to scream (to the Universe, not to Abby), "Are you fucking kidding me?"

Instead, I said, "Thank you. I'm so sorry for all the trouble."

"I'll get back to you as soon as I get it all figured out," she said in such a convincing way that I just knew she would make it happen.

After I got off the phone, my temples were pounding. Why was everything with these dogs always such a heartbreak?

I called Tim and told him what was going on.

"What are we going to do?" I pleaded into the phone, knowing he wasn't going to be helpful.

"Well, I can tell you what we aren't going to do. We aren't going to drive to West Virginia to get them."

"Her," I corrected.

"Them," he insisted, adding, "I told you we should have brought her body home with us."

The fact that he used the word "body" made me feel uncomfortable. I hated being brought back to thinking about that terrible day. Tim wanted to bring her home with us, but I refused, knowing it would have traumatized me even more. Where would we have put her? Not in the open bed of the truck. But also, not inside with us. Plus, it was the middle of winter, and the ground was frozen, so it's not like we could have buried her properly at home anyway.

Tim then said, "Why do they have to tell the courier what's in the box?"

"They can't lie!" I squealed.

He quipped back, "Well, the breeder lied about her age to get her across the border without a rabies vaccine when we bought her. It wouldn't be the first time she's crossed the border on false pretenses."

In spite of the morbid subject matter, I did find his observation a bit amusing.

"We can't ask them to do that, Tim. Not after all they have done for us."

The next day Abby called and cheerfully reported that she was driving around with Raisa on the dashboard of her car, trying desperately to find a courier.

"None of them will take her," she said, her accent sounding so sing-songy that her grim revelation was somewhat minimized.

"I have an idea," I told her.

"There is a shipping outlet just across the border in Lewiston where we pick up packages. Can you ship her there and we can drive across and pick her up?"

"That's a great idea," Abby said, adding, "Send me the address and we'll get your girl back to you."

It felt extremely weird tracking a package that contained the ashes of my dead dog, but I needed to know it had arrived before sending my parents to pick it up. They were big fans of the casino in Niagara Falls, New York, and had volunteered to combine a trip to the Seneca Resort and Casino with a stop at the shipping depot in Lewiston on their way home.

When my parents arrived back at my house to make the sad delivery, my dad waited in the car, obviously trying to avoid any type of emotional situation that may erupt. He thought the whole set of affairs was ridiculous, even though he would never tell me so.

I opened the front door, and my mom, not saying anything, handed the package to me, giving me a sad look.

"Don't open it while we're here," she said, stepping inside briefly to hug me, and then turning to leave, saying, "Call me later."

I peered out the door and waved to my dad. He lowered the car window and waved back. I yelled, "Thank you," and he just nodded before putting the window back up as my mom got back into the car.

Back inside, I set the unassuming and surprisingly small cardboard box on the counter and briefly debated whether to wait for Tim to open it.

Deciding not to make an event out of it, I grabbed some scissors and sliced through the clear tape that was holding the cardboard flaps together. I removed the object on top and carefully unrolled the bubble wrap, revealing a ceramic urn encased in a translucent mesh bag covered in a pattern of little black paw prints. I slid the urn out of the bag and was taken aback at how small it was. I set it on the counter and looked at it. The style suited her. It was slim, white and elegant in its simplicity. Just like Raisa. I wondered if Dr. Radcliffe picked it out or if it was just the standard one that everyone got.

The box also contained a sturdy black take-out food container. I pried off the clear lid to reveal a flat piece of clay in the shape of a circle that held the imprint of Raisa's paw. Above it, her name was stamped inside two little heart imprints. When I picked it up, a folded piece of paper with typed instructions fell out, telling me I had to bake the clay disk in the oven. As I ran both my thumbs over the imprint, an intrusive thought popped into my mind. Which one of Raisa's little paws did they use to make it? Surely not the one from the broken leg? I immediately tried to suppress the morbid vision by quickly sealing the disk back into its container, which is when I discovered that there was still something else in the cardboard box, tucked away under the crinkled packing paper.

Rolled up in a cylindrical shape was the little pink t-shirt with the butterfly on it that Raisa was wearing when I last saw her. My chest tightened at the sight of it.

Feeling suddenly queasy, I carefully packed all the objects back into the box, and walked the ominous package upstairs, pulling some sweaters off a shelf so I could hide it away with all of the other items I still couldn't bear to look at: Her black break-away collar and matching harness that still had some white tinsel fur attached. Her favourite toy - a stuffed replica of Santa's Little Helper from The Simpsons that she used to joyfully prance around the house with. The unchewed rawhide bone she had with her on the last fateful trip. Each of these items held a piece of Raisa's essence, and now her very essence was sitting there amongst them.

As I arranged the folded sweaters back in front of the sacred objects, I realized that the delivery of Raisa's ashes had caused my emotions to shift. I thought having her home would bring a sense of closure, but it didn't.

I felt unsettled. Disturbed. A bit angry even. How could I lay her to rest when there were still so many big broken pieces to her story? How could I write about what happened to us when I still didn't fully understand why her bones kept breaking ... why so many leg breaks were happening in the breed in the first place?

I still had a very strong gut-feeling that there was a hereditary disease behind it all, but my analytical lawyer brain knew there was a big difference between intuition and actual evidence.

It was driving me crazy that the breed club and breeders were still brushing the leg breaks off as freak accidents and bad luck. It bothered me even more that they continued to defame me as a crazy person for suggesting anything different. It sucked that I didn't have a deep enough understanding about dog breeding, veterinary medicine, or genetics to refute them. What sucked even more was knowing that if I didn't do anything, then all of my hard work would eventually disappear behind the vast expanse of their skepticism, and everything I had already done on the subject would be in vain. I hated the thought of wasted time almost as much as I hated injustice when it involved animals.

Reaching back through the sweaters, I blindly located the cardboard box. I slid it back out, and opening it, put my hand over the bubble wrapped urn, as if it were a Bible. Every fibre of my being was telling me that I needed to keep going with my research; that I was onto something monumental. Was it Raisa's energy I was feeling? Who knows. All I do know is that the little white urn wasn't just holding her remains – it was also motivating me to keep going. Despite its diminutive size, that little piece of porcelain became a big physical reminder of all my unfinished business, evoking feelings that helped me to realize that in order to bid my girl a peaceful farewell, and to finally feel at peace myself, I needed some answers.

Before returning the box to its secret sanctuary, I made a silent vow to Raisa that I wouldn't bury her remains until I could properly finish her story. This time I wouldn't get bullied; or sidetracked; or stuck. I resolved to track down the origin of the horrific health problem that took her from us, no matter what.

This of course meant that the book-writing would have to be put on hold so I could focus all of my time and energy on returning back to researching leg breaks. Tim was going to kill me.

32

FORBIDDEN LOVE

IN THE DAYS THAT followed, and with my lawyer spirit re-ignited, I returned with full force to my personal crusade to get to the bottom of silken windhound leg breaks. Reminiscent of my eleven-year-old self who became outraged about the wrongful death of my best friend Duchess, my raw heart was once again taking a back seat to a ridiculously strong desire to rectify a perceived injustice to a dog.

The first item on my agenda was to revisit the data as it related to inbreeding. I needed to understand, first the scope, and then the science surrounding this issue in order to move forward any further.

When Tim got home from work, he found me in the bedroom, sitting on the floor in front of the giant diagram of taped-together canine family trees.

"Oh noooo!" he said so loudly that the big dogs bounded up the stairs to see what was going on.

"I thought we agreed you were done with all this shit?" he said, dressing me down with a scowl.

"I thought so too, but I can't finish writing our story until I sort this inbreeding thing out once and for all."

He just sighed.

"See this guy here?" I said, pointing with the tip of my capped orange highlighter to one of the names in the middle of the chart.

"He looks colourful," he said, in relation to the rainbow of highlighted lines jutting out from the name of the dog which was written with red magic marker: "Unbreakable."

"He's related to so many broken dogs."

"And his name is Unbreakable?" he asked, laughing a bit. "Did he break?"

"Not that I know of; but he had over 50 descendants that did."

"That's crazy," he replied, and then surprisingly started looking a bit interested in my diagram.

"He's Maple's grandfather."

He raised an eyebrow as I continued on. "And he's also Raisa's great grandfather on both sides of her pedigree."

"Good ol' Grandpa Breakable. Is he the source of the leg break gene?"

"His name is Unbreakable, not Breakable, and I haven't found a leg break gene. And no, he isn't far enough back in the pedigrees to be the source of the problem, although he's obviously a big contributor. He's what they call a popular sire."

"Do you remember a dog named Chastity?" I asked, moving my highlighter to point to another area of the diagram.

"No ... should I?"

"Her broken leg was fixed by Dr. Radcliffe before we went to West Virginia for the first time."

"Ok, that doesn't narrow it down."

"True. Sorry. Well, she was one of the breeding dogs from the same kennel that Kim got Maple's mother from."

"I still don't remember her," he said.

"You must recall me telling you about the breeder that asked the silken windhound community for money to pay Dr. Radcliffe's bill to fix her dog's leg?"

"Oh, right. You didn't give her money, did you?" he said, looking straight into my eyes to make sure I would tell him the truth.

"No, but Chastity, the dog with the broken leg, had a sister that broke a leg too, and I did make an online donation to help pay for that one."

"But that dog wasn't owned by a breeder, was it?"

"Yes," I admitted, and then winced, knowing I was about to hear a rant.

"Wait. So, let me get this straight. These breeders are selling puppies to suckers like us for, what, over $2000 USD, and then asking for money when their own breeding dogs break their legs? Where's our money?"

"Some are selling pups for $4000 USD, and yep, I know, it stinks. One breeder even did a GoFundMe twice. Same dog broke both front legs at different times. Two separate online fundraisers to pay the vet bills."

"That's nuts."

"At least she rehomed that dog, although it broke a leg again. Chastity's breeder paid Dr. Radcliffe with donations and then bred Chastity and sold the puppies."

"Ok, so why are you still pointing to her name?" he said, as I watched his eyes follow the highlighter I was still waving back and forth over Chastity's name on the chart.

"Unbreakable is Chastity's uncle."

"So, she's related to our dogs?"

"Yes, but that's not why she's so interesting."

I gestured to the bed. "Sit down, I want to tell you a story."

Tim reluctantly but obediently sat down, knowing he wasn't getting dinner until I was finished. The big dogs jumped up on the bed and Tim started rubbing their tummies as they were lolling around beside him as I began my lecture.

"Chastity's mother was named Sunset *(I point to her name on the chart with my highlighter)*. Her pedigree shows that she was mated to her half-brother to get Chastity. So, Chastity resulted from a brother to sister mating."

"Gross," he said.

"Oh, it gets grosser," I replied.

"Mother Sunset was also bred to her littermate brother, and guess who he is?"

I didn't wait for him to answer, as I slid the capped highlighter back over to where it was originally. "Unbreakable! ...and Mother Sunset was bred to her own father too."

"Disgusting," he blurted out as he started to get up from the bed.

"I'm not done!" I said, insisting that he sit back down by waving my highlighter at him.

"Before Chastity broke her leg, she had a litter of puppies when she was only a year and a half old."

"Isn't that young?" Tim said.

"That's not the issue," I replied. "Inbreeding is. The father of those puppies was Chastity's littermate brother."

"Gross," he said again.

"A few months later, Chastity broke her leg. Let me read you what the breeder posted online," I said, grabbing a piece of paper from a file folder labelled "Inbreeding."

"So, if somehow, I could borrow the money to get the surgery done, at some point I would be able to pay it back, although it would be slowly. Or if you'd like a pup from Chastity, we could work that out too...I'm willing to do nearly anything to get this done."

"Unreal," Tim said.

I put the sheet of paper back in the folder and continued on with my story, telling him how Chastity gave birth to another litter of puppies not long after her leg break, and only 10 months after her previous litter was born.

"That means Chastity was bred right after Dr. Radcliffe surgically repaired her broken leg," I declared.

"The surgery that other people paid for," Tim said flatly.

"Correct." I continued on, "Once again, the father of Chastity's puppies was her littermate brother."

I paused for dramatic effect, and then revealed the best part of the story.

"One of the puppies was given the registered name 'Forbidden Love.'"

"Come on," he said, laughing a bit.

"Yep," I continued; "The breeder called it The Love Litter. "One of the other pups was named 'Love Renewed,' I suppose because Chastity had renewed her love with her brother to make it."

"You're making this up!" he said.

"Nope. The other puppies were named: Love Abiding, Love Conquers All, and Deepest Love."

"That's so disturbing," he grimaced.

"I know. And let's not forget that the mother dog's name 'chastity' itself means refraining from sexual activity that is considered immoral."

Tim just stared at me in disbelief. I continued on.

"There's more. Chastity was just her call name. Her registered name was 'High Fidelity;' do you know what fidelity means?" I didn't wait for him to answer. "It means being sexually faithful to one partner. Which in this case was true ... she only mated with her brother."

He asked, "So, was the breeder trying to be funny?"

"I have no idea. It's not funny though. It's sad. Chastity was bred before her broken leg was even healed. You remember how pathetic and vulnerable ours were while they were recovering from a bone break? Can you imagine breeding them?"

"How do you know that?" he asked.

"Well, four months after having that litter of puppies, which was six months after Dr. Radcliffe fixed her leg, her breeder posted online that Chastity hadn't recovered from her leg break and was still limping about half of the time."

"Why would you breed a dog that had just broken its leg?" he asked.

"No idea. Money, I assume, but lots of the broken dogs in my study were bred. In fact, one breeder even bred one after having its leg amputated."

"Male?"

"Nope. It was a tiny female."

"That's so messed up."

"And get this. According to the pedigree database, Chastity was bred for a third time and I bet you can guess who the father was?"

I didn't wait for him to answer.

"Yep, the same brother again. And, Chastity was over nine years old when she gave birth."

"How do you know all this?" he said.

"I found it online. I used the Wayback Machine to look at the breeder's website from when she was selling the pups."

"What the hell is the Wayback Machine?" he asked.

"It's a tool that lets you search back through older versions of websites so you can see what's been deleted."

"You're insane. And I'm hungry. Let's eat."

There were more disturbing silken stories that I wanted to share with Tim, but I knew I had lost his attention to hunger, so I grabbed my inbreeding folder and followed him downstairs to make dinner.

After we finished eating, and because I knew I had his undivided attention again, I grabbed my folder, and when I sat it on the table, he said, "Oh, no."

"Oh yes!"

"There's more?"

"Oh, there's lots more," I said, telling him how I was no longer under the impression that only back yard breeders were inbreeding dogs. In fact, many of the well-known, reputable and well-respected breeders within the silken windhound community were doing it.

Tim wasn't surprised. He was, however, surprised when I started reading him some of the comments that those breeders made about it.

The owner and breeder of Chastity said on Facebook when questioned about the ethics of breeding close relatives and littermates: "I think that even close inbreeding is simply a breeding tool."

In the same exchange, the silken windhound breed founder wrote: "Breeding close relatives does not create genetic problems...close breeding does not automatically cause a deformed or dysfunctional dog medically."

Another wrote that inbreeding can be a great tool to those who know what they're doing and how to use it. Someone else added, "At this point all silkens are very very related but they are also very healthy."

I asked Tim if they were right: "Can you inbreed like this and get healthy dogs? If so, how could this be?"

"They're not right," he replied. "Our dogs aren't, I mean, weren't, well you know what I mean ... not healthy."

"But is it because of inbreeding?" I wondered.

"Probably," he said.

"Well, I'm going to find out."

"How?" he asked as he started carrying the empty dishes to the kitchen.

"I've already started. I'm part way through an online course in canine genetics."

Tim started loading the dishes into the dishwasher, and with his back turned to me it felt like I was talking to a wall.

When he didn't react about my revelation that I was taking a genetics course, I cleared my throat and then said to his back, "You've heard the phrase 'follow the money,' ... well, I'm going to follow the pedigrees ... right back to the beginning."

"The beginning of what?" he said, turning to face me.

"The breed." I replied, stepping backwards, but still facing him.

"I thought you already did that?" he asked, towering over me.

"I did. But I never found the real beginning. Besides, now I know what I'm looking for."

He just stared at me, but I could tell from the look on his face that he was tired of the subject matter. I just couldn't help myself though. I kept going; pushing my luck, as usual.

"Want to hear about the canine genome?"

"Nope," he said, and then turned and walked out of the kitchen.

And that was that. Tim was clearly done talking about or listening to anything to do with silken windhounds or dogs or genetics.

But I was just getting started — on a journey back in time to unravel the mysterious history of the silken windhound breed. Right back to its beginning; in order to figure out why so many of them were so related to one another, and whether and how the issue of inbreeding might relate to the leg breaks.

33

BRANCHING OUT

I AM SOMEWHAT EMBARRASSED to admit that prior to this point I hadn't realized that the silken windhound breed actually had a beginning.

I obviously knew that Maple and Raisa were part of a rare breed, but I never really thought about how the breed came into existence in the first place. I knew there was a breed founder, but I figured she "found" a breed that nobody knew about; that somehow, she discovered a smaller version of a borzoi. After all, the dog community called her the "breed founder" not the "breed creator."

Imagine my surprise when I discovered that silken windhounds were a fairly recent human invention. In fact, by revisiting the pedigrees of my own dogs, I was able to determine exactly how recent. Maple's family tree only went back eight generations. Raisa's, just nine. A little more searching revealed that the entire silken windhound pedigree database had no litters recorded before 1985.

Hoping to understand why the pedigrees only went back so far, I began researching the names of the dogs at the beginning: Windsprite Autumnal Xenon, Windsprite Autumnnal Jazz, Windsprite Autumnal Woodwine ... wait ... why did they all start with Windprite? Whose kennel was this?

When I typed "Windsprite Kennel" into the google search bar, I couldn't believe what popped up. I grabbed my phone and called Heather but she didn't answer, so I ran outside to find Tim. This couldn't wait.

I located him about half way between our house and the road, where he was busy levelling the gravel that had been plowed off our long driveway during the harsh winter. Jumping in front of his tractor, I began waving both arms at him jumping jack style. He stopped the tractor, looking worried, probably thinking I was in the midst of some kind of dog emergency.

Over the sound of the old orange Kubota's chugging diesel engine I yelled, "They're longhaired whippets!"

"What?"

"Turn the tractor off, I have to tell you something important!"

He looked annoyed, as he turned off the engine.

I repeated it again. "They're almost all longhaired whippets."

"What are you talking about?"

"At the beginning of Raisa and Maple's pedigrees. None of the dogs are silken windhounds."

"I'm confused," he said flatly, with a look that really meant, "I don't care."

"I googled the names of the dogs at the beginning of the pedigrees and I found out they are almost all longhaired whippets."

"Isn't that what Heather has?"

"Yes! That's why Puzzle looks so much like our dogs. They're related to him!"

"And guess what else?"

Tim raised an eyebrow, which I took as a vague cue for me to continue.

"That famous silken windhound they all talk about, you know the one, it's in all the breed propaganda – it supposedly lived to be twenty years old. Well, it isn't a silken windhound at all. It's a longhaired whippet! Boston Legacy, that's her name; she was a longhaired whippet!"

Tim brusquely told me that he had to get back to work, clearly not appreciating the gravity of the revelation that had so radically redefined my understanding of our own dogs' identities.

I literally skipped back to the house, feeling immensely satisfied with what I discovered. I now finally understood what had been preventing me from tracing the leg break problem back to just one silken windhound ancestor ... the pedigrees just didn't go back far enough. If there was a genetic mutation causing the problem, then it must have pre-dated the creation of the silken windhound breed.

This revelation, while exciting, created a new challenge for me. If I wanted to unearth the potential source of the problem, then I had to learn about the origins of yet another dog breed. Given how much time and effort I had already put into learning about one breed, this felt like a daunting prospect. But that wasn't going to stop me.

With the promise I made to Raisa's memory at the forefront of my mind, I began diving into the background of the longhaired whippet breed. Truth be told, once I got started, I was actually quite interested in learning all about those charming little dogs that looked so much like my own.

34

THERE'S A SKELETON IN MY CLOSET

W INDSPRITE. THE NAME OF the first longhaired whippet kennel was so fun and whimsical, but the mere mention of it, I learned, could still garner heated debates on social media. In fact, even the longhaired whippet "breed" itself made some people so angry that they chucked bricks through windows.

This drama in the dog world all started with a very interesting character; a cultured but eccentric American dog breeder named Walter A. Wheeler.

Surprisingly, there was quite a bit of information about Mr. Wheeler and his dogs on the internet. There were also books and magazine articles, many of which I collected with the help of Amazon and eBay. The Longhaired Whippet Association website (which I pulled up on the Wayback Machine) included a link to an official biography, which is where I pulled most of this information from.

Born in Houston in 1924 to a musical family, Mr. Wheeler learned to play the cello and took dance lessons from a young age. During his years in primary school, he kept exotic chickens and other pets. When he was 13 years old, he started breeding terriers. At 14, he performed professionally in a trio with his mother who was a concert pianist, and his brother who was a violinist. He bred his first litter of Shetland sheepdogs (shelties) when he was 15 years old.

In 1943, at the age of 18, Mr. Wheeler sold all of his dogs to register for service in World War II. After the war, he went to Harvard University until 1950 earning several masters' degrees. He then taught at a Boston private school.

Mr. Wheeler bred whippets beginning in 1957. The whippet breed strongly resembles small greyhounds. Like greyhounds, whippets have short hair. Or at least, they are supposed to have short hair. The subject of whippet hair length is what got Mr. Wheeler blacklisted in the purebred dog world. In fact, he made the proverbial fur fly by claiming that he discovered an unknown recessive gene that resulted in a longhaired variety of whippet, which was the beginning of what can only be described as a scandal.

In 1958, Mr. Wheeler coined the term "Windsprite" (his kennel name), after seeing his first "fuzzy" whippet puppy. He alleged that some whippets needed their coats shaved to appear smooth. His longhaired whippet project began by using relatives of that fuzzy puppy and one of his own whippets, which he described as "a show ring champion with a lion's mane and squirrel's tail that had to be trimmed for showing."

Mr. Wheeler reportedly inbred dogs intensely to populate his longhaired whippet project into the 1970's. He went public with his results in 1981 by publishing an article in "The Whippet" magazine.

It didn't take long for the purebred "smooth" whippet enthusiasts to react, accusing Mr. Wheeler of lying about the background of this new variety of whippet. You see, Mr. Wheeler also reportedly had borzoi and sheltie dogs at his kennel. There were rumours that he had used one or both of these long-coated breeds to produce his longhaired whippets. Mr. Wheeler vehemently denied the allegations.

The American Kennel Club (AKC) initially registered the longhaired whippets as purebred whippets. However, the purebred whippet folks from the American Whippet Club carried out an investigation in 1982, which concluded that the longhaired dogs were not purebreds, and as a result, the AKC deleted them from their registry and Mr. Wheeler was expelled from the American Whippet Club.

Despite the departure from the AKC, Mr. Wheeler and his followers still continued to breed longhaired whippets, and two groups of fanciers emerged: Walter Wheeler and a group who insisted that longhaired whippets were purebred whippets with a recessive gene for long hair, and a second group who believed longhaired whippets were created by using another breed and therefore were not purebred whippets.

The story then gets even more interesting (and confusing) as it becomes intertwined with the silken windhound breed.

Sometime in the 1980s, a borzoi breeder in Kentucky named Francie Stull purchased a few of Walter Wheeler's longhaired whippets and she started showing, breeding and selling them. She nicknamed them "silken windsprites," presumably on account of the backlash.

Years later, in 1998, Ms. Stull was reportedly ordered to cease and desist from using the name silken windsprite, because Walter Wheeler took exception to the use of his kennel name. It was then that Ms. Stull started using the name silken windhounds for the dogs she was producing.

It is unclear where Ms. Stull stood regarding the origins of Mr. Wheeler's dogs. In the earliest version of her kennel website that I could find (January1999), she stated that whether the long-haired trait had lain dormant in the whippet breed or had been more recently introduced was irrelevant once she took those "proto-type silkens" and combined them with "some of the finest borzoi lines available, and … an equally fine whippet line." Ms. Stull's stated vision: " … what we wanted was our beloved borzoi, only smaller!"

Now I understood why I never knew about the longhaired whippet origins of my own dogs. When I was originally searching for a type of dog to fit our lifestyle, I focused on the fact that a smaller version of a borzoi - my dream dog, existed. At that time, I didn't think much if at all about the logistics of how a giant breed was made into a miniature version. All I cared about was that the breed looked like a borzoi and was reportedly exceptionally healthy and long-lived.

Getting back to the hairy situation with the longhaired whippets, a number of years later, DNA analysis was applied to the ongoing dispute putting an end to the belief that there was ever a recessive gene responsible for the long coat.

In 2004 a paper was published by the National Academy of Sciences, based on DNA research done at the University of California Davis. It revealed that longhaired whippets carried a defective gene not found in the whippet or borzoi populations. It was, however, found in the Shetland sheepdog breed, therefore proving that there was sheltie (or some type of herding breed) in the background of the longhaired whippet, and therefore also in the silken windhound. Interestingly, this is the same defective gene that caused Maple's drug reactions.

When Mr. Wheeler died in 2013, his breed in North America was still called the long-haired whippet. In Europe, it was called the silken windsprite. Francie Stull was calling "her" breed the silken windhound. In 2017, the International Longhaired Whippet Club officially changed the name from longhaired whippet to windsprite.

Are you following this? If not, here is a recap: The former longhaired whippet breed is now officially called windsprite … except in Europe, where it's called silken windsprite … except in Germany, where the name was recently changed from silken windsprite to windsprite. Ms. Stull's breed, which is based on longhaired whippets that she originally called silken windsprites, is now called the silken windhound. Confused yet? Well, hold onto your hat, because it gets even worse.

Once genetic testing became commercially available to pet owners; DNA results revealed that both the longhaired whippet/windsprite breed and the silken windhound breed had whippet, sheltie and borzoi in their genetic make-up. In fact, the largest dog DNA database in the world uses only one category for both breeds. I inquired about it and was told: "… we tried to detect the windsprite/silken windhound separately, however, it didn't work because they are recent breeds added to our database that are a mix of similar breeds."

Despite all of this, both of these rare breeds still exist as separate entities, with their own separate breed clubs and registries. Neither have gained acceptance into the Canadian Kennel Club or the American Kennel Club. Breed enthusiasts from both breeds claim the breeds have gone in different directions, with the windhounds being more borzoi-like due to Ms. Stull's influence, and the windsprites being more whippet-like due to the ongoing backcrossing to smooth whippets.

It took me awhile to get the whippet/windsprite/windhound narrative all sorted out in my head. It was like a dog breed brainteaser. When I shared the details with Tim, he bluntly stated, "Interesting. But does it matter?"

"What do you mean?"

"Are the longhaired whippets breaking their legs too?" he asked.

"They don't use that term anymore. They're called windsprites now."

"Whatever. Are their legs breaking?"

He had a point. I had become so wrapped up in all the historical dog drama that I had lost sight of the most important subject. Broken legs.

A profound sense of déjà vu quickly settled over me as I came upon one after another set of circumstances that sounded eerily familiar, as I was browsing through social media groups devoted to the longhaired whippet/windsprite breed:

"My poor baby jumped off the bed and broke his leg;"

"Mine was less than a year old and broke his leg jumping off the couch;"

"[Mine] broke one leg at six months old and one at thirteen months. Did not take much, which led me to believe that his bones are not very strong. His father also broke two legs;"

"My own had a broken leg at seven months, his mom had two broken front legs, and multiple other cases;"

"I know four LHW/silken windsprites with broken legs only in this year over here in Germany. There were more broken legs in the last years;"

"... very young windsprite male ... broke both legs twice from accidents and now has plates (implants) in both front legs;"

"... in Europe there are whispers of a long lineage of windsprites breaking legs too easily."

I contacted a windsprite breeder in Germany and was surprised how quickly she confirmed that yes indeed, some windsprites in Europe were having problems with leg fractures. She even admitted there was a certain line of dogs where fractures were occurring more frequently, indicating, "There is currently no medical explanation for the fractures, many are also due to accidents."

Finding so many similar scenarios manifesting in two very closely related breeds strengthened my belief that the condition just had to have a hereditary origin. What really cemented this belief though, was when I came across some statements made (more than once) by the most prominent person in the silken windhound world - the breed founder herself.

I almost fell off my chair when I read Francie Stull's declaration that EVERY (her capitals) longhaired whippet that she brought home from Walter Wheeler to create the silken windhound breed, except for one, had broken a leg - some by just stepping off the front porch. Wow. This sure seemed like a smoking gun to me.

In a different post, she reported that when she was visiting Walter Wheeler, "He handed me a tiny little female ... tragically, she jumped off my lap and broke her leg when she hit the floor."

Holy crap! Now I knew for certain I was onto something. A little more digging into the history of those early longhaired whippets led me to another exciting discovery. While I was leafing through a book of historical documents that I had obtained on the internet about the longhaired whippet breed ("Windsprite Chronicles, No. 2"), I came across a black and white copy of an old photograph depicting Walter Wheeler at a dog show in 1976.

In the photo, Mr. Wheeler was kneeling beside two matching sleek longhaired whippets. It wasn't the picture itself that turned out to be monumental though. It was the faint description in tiny print below it. So tiny in fact that I had to use a magnifying glass to read it. Shivers went down my spine as I read how one of the dogs depicted in the photo had suffered a broken front leg ... in the show ring!

How does a dog break a leg while being walked on a short leash?

Oh my God. Could this be the elusive common ancestor I'd been searching for? This dog was way further back in the pedigrees than all of the broken-legged dogs I knew about. Wouldn't it be amazing if I could trace its descendants through a web of dogs with broken legs all the way to my own?

I grabbed my laptop, opened the pedigree database for the longhaired whippet/windsprite breed and held my breath as I typed the dog's registered name into the search bar.

Dammit. Nothing came up. The dog wasn't in the database. I guess I shouldn't have been surprised. I knew there were gaps in the old pedigrees, and sadly Walter Wheeler was no longer around to interview about it. I was stumped, with no way to connect that showring leg-breaker to any silken windhound descendants.

When Tim got home, he asked why I was moping around. I showed him the photograph and explained how disappointed I was, having come so close to finally cracking the case.

He said, "What about the other dog?"

"Huh?"

"There are two dogs in the picture. It says they're littermates. Did you check the other one's pedigree? Wouldn't they be identical?"

Bingo! He was right. It was in there. While I couldn't see the broken dog's descendants, at least now I could see who his ancestors were.

Right away, I noticed that both parents of the show ring dogs had the same mother, which meant that their two grandmothers were the same dog!

It took a few hours of cross-referencing pedigrees from the silken windhound pedigree database and the windsprite breed archive, but it was all right there in black and white. That double-grandmother, born five decades ago, was in the pedigree of every silken windhound that had broken a leg!

This just had to mean something. But now what? Did the problem go back further than the double grandmother? Her family tree went back to purebred "smooth" whippets, but I just wasn't seeing anything in the whippet social media groups that looked like the leg break trends I was seeing in the windhounds/windsprites (legs breaking easily, multiple leg breaks, runs in families, etc.).

Then it hit me – the secret sheltie!

Up until this point, I had been monitoring the whippet and borzoi social media groups for any leg break patterns that matched what I was seeing in the silken windhounds. For whatever reason (maybe because it isn't a sighthound), I never thought to do the same for the sheltie breed. As it turns out, I should have. After all, it was the sheltie genetics that brought in the mutation that almost killed Maple. Also, some silken windhound breed club folks commented on social media that the DNA data showed that ALL male silkens were descended from a single dog … and that dog was a sheltie.

I felt like a bloodhound on a trail. I had gone from leg breaks in silken windhounds to leg break in windsprites and now I was looking for leg breaks in shelties.

I eventually discovered a database that listed hereditary diseases common to the sheltie breed. Unfortunately, leg breaks weren't listed, but interestingly, Osteochondritis Dissecans (the condition that caused Maple's lameness and necessitated two major orthopedic surgeries on her shoulders) was. Wow, now I knew that she probably inherited more than just a mutant drug sensitivity gene from that secret sheltie ancestor.

I kept digging into sheltie health information, and was just about ready to give up when I came across an article written by a long-retired sheltie breeder that literally took my breath away.

The article was titled, "The Importance of the Bitch in the Breeding Program." It was written by Tom Coen, a sheltie breeder. This paragraph gave me goosebumps when I read it:

Thirty-five years ago, I had a bitch shipped in for breeding who possessed the most beautiful eye and skull that I had ever seen. She was unknown due to a crooked front leg that she had fractured during puppy hood. No problem, I thought, as I was interested in the genes for skull and eye. I acquired a daughter from the breeding and at four months of age she broke her front leg but went on to be a very influential producer. She would have had more champions herself but one of her best daughters broke her leg as a puppy – a statement on the inheritance of physical weaknesses.

Wow. Wow. Wow. Broken legs that spanned three generations. A breeder who admitted the problem was inherited. In a breed that was in the ancestry of my own dogs and every silken windhound that had ever broken a leg!

Could it be that the sheltie dog (or dogs) that Walter Wheeler used to create the longhaired whippet came from this line of shelties that was prone to leg breaks?

I wondered if these two breeders knew each other? After all, it appeared that they both lived in Massachusetts and were both showing dogs at the same time. In fact, they both bred shelties. The Westminster Kennel Club website had a bio for the sheltie breeder, who is one of their dog show Judges, and it revealed that Mr. Coen whelped his first litter of shelties in 1964 when he was in high school. The timeline worked.

I reached out to find out if he had ever sold a dog to Walter Wheeler, but I never received a response. It didn't really matter though, since I now had enough evidence to satisfy myself about the origins of the leg breaks.

There were a whole lot of "ifs" and "maybes," but when considered collectively, there was a preponderance of evidence supporting my theory that leg breaks in silken wind-hounds were hereditary and caused by a genetic mutation. I couldn't wait to tell Tim!

35

IT'S ALL RELATIVE

"**S**o, you're done," Tim said. "Finally."

"Nope."

"Why? You've got your evidence. You have your answers. It's time to put a bow on it and move on with your life."

"They're just going to brush it off."

"Who?"

"The breeders and the breed club."

"Why do you care? And how can they brush off the fact that you traced a health problem back through a whole pile of related dogs that have broken their legs, right to the beginning of the breed?"

"Well, first off, the sheltie thing is just a longshot. I have no proof that those broken legs are related."

"But you have all those longhaired whippets that broke their legs?" he said. "They literally created the silken windhound breed. And that really old one that broke its leg in the show ring. There's your proof."

"They're just going to say it doesn't mean anything because the longhaired whippets are inbred too."

"Why do you care what they say? They're never going to agree with you anyway. You know that."

"True. But I still have one thing left to figure out."

"What's that?"

"Inbreeding."

"What's to figure out?"

"Its role in the leg breaks."

"Isn't it obvious?"

"To me. Yes. To you. Yes. To them – nope!"

I could tell Tim didn't understand what was motivating me to continue on with a crazy crusade that had already consumed several years of my life. I don't even think I understood what was behind it myself.

I just knew I wasn't finished. Not yet. Probably because I still felt confused about the extent to which inbreeding played a role in the leg breaks. For me, it was the last piece of the puzzle, and I couldn't put an end to my research until I had it in my hands.

Over the years I discovered so many instances where closely related silken windhounds suffered from broken legs. I mean really closely related. There were way too many of them to be a coincidence.

There was a breeder in California who vehemently denied that there was anything wrong with the breed after one of her breeding dogs broke its leg (it was amputated), and three of that dog's offspring from the same litter went on to break their legs, with one of them even breaking both front legs, and another breaking the same leg twice requiring an amputation. When I reached out to her, she said this: "Ignoring the fact of accidents and science. You can quote statistics all you want but that doesn't make fact. Take your unscientific study and just go away."

Then there was Heather's dog Fable. Poor Fable suffered multiple breaks to her front leg, an amputation and then she broke the remaining front leg, which resulted in her death. Imagine how Heather felt when I told her that I discovered that the exact same series of events happened to Fable's mother?

Even with Raisa; her family was full of dogs that also broke their legs. Her grandfather broke a leg, and three of that grandfather's offspring also broke legs (one broke both front legs). Two of his grandpuppies broke legs (one being Raisa with multiple leg breaks), and one great-grand puppy broke too. Her grandmother broke a leg too, and she had seven descendants that broke their legs.

The insidious problem ran in families; that I was sure about. Yet every time Heather and I questioned whether the cause of the leg breaks might be hereditary, we were told by prominent members of the breed club that all silken windhounds were closely related

- that any family connections between the broken ones didn't mean anything. Even the person who conducted the Survey Monkey reported that, "silken lines converge so quickly in the pedigrees that no definitive family links could be found."

It boggled my mind that the official response to the questioning of whether a health concern was inherited was a dismissal based on the premise that the whole breed was inbred.

How could this be? I was even more confused about these statements now that I knew the breed was only a few decades old - a relatively recent mixture of several different breeds. Shouldn't this make them less inbred than regular purebreds; you know, with hybrid vigour and all?

As I was looking for answers about why silken windhounds were all related to each other, I happened to come across a personal account by the very person who founded the breed. On YouTube of all places!

Francie Stull published a video of a lecture she gave at an annual gathering of breed fanciers called Silkenfest. It was titled, "A History of the Genetic Diversity of the Silken Windhound Breed," and it contained a gold mine of information.

As I began watching the video, I was immediately struck by Ms. Stull's charming demeanour. She appeared to be in her 60s, with dirty blonde curly hair that sat on her shoulders behind big dangly earrings. Her tunic shirt was eggplant coloured, and she had painted fingernails to match. Using really fun words like "serendipity" and "boom," she smiled frequently as she offered up personal anecdotes while transporting her live audience back to the early 1980's when she travelled the globe to purchase some of the dogs that she used in the formation of her new breed. With a folksy manner, Ms. Stull intimately recounted her early struggles, holding herself out as both a geneticist and an artisan, saying: "I produce art out of bone and muscle and coat ... and genetics are my medium that I use to sculpt them."

Despite her interesting stories, and there were many, I was not distracted enough to overlook her revelation that there was an incredibly small number of "original stock" used to create the silken windhound breed.

Using the information from Ms. Stull's lecture and combining it with my own pedigree research, I concluded that it was likely that only 10 dogs formed the foundation of the breed when the studbook was closed: six longhaired whippets, three borzoi, and one "smooth" whippet. The silken windhound studbook (registry) was officially closed in the year 2000, meaning that only those 10 dogs and their offspring could be used to populate the entire breed. This was done to achieve purebred status, since most kennel clubs insist on a closed studbook.

In order to understand the magnitude of this, try to imagine those 10 original dogs being put on an island with no other dogs. As they reproduced with one another, their population would increase but the genetic material would not. In fact, it would decrease. When the population grew to a few thousand individuals, all of them would only have the genetic material from just those original 10 dogs. Now, take away the island and you have the silken windhound population – a genetic island. I learned from a population genetics standpoint; this process is called "founder effect."

To be fair, I have since discovered that even though the silken studbook is officially closed, the breed club has added a few more borzoi and a few more whippets over the years. However, according to the breed founder, those few additions haven't actually produced dogs that are less inbred than regular silkens, presumably because their offspring were bred right back into the already inbred silken windhound population. Plus, even if you consider those later additions as founders, the founding population of the breed is still incredibly small (less than 20 dogs).

To make matters even worse, Ms. Stull also revealed in her lecture that the founding dogs were already very inbred to start with, describing the longhaired whippets that she obtained from Walter Wheeler as "genetic clones" of one another. Other sources I looked at confirmed this. For instance, the man tasked with investigating whether Walter Wheeler's longhaired whippets were purebreds (Charles E. Billings, M.D.), said this about them: "The supposed pedigrees of these dogs showed incredibly narrow line breeding from a very small number of dogs. It is known that a very extensive elimination of litters took place, partly because of particularly severe genetic defects and malformations."

Ms. Stull stated that several of the borzoi she used were also quite inbred. She chuckled when she revealed that one of them had the same dog for all four of its grandmothers (I'm assuming she meant great-grandmothers, since a dog, like a person, only has two grand-mothers). She spoke candidly in the lecture about the intense inbreeding she did; and in particular about the brother-to-sister pairings that she used in her breeding program, noting that the offspring from those unions is behind the breed "big time."

While Ms. Stull seems to acknowledge that there isn't enough genetic diversity in the breed to be sustainable, she says that there isn't a problem "yet" because of the purity of her lines:

And you can breed tightly, you can inbreed, you can do it if the dogs are good enough. Okay, if you've already pulled out the garbage health-wise, inbreeding does not necessarily cause destruction of your dogs. You can inbreed for a long time if you start with the really really good healthy dogs. And Walter before me and I myself spent generations purifying these lines. So, you guys have healthy lines but you don't have the genetic diversity to hold it very long, okay?

Over the years, I noticed a number of silken windhound breeders using this "purity of lines" explanation to justify breeding close relatives together. A prominent silken windhound breeder who later became the president of the breed club, said this about the longhaired whippet founder, who she claimed to know personally:

Walter kinda serves as a bizarre health screen because he functions a lot like natural selection would in the wild. He has a really high euthanasia rate in his breeding program; he puts down any dog with problems, even if they are slight. He will put down newborn pups. Also, because of his haphazard care of his dogs, the weak tend to die off due to starvation or dehydration. So, the dogs that are left tend to not have any problems, at least in regard to health.

Were they right? I remembered learning in high school biology that inbreeding could result in severe health and reproductive issues. Was this "purity of lines" thing a way to get around it? A hack on Mother Nature?

I am undoubtedly over-simplifying here, but in the spirit of avoiding a really long boring technical explanation, I can tell you emphatically that the answer is no; they aren't right. And here's why, using the simplest breakdown I can muster from what I have learned.

The majority of genetic diseases in dogs are caused by recessive mutations (meaning you need two copies for the disease to manifest). A genetic mutation is essentially just a broken gene that can't do its job. Every single dog, even those that look healthy, carry a number of them. Most of the time, these broken genes are harmless, since a particular disease will only affect a dog if it inherits two broken copies (one from each parent). Dogs with unrelated parents almost never inherit two broken copies of the same gene, meaning that even if they get a broken gene from one parent, they will get a working copy from the other. This is how harmful recessive genes can lurk undetected and usually quite benignly in a population that is not inbred.

On the other hand, close relatives are much more likely to share the same harmful recessive genes, so when related dogs are bred together, two broken genes are more likely to pair up and "boom," a disease shows up; sometimes from seemingly out of nowhere. "Purifying the lines" won't stop this from happening, because harmful recessive genes are always lurking like timebombs waiting to go off.

But what about health screening I wondered? When I first read about the silken wind-hound breed, I was so impressed to find out that many breeders were testing for genetic conditions. Sadly, I found out that they are only able to screen for the few conditions that have a genetic test for the mutation. There are far more genetic diseases that can't be tested for. Thus, the elimination of bad recessive genes will never be complete. Common conditions that silken windhounds are prone to, like allergies, do not have DNA tests. There aren't tests for complex diseases like cancer, autoimmune disease, neurological and cardiac diseases, all of which are in the silken windhound population.

So how does all of this relate to broken legs?

Well, if the problem is, as I suspect, caused by a recessive genetic mutation, the fact that all silken windhounds are related to one another increases the chances of a dog inheriting the faulty gene. In fact, in a small gene pool like silken windhounds, the chances of two broken genes meeting are even greater. And get this - the stakes get higher in direct relation to how inbred the dog is.

So, I bet you are wondering ... just how inbred are silken windhounds?

You may be surprised to hear that I am able to answer that question, and with a remarkable degree of accuracy.

36

INCEST IS BEST

I SURE WISH I had known about the concept of COI before we bought our dogs. In fact, finding out about this "inbreeding calculator" has altered the trajectory of my research and forever changed how I think about dogs.

The coefficient of inbreeding (COI) quantifies how inbred an individual is by measuring how related its two parents are to one another. Breeders have traditionally used pedigrees to measure it, with a calculation to determine the probability that a dog will inherit the exact same gene from the exact same ancestor. If you look back through your own family tree, you are unlikely to see the same ancestor twice. That would give you an inbreeding coefficient of zero. When I went back through my own dogs' pedigrees, I saw so many ancestors appear more than once. In fact, one of Raisa's female ancestors appears 25 times in an eight-generation pedigree!

As you can imagine, calculating inbreeding coefficients using written pedigrees and a mathematical formula is quite complicated and depends heavily on the accuracy of the recorded data. Thankfully, COI can now be determined genetically using a dog's actual DNA, which is an easier and more accurate way to obtain much better information about the actual genetic composition of a particular dog.

A "cutting edge" consumer DNA testing company called Embark uses what it describes as the gold standard for measuring inbreeding. I couldn't wait to give it a try.

I ordered the Embark DNA kit online. A few days later, Amazon delivered a package containing a sleek Tiffany-blue coloured box holding an activation kit, a swab, a return package, and instructions.

Maple eyed me suspiciously as I opened the kit in front of her. I think she knew something was up, but her ears perked up when I set the box down and obtained a piece of cheese from the fridge. I set the cheese on the edge of the counter and Maple kept her eyes glued to it for the entire 60 seconds that I spent scraping the little brush around the inside of her cheek. While unhappy about the indignity of it all, she was quite thrilled to receive the reward when it ended, along with praise for being such a good girl.

I dropped the swab into the collection tube, popped it into the return package and immediately delivered it to our community mailbox. It felt so weird sending something as intimate and valuable as DNA through the regular mail. As I checked the chute to make sure it slid down, I said a little prayer that it would make its way where it needed to go.

It took almost a month to get the results back, and when I did, the exciting subject line of the email said: "Maple's Results Are Ready!"

I clicked on the "Review Results" tab, which prompted me to sign into the account I had already set up.

The next screen said "It's time for your pup's reveal!" Gosh, this was exciting.

I had to click a few more tabs to get to the section I cared most about. Under the "Health" heading, there was a section called "Genetic Diversity" which is where I discovered that Maple had a coefficient of inbreeding of ... dum da da dummm ... 24%.

What did this number mean? Was it good or bad? I had no idea. The Embark website declared that studies show that excessive inbreeding can have a profound impact on a dog's health and lifespan. But what is considered excessive?

I turned to The Institute of Canine Biology (ICB) for answers – an organization that describes itself as an independent, international consortium of canine biologists. The ICB had a number of useful articles about inbreeding on their website. One called "Understanding the Coefficient of Inbreeding" stated that:

The deleterious effects of inbreeding begin to become evident at a Coefficient of Inbreeding (COI) of about 5%. At a COI of 10 %, there is significant loss of vitality in the offspring as well as an increase in the expression of deleterious recessive mutations... So, in terms of health, a COI less than 5% is definitely best. Above that, there are detrimental effects and risks...

Yikes. No wonder Maple had so many health problems. Wondering how her score compared to the rest of her breed, I reached out to Embark and they advised that the average for all silken windhounds tested was 28% with a sample size over 1000 dogs. Holy cow – her high inbreeding level was lower than the average for the breed.

A silken windhound breeder made an inquiry on Facebook as to what breeding lines were represented in the Embark data. The chair of the health committee replied, "There aren't really true lines...they all collapse into closely related pedigrees pretty quickly.

We have very few silken windhounds with a COI lower than direct brother to sister breedings."

When I first read that statement, it sounded shocking, although I have to admit that I didn't understand exactly what it meant.

I have since learned that mating littermates together would produce puppies with a coefficient of inbreeding of 25%. You would get the same percentage when mating a mother dog to her son or a father dog to his daughter!

Wow. This was so crazy. I knew that Maple's parents weren't littermates (or a parent/offspring pairing), so why was her inbreeding coefficient so high? In fact, why were all the silken windhound COI scores so high? I could see from the Embark data that a few even clocked in at 50%! How was this even possible?

It turns out that the sky-high COI in silken windhounds reflects the cumulative effects of inbreeding over the years. Generation after generation of inbreeding has compounded the problem, meaning that the average inbreeding level of the breed is actually higher than what is produced from mating mother to son, father to daughter or full siblings together! Looking back at how the breed was created with so few founding dogs; how soon the studbook was closed; and how much inbreeding has taken place, I guess I shouldn't have been surprised by these numbers. But I was.

I did learn something else that surprised me even more though. Something that made me realize that I was very close to being able to finally feel like I knew enough to end my research phase. For it wasn't just leg breaks. It wasn't just silken windhounds. There was a much bigger issue at play that was systemic in nature, and it all boiled down to how we, as humans, treat the animals that are supposed to be "man's best friend." And it sickened my stomach.

37

WE ALL HAVE BLUE BLOOD

A S YOU CAN PROBABLY appreciate, there was a fair amount of rage that followed my discovery about the highly inbred state of my dogs. Of course, rightly or wrongly, I blamed all of their health issues on it.

"But how do you know their problems are because of inbreeding?" my mom asked me at a family dinner. We were the only ones left sitting at the table, since I had already driven everyone else away with my obsessive and relentless rants about dog breeding.

"Easy. Maple has four genetic disorders. I may not be able to prove the bone breaks are related, but her outie-bellybutton hernia, the drug-reactions, and her bum shoulders are all inherited conditions. Plus, I also found out that she is a carrier for a condition that causes blindness."

"How do you know this?"

"From her DNA test. Wanna hear something even crazier?" I asked.

"Sure," she said eagerly, although her voice was a little too high pitched, tipping me off that she was only merely pretending to be interested because she loved me and not because she actually wanted to hear anything else about the subject of purebred dogs.

I took a long slow sip of my wine, set the glass down on the table dramatically, and then laid it on her.

"ALL purebred dog breeds are inbred. And the majority of them are highly inbred. Just like silken windhounds."

Looking contemplative, my mom countered with, "Aren't farm animals inbred too? What about race horses? I bet they're really inbred."

Dammit. Every time I thought I had the whole inbreeding thing figured out, something else popped up that threw me off. I hated to admit it, but I had no idea about whether and how inbred farm animals and race horses were, although I suspected she might be right.

It was at this point that Tim returned to the table and said, "She used to be obsessed with leg breaks. Now she's obsessed with inbreeding. Don't encourage her."

I was obsessed with inbreeding. It was true. I had been reading everything I could find on the subject.

The following day, I looked up inbreeding levels in livestock and even race horses. I was surprised to find out that neither were as inbred as purebred dogs. Not even close. In fact, I discovered that in racehorses, an inbreeding coefficient of 5% is considered high. I also learned that the mating of first cousins produces an inbreeding coefficient of 6.25%, which is forbidden and even illegal in some human societies. Zoos don't like to go over 10%. The Institute of Canine Biology said that a COI less than 5% is definitely best. Now that I had a good frame of reference, I was able to say with confidence that inbreeding levels in other species paled in comparison to purebred dogs.

In fact, according to a recent article in the journal Canine Medicine and Genetics, the average inbreeding level of most breeds was close to 25% - well above what is considered safe for either humans or wild animal populations.

As a lifelong canine enthusiast, how did I not know this? Thinking back, I guess I kind of knew that some breeds were "high strung" and others were prone to certain diseases, but I never attributed the problems to inbreeding. But I should have. Because inbreeding dogs renders their offspring susceptible to a myriad of genetic disorders, deformity and weakened immune systems. There is even a well-documented correlation between higher levels of inbreeding and shorter life spans!

But why? Why were they so inbred? After all, we sure don't tolerate it in humans. In Canada, for instance, if found guilty of incest, a person could be imprisoned for up to 14 years. In some US states, the penalty for committing incest is life imprisonment. The Criminal Code of Canada defines incest as having sexual intercourse with a blood relative that is a parent, child, brother, sister, grandparent or grandchild. Half-siblings are included. The practice is prohibited due to the significant risk of genetic abnormalities that can lead to severe health issues, including both physical and mental disabilities, which may hinder the offspring's ability to lead normal lives. The law seeks to prevent these risks and ensure the well-being of all parties involved.

Human inbreeding. Blech. The very thought of it turned my stomach. My revulsion was visceral, probably because of the universal moral and legal taboo which is reflected in depictions of inbred people as deviant and even deformed.

I thought about the notorious Spanish king with his "Habsburg jaw." Scientists have determined that he (Charles II) had an inbreeding coefficient of 25%... coincidentally, the same as the average for most dog breeds!

It saddened me to think about how our beautiful Maple was as inbred as one of the most inbred people of all time. Raisa had something in common with the highly inbred monarch too. They both had a grandmother who was also their aunt. This would be funny if it weren't so tragic, especially given that Raisa's Aunt Grandma Sandy also broke her leg. Oh, and to add another sad but funny twist, Aunt Grandma Sandy is Maple's aunt too!

In humans, close inbreeding is considered immoral, illegal, and dangerously risky for the health of a population. It evokes disgust. Yet, when dogs are incest-bred, we call it pure breeding, with the resulting "purebred" offspring regarded with quality, not revulsion. It is normalized by dog breeders, condoned by consumers, and even required by governing bodies like the Canadian Kennel Club and the American Kennel Club, who insist on closed stud books, ensuring that every dog in a registered breed is related by design.

Discovering that all dog breeds were invented by humans, and not really all that long ago, I wondered why we use the word "breed" for related dogs, when really, they were all just big families?

My research journey sure had taken me on an interesting ride. By diving into a health problem in my own dogs, I had discovered a far greater issue: that the entire current modern dog breeding system was basically in a crisis; and that at the heart of it all was inbreeding.

I called my mom to reveal what I had found out.

"I have some interesting information for you," I announced.

"Is it about incest?" she replied, which made me laugh.

"Kind of. But it's more about the Victorians."

"Oh, you mean how Queen Victoria's kids had hemophilia from inbreeding?"

"No. This is about dog breeds," I replied.

"Didn't she have corgis?" she said.

"No! That was Queen Elizabeth. I'm not talking about the Royals; I'm talking about the Victorian time period. I just found out that it was the Victorians that invented dog breeds."

"I thought dog breeds always existed?" she said.

"I did too. But they were invented. By the Victorians mostly. Dogs were domesticated from wolves thousands of years ago, and since then, people have been breeding 'types' of dogs, but mostly for things like working abilities or companionship. It was the Victorians that changed all that."

"What were they breeding for?" she asked.

"Shits and giggles," I said, which made her giggle. "No, really, it's not funny. It's kind of frightening. They were breeding them to exhibit and win ribbons. Our whole modern dog breeding system goes back to the Victorian obsession with pure bloodlines. And eugenics. Using selective breeding to create the perfect specimen ..."

"Snobbery!" she interrupted.

"Well, yes. It was the Victorians that started dog shows, after all."

"Like the Westminster," she said, proud that she knew the name of something from the world I was now immersed in.

"Correct. It's because of them that our current dog breeding system is so screwed up."

"The dog shows or the Victorians?" she asked.

"Both. Dog shows are basically just beauty pageants. But it was the Victorians that started the closed stud book thing – you know, closing the gene pool off, usually with not enough founding dogs, and then the requirement that all dogs of a particular breed look alike, which of course requires inbreeding."

"A recipe for disaster," she said.

"Exactly!" I replied.

"What does eugenics mean? Isn't it something to do with Hitler?" she asked.

"Yes, it means selectively breeding for desirable traits and breeding out undesirable ones. The Victorians used eugenics to try and 'purify' both humans and animals. To breed for perfection."

"So, dog breeds are like Royal families with blue blood." she stated.

"Yep. But the Royals did it to consolidate power. The Victorians did it because it was fashionable to have a dog that looked a certain kind of way."

"Is that why French poodles look so fancy?" she asked.

"It sure is. To the Victorians, breeding dogs was a like a fashionable competitive sport. They wrote up 'breed standards' to catalog how each invented breed was supposed to look, and formed kennel clubs and dog shows to govern these blueprints for perfection that each breed must conform to."

"Snobby," she said.

"Yep. The same breed standards exist today, which is why so many breeds are in trouble. And get this – some of the traits they select for to make a breed unique are actually genetic mutations."

"I don't understand," she said.

"OK, you know how you love Game of Thrones?" I asked.

"Oh, yes!" she said.

"Well, wiener dogs have those incredibly short legs because of a genetic mutation. Just like Tyrion Lannister."

"They're dwarfs?"

"Yes! Which is bad enough in itself, but it also comes along with a bunch of serious health issues that can impact their quality of life like arthritis and spine issues that cause back pain."

"And breeders do this on purpose?"

"Yes! Isn't it crazy? They are deliberately selecting a skeletal deformity; breeding this genetic mutation so that all wiener dogs will have the super short legs that are mandated by the breed standard."

"Seems cruel."

"I know. I figured their weird body shape just existed naturally, but they were made that way on purpose. Just like dogs with smooshed up flat faces, like pugs."

"I think they're so ugly."

"I know you do, but lots of people think super short snouts are cute, and breeders select for genetic mutations to get them to look that way. It is sometimes called torture breeding because their deformed faces can make them susceptible to really severe health problems. Some even have to sleep standing up because they can't breathe when they lie down."

"So, what are silken windhounds bred for then?" she asked.

"They were invented to look like a miniature borzoi. And the weird thing is, there's even talk of an unknown gene that made their body size smaller."

"You've lost me."

"Okay, well, the breed founder says that the founding borzoi she used to create the breed carried a 'miniaturizing gene' which allowed her to make her new breed smaller more quickly."

"So, what's the problem?"

"They break! Or at least some of them do. While trying to isolate this 'miniaturizing gene' as she calls it, three young dogs all broke their legs at her kennel. One broke BOTH its front legs."

"Wow."

"Yep, and she also stated that she wasn't planning to remove those dogs from the breeding pool."

"How do you know this?"

"Facebook."

"So, you think this miniaturizing gene is what gives them fragile bones?"

"No. But I do think the problem is genetic. And inherited. Let me explain. This is important, so pay attention."

"I always pay attention to you!"

"Okay, I am certain there is a mutant gene at play, but I don't think it came from a borzoi. I truly believe the gene came from Walter Wheeler's highly inbred longhaired whippets. I think it was a super rare recessive gene that existed in some shelties and when Walter added the sheltie genetics to his whippets to give them long hair, he introduced the leg break gene to the longhaired whippets. Inbreeding them so severely then spread it through the population, and that's why Francie's longhaired whippets from Walter Wheeler all broke their legs so easily."

"Wow, it sounds like you've got this all figured out."

"I feel like I have, but genetics is complicated, and I still don't know enough. I never will. Who knows, maybe I'm wrong about where the gene originally came from, but one thing I am certain about is that the propensity for broken legs must be caused by an inherited genetic flaw, and maybe it's something like the brittle bone disease in humans."

"There's a brittle bone disease in humans?" she asked.

"Yes, it's called osteogenesis imperfecta. It's a genetic disorder that causes a person's bones to break easily from little or no apparent trauma."

"That sounds exactly like what happened to Raisa!"

"Yep. It's in some dog breeds, but the mutation is different for different breeds, so the genetic tests that exist won't tell us if silken windhounds have it."

"So, how will you figure it out?'

"I won't."

"What? Why? You can't give up now!"

"There's nothing more I can do at this point, mom. The only way to move forward would be to convince the breed club to hire experts to identify the mutation, if there is one, and that's never going to happen."

"Why?"

"Because they hate me."

"But that shouldn't affect them wanting to solve a health problem?"

"Sadly, yes it will. And here's the thing: I've come to realize that even if the leg break gene is identified and a screening test is developed, if the breeders start removing affected dogs from the gene pool, then the inbreeding situation will get even worse, meaning that the genetic diversity of the silken windhound population will tank even more, resulting in even more genetic problems in the long run."

"So, you wouldn't actually be helping the dogs."

"Exactly. The leg breaks aren't the big problem. They are my big problem, but overall, in terms of the breed, they are merely a symptom of a far more insidious and systemic issue. The elephant in the room is the lack of genetic diversity that has resulted from inbreeding in a closed population. And that's not going to stop, even if the leg break gene is discovered."

"So, you're done then?"

"Almost. I have three things left to do," I paused, but she didn't say anything, so I continued. "First, I'm going to write my book about all we went through with our own dogs."

"That's exciting."

"I know! I'm excited too. Then, I'm going publish my data on leg breaks. All the stuff that Tim says is too boring for the book. Statistics and all that. I'm even going to create a website so I can hopefully avoid some of the vitriol of social media."

"That sounds like a lot of work."

"It will be. But I'm looking forward to it, actually. I've already bought the domain name: silkenwindhound.ca to publish the website. Then when I'm done all of this, I can finally put the topic of silken windhound leg breaks on the back burner and get on with my life."

"That's only two things," she said.

"What?"

"You said there were three things you had left to do."

"Oh, right. The third thing I'm going to do right away. I'm going to bury Raisa's ashes. I think I'm finally ready."

"Ready for what?" she asked.

"Ready to lay her to rest. Because now I finally truly understand what happened to her. For years, I've literally been twisting myself up in knots, blaming myself for her health problems, and for Maple's too. Was it their diet? Exposure to chemicals? Pesticides? Too much exercise? Too little? Now I know without a shred of a doubt that their health problems happened because of inbreeding. I mean, other factors may have contributed, but inbreeding is what made them so susceptible in the first place."

"Raisa was like a tiny little Royal princess, whose blood was much too pure," she said.

"Yes. Exactly. You've hit the nail right on the head. She was so beautiful and perfect on the outside, but oh, so broken on the inside."

"Just like you!" she said.

"Not anymore, mom. I'm not broken anymore. Putting all of this dog stuff together has put me back together. I'm in a good place now."

"Well, I'm proud of you. Do you know that? You ended up exactly where you needed to be, and that makes me happy."

"Me too, mom. Me too."

38

RESTING IN PEACE

GROUPS OF DAFFODILS WERE blooming all over our property, looking like nature's own premade bouquets whose sole purpose was to decorate our forest floor. April was a magical month and with the woods waking up, it seemed a fitting time for the official farewell. Unfortunately, though, moving my little girl to her final resting place did not go remotely as planned. Or at least not how I had planned it.

With Tim in charge, the internment turned out to be more of a practical affair than the canine funeral I had imagined it would be. While perfectly happy to discuss topics like the best location for the new pet graveyard, Tim had zero interest in memorializing its first occupant in any kind of ceremonial way.

"Why open up old wounds?" he said, adding, "I don't understand why you purpose-fully want to make yourself feel sad and shitty."

"It's your attitude that's making me feel shitty," I snapped back. "Why are you treating this like an unpleasant task?"

"Because that's what it is!"

I knew where this this conversation was heading, and that if I kept going, it would make the whole ordeal even more upsetting. In fairness, I suppose Tim didn't understand what a monumental occasion this was, since for whatever reason, I never shared the connection between saying good-bye to Raisa and completing my leg break investigation. As far as he was concerned, we had simply been waiting for the frost to come out of the ground so he could dig a hole.

After we gently lowered the soft blanket that was wrapped around the menagerie of Raisa's earthy effects into the hole, I said a few words. Very few. And nothing overly emotional since the grave digger was standing behind me with a shovel full of dirt, making it known that he was ready to fill the hole back in.

For the rest of the day, I was overcome with disappointment about how the non-funeral went down. That evening, I sat down at my computer and let my thoughts flow freely as I typed out all the things I wanted to say to her. A love letter of sorts. But also, a final good-bye. I didn't stop myself from making it as raw and vulnerable as it needed it to be, because this time I knew I would be delivering the words when I was alone.

The following morning an intense beam of sunlight streamed in through my bedroom window and woke me up. It was very early and Tim had already left for work. I tried to go back to sleep, but the birds seemed to be singing louder than usual, which I took as a sign that it was time to get up and begin the important day in which I would be delivering my eulogy.

As I sipped my morning coffee, I planned how the morning would unfold. Working from home allows me this great privilege, and I don't take one single peaceful morning for granted. When I was based out of a high-rise tower, even sitting in my prestigious corner office didn't make up for the fact that almost all of my days began in a frenetic and mostly stressful way. My time spent at the law firm always seemed driven by other people's agendas. Now that I was in charge of my own schedule, I did things differently. Slower.

Before leaving the house, I peeked in on Maple, but she was still barnacled to the bed, showing absolutely zero interest in joining us outside. She didn't know, and probably didn't care, about the auspicious occasion that was about to take place after I had finished walking the dogs. I stroked her long pretty head and kissed the top of it. Gently lifting up one of her silk-fringed ears, I whispered into it that I would deliver her special breakfast when I was finished outside.

As I headed into the basement, the big dogs were both at my heels, jostling each other around as they raced to the back door. They paced and whined while I pulled on my rubber work boots and donned my plaid shirt jacket; the utilitarian items of clothing that had replaced the high heels and tailored suits that used to comprise my daily uniform. When I opened the door, they blasted out to search for the smells that had been left behind by the wild canines that hunted on our land the night before.

As I stepped outside, I breathed in the fresh spring air as I started to walk. Beginning each day this way brings me great pleasure. It provides the dogs with lots of exercise and provides me with plenty of time to think. And today my thoughts are deep and heavy, given what I am about to do, and all that has led up to it.

I begin to reflect on how much has changed in our lives, and how so much of it happened because of the silken windhounds. Love and fear: probably two of the strongest driving forces in change. And both came flooding into my life in equal measure when we brought home Maple and then Raisa. Love came first of course; and right along with it came a primal instinct to protect and shield them from harm. But when I found myself unable to do that, it broke me. At the heart of it all was the fear that was always lurking in the shadows, constantly reminding me of their fragility. It debilitated me; fracturing the path I had been travelling on my whole life.

But I wondered, would my path have changed in any event? Was it the love for my dogs and my anguish over their horrific propensity for broken bones that unravelled me? Or were they just the proverbial straw that broke the camel's back? Maybe the camel's back was eventually going to break anyway?

Hmmmm, it was a tough call, but looking back at all "the evidence," I didn't think I would have crashed psychologically if it weren't for the dogs. After all, prior to owning them, I was functioning at an extremely high level in a ridiculously stressful profession. No. It was definitely the dogs that took me down. Had I never brought them into my life, then things would have undoubtedly just continued going along in the same direction. There would have been ups and downs, but just the usual ones, and probably nothing nearly as devastating and damaging to my psychological wellbeing.

As I kept walking and kept thinking about it all, I suddenly realized that maybe it wasn't just the silken windhounds that were fragile because of the way they were made. Maybe I was too. Just like them, perhaps I had a pre-existing vulnerability that made me more susceptible to injury, even though my injuries weren't as obvious as their broken bones. My reaction to what happened to my dogs was extreme -- I acknowledge that. It disrupted my ability to function in both my personal and professional spheres. Most people probably wouldn't have experienced such debilitating symptoms, but most people probably aren't as deeply sensitive to the suffering of animals as I am.

There's a legal doctrine called the thin skull rule. It's meant to protect the fragile and the vulnerable. It dictates that if you harm someone, you're responsible for all the harm caused, even if the person was more fragile or delicate than usual to begin with.

It suddenly dawned on me that I was a thin skull. My severe reaction to the broken bones of my dogs was an inevitable consequence of the profound love I felt for them, combined with the immeasurable burden of caring for them and worrying about their wellbeing.

Did this mean that someone was responsible for the harm I suffered? I wondered if there could be any legal liability? Should there be? This was, of course, my litigator brain kicking in; cutting through the raw emotion that had been ruling my thinking for the past few years. And it sure was taking me to an interesting place.

Maybe the breeders were at fault for producing the dogs that caused my suffering? After all, even though silken windhounds are living creatures, they are still products. Furthermore, by design, they are long-legged, wispy, exotic-looking creatures, and due to how they are bred, some of them have an inherent flaw. I realize that nobody intentionally sets out to breed dogs with brittle bones, however inbreeding them to such a ghastly extreme to get them looking this way is what made them susceptible to the condition in the first place (and also to other serious and chronic illnesses).

The more I thought about it, the surer I became that a Court could be convinced that breeding defective dogs is negligence. After all, breeders know, or ought to know, that inbreeding so intensely in a closed population will lead to health issues and shortened lifespans in some of the animals they produce. And we're not just talking about the "usual" inbreeding that takes place in domesticated species. These are dangerously high levels of inbreeding. Levels that can be accurately and easily measured with genetic COI tests. Levels we deem unsafe in humans, with practices that we even consider illegal.

But here's the problem. Lawsuits involving damages to dogs aren't worth much. Dogs are considered property, so the financial exposure for producing a defective one is really only limited to the cost of the dog. There isn't any meaningful legal remedy for a dog that gets sick as a result of bad breeding (that I know of).

But what if a lawsuit was brought seeking damages for the person who owned the sick dog? An owner like me who suffered damages, some of which can be easily quantified (like vet bills and travel expenses), but some that are less discernible (like pain and suffering, loss of quality of life, future wages and emotional distress). Now we're talking about a significantly higher number!

Many of the owners I interviewed also suffered psychological injuries as a result of looking after a dog with a serious and expensive health issue. In fact, I recalled reading several articles about how caregiver burden in owners of a pet with a chronic or terminal disease was similar to what happens in human caregiving, with symptoms of higher stress, anxiety, clinical depression and a lower quality of life than owners of healthy pets.

Breeders ought to know that when they sell a dog with a serious inherited condition to a person like me (who treats their dog like family or even in some cases as their child), then it is reasonably foreseeable that the owner could be harmed as a result of caring for the dog and by watching them suffer. In which case, legally speaking, the product is not only defective; but also, dangerous.

I thought about other consumer goods that cost roughly the same amount of money as a purebred dog. If I bought a refrigerator that turned out to be a lemon, I could return it and get my money back. But what if the refrigerator didn't just break, but it exploded as a result of faulty engineering and I was injured because of it? I could sue the manufacturer to hold them responsible for my personal injuries, meaning that my damages would go way beyond just the replacement cost of the refrigerator. This type of lawsuit might also influence the whole refrigerator industry, eliminating, or at least substantially reducing the risk of exploding refrigerators. After all, sometimes it takes a lawsuit to overcome the entrenched interests of those profiting from the production of a product.

Maybe this is exactly what is needed when it comes to dogs? A few successful lawsuits might actually result in some meaningful changes to the harmful modern dog breeding practices put in place by the Victorians that are still being followed today, to the detriment of so many dogs and so many people who love them.

As I was nearing the end of my walk, I started to think that perhaps this was the silver lining to all that we had been though with our dogs. That while my fear for their wellbeing had unraveled me, it was my love for them that led me back to where I needed to be. To a place where I probably should have been all along, both literally and figuratively. Back to the essence of that small town girl that loved nature and loved dogs ... all dogs; not just the pedigreed ones. That little girl that wanted to help animals. That little girl who believed in justice. That nerdy girl who went to law school and became a lawyer, hoping to do something meaningful for animals.

Maybe having my meticulously ordered existence blown up so spectacularly was exactly what was supposed to happen, because amidst all the turmoil, I finally found clarity, and maybe even my true purpose. It was, after all, my love for Raisa and Maple that compelled me to conduct research and eventually weave together this narrative that speaks not only to what happened to my dogs, but also to the deeper truths I unearthed about myself and most importantly, about a broken system that is in dire need of reform.

I thought about what Dr. Seuss said in "The Lorax": "Unless someone like you cares a whole awful lot, nothing is going to get better. It's not."

And who knows, maybe one day I will represent, or at least inspire, the first successful plaintiff in a trial that will result in justice; not just for the caregiver of the compromised canine, but for all the defective dogs and for all the damages that we've heaped upon them in the name of purity.

39

EPILOGUE TO A DOG

OUR WALK ENDED AND we were back to where we started - at the basement door. But my work outside wasn't finished, so after putting the big dogs back inside the house (I didn't want any distractions), I retraced my steps but in the opposite direction until I reached the middle of the property, where I veered off the trail and headed up the steep hill we call the mountain.

Pushing the skinny sugar maple saplings aside, I wound my way through the big hemlock trees to the place at the top of the mountain that we chose for Raisa's grave. Purposefully away from our everyday walking trails, I thought it better to have a location where I could intentionally enter the area and that state of mind, rather than have it take me by surprise, the way it does when the song "Raise Your Glass" by Pink does sometimes when I unexpectedly hear it on the radio while I'm driving.

We marked Raisa's grave with a flat stone with her picture on it. She is buried a few feet away from the trunk of an elm tree that forks in two at about six feet up. One day Maple will rest here too. I can't think about that right now though. This moment is about Raisa.

I take my phone out of my pocket and punch in my password. Billy Joel's song, 'Lullabye' is cued up on YouTube.

I press the play arrow, and sad piano music begins, followed by the opening lyrics ... "Goodnight my angel, time to close your eyes." One of the first images in the video is a white feathered wing. I set my phone down on her gravestone and close my eyes, conjuring up an image of her; vibrant and happy. This is how I want to remember her.

As soon as the song ends, I take the piece of paper out of my coat pocket that holds the words I wrote to her. I unfold it, and as I begin reading, all the lingering sadness that I have been carrying around with me for so long is finally released. I am truly at peace with myself .... and now it is time to let Raisa rest in peace too.

Dear Raisa,

I didn't know when we got up together in West Virginia on that fateful morning that it would be for the final time. I wish you could have told us what to do when we were faced with the terrible decision that ended your life. Please know that I couldn't keep you suffering in this world just because I couldn't bear to not have you by my side.

I regret that I didn't get to say a proper good-bye to you or send you out of this world in a way that was more peaceful for you. But I am thankful that Dr. Radcliffe was there when you took your last breath. I know you liked him.

Though I feel much guilt over the decision we made, I keep reminding myself how I devoted so much of my energy to you; always trying to ensure that your little soul was fulfilled as much as possible, despite the restrictions that we had to put on it. Before making any decisions about your care, I always put myself into your place and would think about what I would want if the roles were reversed. It is such a heavy burden to carry when we control the destiny of someone we love.

I used to hate the term mother being used in relation to dogs, but I know now when it came to you, I had the soul of a mother – I was your mother in spirit and in practice. It was your face that greeted me every morning when I woke up, and every time I returned home. Like the love a mother has for a child, I was able to experience a love that had no boundaries. You were dependent on me for food, shelter and love, and you wanted to be with me above anything else. As it turns out, I was dependent on you too. It was a version of motherhood that was true to me.

Raisa, you have taught me that love is fleeting, and that when you have it you must make the most of it, being intensely in the present by living in the moment and enjoying the simple routines of the every day. For the five years you were here with me, my daily life was enhanced by your presence, and I will miss our everyday together: your tail wags, your sweet kisses, your smiling face, and your melty eyes that looked at me like you wanted to drink me in. I will miss the feel of your corn silk hair under my fingers and the pattern of sound that your feet made when running to greet me every time I arrived home. I will always remember how it felt like butterflies landing when you jumped up on the bed to join me for the night. I will miss your sweet muffled barks while you dream beside me. Please come back to me in my dreams and greet me as you greeted me in life, with your tail sashaying from side to side in such an enthusiastic way that it wagged your whole delicate body.

I hope you can somehow know that you are still my muse, my quiet heroine. You took every medical treatment given to you with the greatest dignity, trust and good humour. You were fierce yet feminine, elegant but playful, and you chose joy in your life, even though it was a compromised one almost right from the start. You still inspire me to look at the bright side of every situation, knowing that you stayed happy and resilient even as your genetics let you down. Because humans let you down by engineering the defective vessel that carried your most precious of souls. For you were like a unicorn – created to be so beautiful and perfect, but as a result, you were so genetically sick that you were unable to exist in this world. You were ephemeral, with hollow bones full of too much air and not enough substance for this harsh world.

As you know, Raisa, I am not the strongest of humans. I feel things deeply, and like you, I break easily. But now that you are gone, it is your memory that will keep me going, fighting to raise awareness of what took you from me. As a non-credentialed "pet-owner," my pen is the only weapon I can use in this fight. But fight I will, because my grief over losing you has led me to the truth – and it is time to tell the world about your brittle bones and about the fragility of others of your kind, and the fragility of the broken system that creates purebred dogs for human enjoyment. And when the steps ahead are heavy and difficult, I will carry you with me in my heart in the same way that I carried your beautiful body when it was broken. I will make sure that your suffering will not have been in vain, for the tragedy of your death is what has given meaning to my fight.

Raisa, the briefness of your life is the sharpest part of my loss; the price I have paid for having fallen in love with an evanescent creature. But loving you has taught me that being stoic and closed emotionally might be safe, but that it isn't living; that loving deeply and openly connects us to another soul and to this world and makes life worth living, even if it hurts. That if I shut down my heart to love, I might prevent some pain, but I will miss out on the wonder of this world.

And it hurt. Losing you physically hurt. For you were my constant friend who bore witness to an important part of my life journey, as I did to yours. But I hurt less now knowing that we did right by you, and it gives me peace to know that somewhere in spirit form you are now running free to your heart's content, without any worry of the mortal problems that prevented you from running freely in this life.

For you were loved beyond measure – you weren't just my pet, you were my world. You were my One.

ACKNOWLEDGEMENTS

I am deeply grateful to the following individuals, whose contributions have been vital in bringing this book to life:

To my mom, who has always inspired me to reach for the stars—your unwavering belief in me has been my guiding light. To my husband, whose faith in my vision gave me the courage to leave behind a lucrative career and devote myself to this project—your support has been invaluable. To my dear friend Sandra, who taught me the importance of critical thinking and the transformative power of the written word—your wisdom and coaching have been guiding forces. To Heather, my steadfast "partner in crime" – your companionship has been my anchor. To Mark, who planted the seed of this endeavour and nurtured it with care—your guidance has been essential. To Dr. Radcliffe, whose skill and compassion have mended my beloved dogs time and time again—you are truly my hero. And finally, to my cherished friends who have cheered me on from the sidelines, serving as first readers and offering invaluable suggestions: David, Michel, Jacquie, Kathryn, Graham, Gerald, Kim, Kristie, Sherry, Sara, John, Deena, Shelagh and Howard—your unwavering support has meant the world to me. A special thank you goes out to my online friends, Brenda and Kathleen, who have provided boundless "virtual" encouragement from afar, as well as kindness when I needed it most.

ABOUT THE AUTHOR

Michelle Stark, a distinguished civil litigator for twenty years, has transitioned from the courtroom to the writer's desk, pursuing her passion for storytelling. Her debut memoir delves into the intricate world of canines, caregivers, and unexpected fragility. Michelle lives on a picturesque Canadian farm with her husband, where they produce award-winning maple syrup and share their lives with several dogs, a flock of sheep, curly-feathered geese, a few hives of honey bees, and according to her husband, "way too many" chickens. Follow her latest adventures at michellestark.ca

Printed in Great Britain
by Amazon